THE UNKNOWN
GERTRUDE JEKYLL

THE UNKNOWN
GERTRUDE JEKYLL

Gertrude Jekyll

Selected and edited by Martin Wood

F

FRANCES LINCOLN LIMITED

PUBLISHERS

'To one who had a verdant heart'

Frances Lincoln Ltd
4 Torriano Mews
Torriano Avenue
London NW5 2RZ
www.franceslincoln.com

The Unknown Gertrude Jekyll
Copyright © Frances Lincoln Ltd 2006
Foreword copyright © Martin Wood 2006
Illustrations copyright © as acknowledgments on page 208

British Library Cataloguing-in-Publication data
A catalogue record for this book is available from the
British Library.

ISBN 13: 978-0-7112-2611-1
ISBN 10: 0-7112-2611-3

Printed and bound in Singapore

9 8 7 6 5 4 3 2 1

CONTENTS

Foreword 6

The Joy of Spring 9

A Summer's Lease 22

Mists and Mellow Fruitfulness 36

The Bleakness of Winter 42

Some Ideas on Garden Planning 50

Around the House 58

Some Thoughts About Colour 66

Roses 82

Wild and Woodland Gardening 92

108 Bulbous Plants and Their Uses

116 Some Hardy Plants

126 Scents in the Garden

130 Climbing Plants

138 Small Gardens

146 Shrubs and Their Uses

160 Water Gardening

164 Some Elements of Design

182 Some Practical Ideas and Solutions

198 Sources
202 Index
208 Acknowledgments

FOREWORD

It has been said, and with ample justification, that Gertrude Jekyll 'changed the face of England more than any, save the Creator himself and, perhaps, Capability Brown'. Just as a Brown landscape reflects the elegance of the eighteenth century, so the idea of a Jekyll garden seems to encapsulate the essence of the Edwardian period.

Gardens are perhaps the most ephemeral of all art forms, for they are an ever-changing tapestry of colour, form and texture, a seemingly never-ending parable of life, death and immortality. A garden is a living picture, but each day we see again a different picture, set beneath a different sky, in a different light, which we enjoy once more and yet anew. No one was more adept at creating such living pictures than Gertrude Jekyll. Over a career spanning some sixty years Gertrude Jekyll designed nearly four hundred gardens. (Ironically, though she was famed for designing gardens attached to beautiful country houses, her career as a garden designer began in 1870 with a window box for a mill boy in Rochdale.) Like most of the gardens created during the twentieth century, they were essentially personal gardens, and once their creator ceased to exist, the gardens tended to become pastiche, and deteriorating pastiche at that, until nature reclaimed what was once her own. Today few of her gardens remain as she originally intended, and only a handful exist in any recognizable form; the only records of virtually all her gardens are plans and old photographs. But their legendary fame endures and, most notably through her collaboration with the architect Sir Edwin Lutyens, the gardens she helped fashion and create have inspired succeeding generations of garden makers.

Gertrude Jekyll's enduring influence has been achieved not only through her spade but through her pen. While her gardens have by and large not survived, and indeed the way we all live has changed out of all recognition and in a way she could never have imagined, by writing she was able to propagate her ideas, challenging the conventions of the period and changing perceptions of what a well-ordered garden should look like. Over her long life she published fifteen books and contributed well over a thousand articles, notes and letters to numerous newspapers, magazines and periodicals. In 1937 Miss Jekyll's nephew Francis Jekyll and George Taylor, then gardening editor of *Country Life*, published a selection of her journalism under the title *A Gardener's Testament*. This selection included only sixty-seven pieces. A treasure trove of work from her prodigious journalistic output was left inaccessible to all but a few scholars or those with a peculiar interest in the subject and a dogged determination to seek out magazines not widely held in today's reference libraries. *The Unknown Gertrude Jekyll* endeavours to make good this loss. Comprising well over a hundred further pieces, it brings together an extensive collection of material. Although by no means exhaustive, it is the fullest selection yet of those pieces that have never been republished.

An editor once remarked that he 'would rather have clipped the wings of an archangel' than cut her beautifully crafted prose, even if it required him to rearrange his whole layout. I can only concur. Here I have merely removed references to photographs, or complex explanations of Latin plant names, which are now meaningless and would serve to confuse rather than illuminate. All the botanical names have been translated to their modern equivalents for ease of reading, although in a few places her explanations of groupings have been retained even though they are old-fashioned. Any editorial comments, which have been kept to a bare minimum, are to be found in square brackets. Unless otherwise stated in the caption, all the black and white photographs were taken by Miss Jekyll and are of Munstead Wood, Surrey, her former home. These, together with the eight auto-chrome photographs and two watercolours, give a unique record of this famous garden. Other illustrations show designs that were influenced by or appear to be influenced by her ideas.

Many of the themes in this selection will be familiar to readers from Miss Jekyll's other works. Some, however, will be quite unknown. Except for *Garden Ornament* and *Old English Household Life* all of Miss Jekyll's books appeared during the Edwardian period: indeed her two most influential books – *Wood and Garden* and *Colour in the Flower Garden* were published in 1899 and 1908 respectively. Her own garden at Munstead Wood gradually evolved over the fifty years she lived there. She added various features, some not mentioned in any of her books, and changed or dispensed with others, and she was undoubtedly emboldened to create further 'dressed ground' following the huge popular success of *Colour in the Flower Garden*, the royalties from which 'warmed the cockles of the depleted exchequer'.

These articles all demonstrate her basic philosophy, which never varied throughout her life: it was summed up by the phrase 'gardening for beautiful effect'. She was fascinated by colour and the use of colour in the garden, and her appreciation of colour was allied to keen observation. She was a friend of the art critic John Ruskin and someone once asked her what she had learned from him. She recalled that Ruskin had once asked her a question: 'What is the colour of the grass over there?' Green, of course. 'No, it's not,' was Ruskin's swift response. 'Were you to paint that grass, green is not the colour you would take from your watercolour box. It would be primrose yellow.' He was, of course, quite right. The moral of the story is always to look, and look again, and more importantly to observe. In all Gertrude Jekyll's writings there is an astute sense of observation that with an evocative prose style creates a wonderfully vivid picture of her subject for the reader.

Although most of her gardens were designed for houses built by the nouveaux riches, with whom she would instinctively have had little in common (she was herself 'old' gentry), she drew much inspiration from the 'little cottage gardens that help make our English waysides the prettiest in the temperate world'. She loved the old country ways and country people, and was interested enough to document their homes and lives in her book *Old West Surrey*, which appeared in 1904. It was to be her misfortune to see this way of life – a way of life that had existed for hundreds of years – disappear into our modern world with all its attendant advantages, tragedies and horrors.

Plants were Gertrude Jekyll's paint, the earth her canvas and nature her inspiration. She remarked, 'no artificial planting could ever equal that of Nature', and that from nature one could learn the 'importance of moderation and reserve, of simplicity of intention, and directness of purpose'. While her interests, her core ideas and thoughts remained constant, she was always experimenting and adapting. It is odd that her name should, in popular perception, be synonymous with the herbaceous border: she did not herself use the term, and it was a style of gardening in which she did not indulge. Her borders were always 'mixed' borders, in which she used any plant so long as it gave the desired effect.

These articles and notes of a great gardener inspire us with ideas for our own gardens in our own time, as well as affording the sheer pleasure of reading elegant prose. They offer a celebration of gardens, garden making and garden writing, and are a testament to what Gertrude Jekyll described as 'the enduring happiness that the love of a garden gives. For the love of gardening is a seed that once sown never dies.'

Martin Wood

THE JOY OF SPRING

LENT HELLEBORES

The Lent hellebores are by no means so generally cultivated as their undoubted merit deserves, for at their time of blooming, from the end of February to nearly through March, they are the most important of the flowering plants of their season, both for size and general interest. They are well suited to some place where wood and garden meet, and are also good at shrubbery edges, for they hold their foliage all the summer and are never unsightly. One would like to plant a whole garden of them in the nearer part of some wood where primroses and bluebells come naturally, in cool soil enriched with its own leaf mould, and to have them grouped with a following of hardy ferns, sheltered by hazels and occasional oaks. In my own garden I have them in the borders of a nut walk, a place that suits them well, for by the time the young foliage is growing the leaves are coming on the nuts and giving just the amount of shade that is most beneficial.

Gertrude Jekyll in the Spring Garden, September 1923. Photograph by Professor John Harshberger of Philadelphia.

I doubt whether any of my plants are the true species. They came originally as a handful of small seedlings from the late Mr Archer-Hind's garden in Devonshire, and were given me by Mr Peter Barr – now many years ago when his nursery was at Tooting. He had just received from Mr Archer-Hind such a liberal gift of seedlings that there were some to spare for a keen amateur. Their original parentage was somewhere within these Caucasian and Near East subspecies of *H. orientalis* – *colchicus*, *caucasicus* and *abchasicus* – with flowers for the most part of a low-toned reddish purple, but some with pure white varieties and many with gradations between purple and white. They vary in height, from compact plants rising about ten inches to more spreading ones whose height is anything from eighteen to twenty inches.

It is interesting to observe the large variety of colouring and marking, for even among the purples alone there is considerable difference, though what is most usual is a finely splashed spotting of a darker colour. In general the purple flowers have a lustreless surface, in many cases with a faint film of plum-like bloom. Their spotting is only on the front or inner side, for turning the flower over, the back shows only a straight veining.

The pure whites are charming flowers. A mature plant carrying a quantity of bloom is a striking object in the still wintry woodland or in some sheltered garden corner; an occasional tinge of green only serves to make the white purer. Sometimes there comes a remarkable break – a pure white flower heavily spotted inside with dark crimson. When this occurs the spots show faintly through to the outside. There are a number of plants showing intermediate colouring. Some have a rather coarse habit of growth, but are well suited for woodland planting; they have large leaves and light-coloured bloom. Some gardeners or growers might think them worthless because of the undecided colouring, but to anyone with a trained colour eye they are charming and full of interest, with their tender flushes of pink suffused with a still tenderer hint of green, and sometimes a thread-like picotee edge or rosy red.

What appear to be petals in the hellebores are not petals but sepals. The true petals are quite small, barely a quarter of an inch either way. They are set in an overlapping ring in the base of the flower, and are like little triangular flattened bags, closed at the mouth and running down to a fine point at their insertion. The age of the flower may be known by the development of the central organs. At first the clear, warm white stamens are closely packed, but as the flower develops those at the outside separate themselves, and the filaments that carry the pollen-bearing anthers increase in length. These are followed by the next, and at the moment of full development they all stand out slightly apart, making a handsome centre to the flower.

It is often thought that the Lent hellebores will not last in a cut state. It is true that if they are put in water without preparation they soon droop and fade, but they last well if they are properly treated. As soon as they are cut they should have the ends of the stalks slit up from one to two inches, and should then be plunged right up to the flower in a pail of water, to stay there all night, or at least for some hours. They can then be arranged with any suitable foliage, preferably warm-tinted berberis, and will last as well as most flowers.

Hydrangeas in tubs at the top of the Nut Walk.

A NUT WALK

A shady nut walk is a pleasant feature in any garden. It may often be arranged so as to lead from one definite portion of a garden to another, or from the pleasure garden near the house to the vegetable grounds or to woodland; and if it is planted with cobnuts or filberts, it will add another to the good harvests of the later year. Where the planting of such a shady walk is in contemplation, it may be well to advise that the nuts should be planted in a double row on each side, leaving room for flower borders. If the path is five feet wide, the inner rows should be thirteen feet apart and the outer twenty-one feet. One row will thus be four feet beyond the other. The nuts should be planted zigzag, so that the outer ones show between the inner. After some years' growth they will arch over the path and meet overhead, so that the borders are in shade in summer but have light enough in early spring for the well-doing of the Lent hellebores, primroses and myosotis, with which they may be planted. These are followed by columbines and the taller campanulas.

   A nut walk so planted has given me much pleasure for many years, with its good display of spring flowers followed by its grateful summer shade. But its well-being was not to be without interruption, for one year I noticed that the foliage of one of the cobnuts was unusually small and looked unsatisfactory, not withered, but shrunk, and the next year all the heavier wood, about two inches thick, was dead. It was cut out, leaving a gap that let in unusual daylight. This trouble began near the middle of the length of the nut walk. The following year the next nearest tree showed the same sign of distress, followed by the death of the older wood. It was only when five clumps had failed in this way that we found out what was the matter. The nuts were attacked by the fungus *Fomes annosus.* They were rather thickly overgrown at the root by seedling *Mahonia aquifolium,* and it was only on clearing away this that we found the enemy. It appeared that as nut after nut, always in one direction, was attacked, the malignant strength of the fungus had increased, so that, whereas the first nuts attacked recovered after the heavier dead portions had been removed, the one that was the latest victim was killed outright. We dug it out and found the whole root in a decayed state and the white strings of threatening mycelium travelling along towards the next. These were carefully followed up and destroyed, and we hope that further danger has been averted. It seems curious that the fungus only travelled in one direction, and that, in the beginning, having attacked a tree once, it did that one no further harm but passed on to the next. Those earliest attacked are growing well again, and have shown no trace of the trouble since the first injury.

A PRIMROSE GARDEN

The present condition of a fine strain of white and yellow bunch primroses is the result of nearly fifty years' careful selection. In the early seventies of the last century I saw in a cottage garden a primrose that had what I then thought an unusually good appearance and colour. It was only a little deeper yellow than a wild one, but it stood up well with its little bunch of bloom, and I asked the owner to keep me the seed. This was sown and for some years there was not much progress. Then came a change of home and an intermediate two years in hired houses while the new house was building. But the primroses and all that I then had of hardy plants went on the same pilgrimage, and as there was a good garden in the last temporary shelter and a nice place for them in the shade of a row of nuts, the primroses began to show a distinct advance. Next year, in the new settled home, a place was chosen in a birch copse, where spaces were prepared on each side of some slightly winding paths. The very poor sandy soil was deeply dug and plentifully enriched with cow manure, and as by this time there was a good store of seedlings, some hundreds of the little plants were ready. In their new home, when blooming time came, they could be better seen and their merit better appreciated. A rigorous selection was made and only the very best plants kept for seed. From about the year 1890 improvement was steady, and every year a larger number of plants of better quality appeared. Every now and then there came a coloured one, sometimes of quite a good red, but these were weeded out, as it was soon found that if the strain of whites and yellows was to be kept pure, no other colour must be allowed to be near them.

Once more the primrose garden had to change its home, but this was only to some nearly adjoining land. The place is not so pretty as in the birch wood, but it has some near oaks for sheltering, and as in the neighbouring copse, where the wild primroses abound, they always seem most happy when accompanied by hazels, some cobnuts were planted for shade in addition to the existing oaks. About the year 1898 there appeared a flower of a much deeper yellow, and from then onwards the yellows came on in steadily increasing strength of colour. The general quality has now so much improved, that whereas in the earlier years of the strain quite 75 per cent were discarded as unworthy, now it is only here and there that a plant is

The Primrose Garden, set
amongst oaks and silver birch.

pulled up as not up to the general standard, for this is now jealously guarded, as the seed goes to the trade and the plants are widely dispersed.

It is interesting to observe, in a strain whose colouring is restricted to white and yellow, the great diversity of habit and appearance of the individual plants, both in flower and leaf. Some look as strong as a prosperous foxglove, but these are by no means the best, for a coarse leaf is commonly accompanied by a tall-stemmed loose flower of what we now consider poor quality. The flowers in general are large, some as much as two inches in diameter, a size that seems almost incredible when we look at it on a two-foot rule; but great size has never been so much valued as other good qualities, such as handsome trusses on firm stems, good colour and the general appearance of a worthy garden flower. Some of the later developments in the whites and pale yellows have a strongly coloured eye approaching the colour of red lead – a useful colour word, standing for what is deeper and redder than anything that can be considered orange and yet just short of what can rightly be called scarlet. These and the strongest yellows appear to please the greater number of people, though my own liking inclines to the tenderer shades, where the colour is not abruptly different, but is gently diffused; still, the eyed flowers are certainly handsome and have also a firm texture.

The primroses vary not only in arrangement and depth of colour, but also in form. Some are flat and distinctly five-petalled to the eye; others, though the petals are actually five in number, have them so wide that they are not only deeply imbricated, but also so heavily frilled or fluted at the outer edge that they look like double flowers. This is very beautiful when it occurs in a flower of pale lemon colour. It is a curious thing that, although the strain is entirely within white and yellow, and that the common wild primrose is certainly its ancestor, the colour of the wild plant – that pale yellow with a hint of green – is the rarest among them. It may be accounted for by the increased substance of the petal, the thicker texture not permitting the greenish translucency.

In judging the merits of the individual plants I do not follow the florists' rule of giving praise only to flowers that are 'thrum-eyed'. The difference between thrum-eye and pin-eye is that in the thrum-eye the anthers form a neat little group above the pistil just within the throat of the flower, while in the pin-eye the pistil protrudes and shows like the head of a small pin. Looking at a single bloom, the thrum-eye has a rather more finished appearance, but the more important thing to look for is whether the whole effect of the plant is good and handsome and distinctly of garden value.

A primrose garden is specially delightful in the late afternoon and early evening. If there is hot sunshine before the leaves of the shading trees are fully formed, the flowers in daytime are apt to droop and look fatigued, but in the cooler late afternoon they stand up and are evidently refreshed. The later hours also have the advantage of the lower, yellowing light which tends to harmonize the masses of colour, and the evening also brings out the delicious scent.

Gardeners are divided in their opinion about the time of sowing the seed: whether to sow as soon as it is ripe in July or whether to keep it till the following spring. The first way may be right in the good loamy soil that is the best for all primroses, but after trying both ways we find that sowing in early spring is best suited to our poor soil, which demands yearly enrichment. The seed is sown in boxes in late February and pricked off in April into open frames or prepared beds, and the young plants are put in their places in July or early August. I only wish I had another garden, or some place at a little distance where I could have a plantation of coloured kinds.

A GARDEN OF SPRING FLOWERS

If a garden for the flowers of the earlier months is to be given all that it deserves it should be in a place of its own, apart from the spaces devoted to the flowers of summer and the later year. It cannot everywhere be so arranged, for often the only chance for the spring flowers is to have them in beds or borders that will be filled later with summer blooming plants. Where this is so it is inevitable that the planting, however well arranged, will have the temporary 'bedding' appearance that is out of harmony with those sentiments of repose and continuity that are such valuable qualities in all good gardening; also the scope in the choice of plants will be necessarily restricted. But in the spring garden, that need not be disturbed,

A planting plan for a spring garden.

The Spring Garden. Morello cherries decorate the main border wall. Note the careful use of 'drifts' in the style of planting. Autochrome colour photograph taken *circa* 1912.

The Spring Garden: another view looking towards a fine *Euphorbia characias* subsp. *wulfenii*.

there is not only a much wider range of material to choose from, but there may be bold groups of some of those permanent plants of large and handsome form that have a conspicuous air of importance and distinction. These are the more to be valued because the large-leased garden plants of springtime are none too many.

As it has been one of my pleasant tasks of late years to puzzle out ways of using spring flowers it may be of use to say something of my own garden, especially as it showed itself in those happier years before the war; and to note certain conclusions I have come to since; for though for three years it has been almost neglected, yet one never ceases to think out ways and means, in the hope that some day it may again be given the attention it deserves.

The spring garden lies a little way apart and yet is easily accessible. There is a long, high wall that was built for the protection of the main summer flower border from the north-west wind. The spring garden lies at the back of this at one end and on its northern side, where the line of the wall is prolonged by a yew hedge which has now grown to equal the ten-foot height of the wall itself. The hedge returns at the farther end and hides some outbuildings. The other sides of the garden have a double dry wall planted at the top; this has now grown into a thick mass of *Rosa virginiana*, and the remaining short side has another wall, barely five feet high but with shrubs outside, so that it also forms a sheltering boundary. Near the middle is a grassy space a few yards wide and roughly circular. Three oaks and two hollies nearly surround the little grass plot, but the ring of shade is completed by some nut trees, filberts and cobs, now grown to a good height. There are two wooden seats, one of them in an arched recess notching into the largest holly.

The main border is against the wall and the yew hedge that forms its continuation. It is twelve feet wide, with a space of two feet next to the wall for access to the back plants, and sixty-five feet long. Near the back and partly coming forward towards the middle of the border are in two places groups of *Veratrum nigrum*, that fine middle European plant of noble foliage; the deeply plaited leaves are over a foot long and about seven inches wide. The flower does not concern the spring garden; it does not come till June, and though the tall spike of blackish purple is then a handsome object, yet the chief beauty of the plant is in the foliage which is in perfection in April. This fine plant alone will give the border a certain impression of solidity and importance, but we have also early growth into large leafage in *Myrrhis odorata*, the old English sweet cicely, a handsome plant with wide-spread, fern-like foliage, crowned with broad cream-white bloom, which is not only good in itself but shows out well among the other spring flowers as the only representative of its large botanical family. There is also Solomon's seal (*Polygonatum multiflorum*) in good-sized patches of its fine arching sprays; it is the large Irish kind, nearly four feet high.

Before coming to the actual flower masses, I should like to emphasize something I have learned of late years and that I now practise with ever increasing confidence. This is the great value of what, for want of a better name, I know as the 'between plants'. Any mass of bloom may be a pleasant sight, but if the flowers have a proper setting their value is very greatly enhanced. Years ago I used to notice, in friends' conservatories, places where many tender plants grown under glass were brought together when in bloom for show, how poor the effect often was – just a quantity of flowering plants put together without any definite arrangement except that the taller ones were put at the back and the shorter in front. I shall hope, later, to have something to say about such places, but what I learned was equally applicable to outdoor gardening, and it set me making search for good between plants for use with the spring flowers.

Two were found whose value can hardly be over-estimated. One is a variety of the common sage with purple-tinged leaves; the other is *Heuchera americana*, the satin leaf, so called because the young foliage, suffused with reddish-brown, and just in young perfection in April, has a satin-like lustre. These two plants are rather freely used for the most part in diagonal drifts, but also singly, outlying, as the planting may require. The purple sage is a charming accompaniment to anything of pink or purple colouring, and the heuchera has proved an admirable setting for the further plants where the colouring is of scarlet, orange and wallflower brown.

To give a general survey of the arrangement, it begins with the double white arabis in front, followed by aubrieta of pale and deep purple; they are not at the front edge only, but also swing back a little way into the depth of the border. I have found, in all border arrangement, that, as a general rule, it is better to plant in what it is convenient to call drifts, running more or less diagonally with the line of the path, rather than in patches of more solid shape. For one thing the whole drift is better displayed as one passes along, and then by having them in this form, when the bloom of one kind is over, it is more easily concealed by flowers of its neighbours on either side. My drifts are anything from five to ten feet long and a little thicker in the middle.

To return to the flowers, at the near end there are daffodils and white tulips, interplanted and sometimes carpeted with forget-me-not and white and yellow bunch primroses, and early irises, both purple and cream white, in a framing of the purple sage, with purple wallflower and a fine form of dark purple honesty (*Lunaria annua*) at the back. The wallflower is repeated after a big drift of the primroses, and now comes one of the groups of the veratrum. Quite at the back there are some patches of the stately crown imperial (*Fritillaria imperialis*), the sulphur-coloured one. Purple sage is used with the tulips, the early pink 'Rosamundi' followed by the taller 'Clara Butt', a flower whose quite pink colouring accords most charmingly with that of the sage. Here there is a front edging of the purple-leaved form of the native *Ajuga reptans*, broken by a few plants of aubrieta which make a pleasant repetition of the colour of the earlier, larger group. The colour now changes to the richer yellow of *Doronicum plantaginium*; with yellow tulips are still some purple iris in the middle, and *Viola gracilis* in the front. Now the main 'between plant' is the heuchera as the yellow flowers deepen to orange, with orange crown imperials at the back and tulips such as 'Thomas Moore', followed by 'La Merveille', all with a liberal interplanting of brown wallflower. This leads to the strong reds of the splendid tall tulip 'Gesneriana Major', with shorter earlier kinds, such as the bright little 'Artus'. As all these have a good setting of the dark satin leaf the eye is pleased by having a break of green leafage of the second group of veratrum, with the graceful myrrhis and Solomon's seal and more of the tall blooming doronicum.

Now there comes a cross path and beyond it the border widens as the main walk swings to the left near the hollies and passes out beyond by an arch in the yew hedge. This wider part is all rich yellow and orange, with kerria, *Berberis darwinii,* red and orange tulips and the dark heuchera, and, at the back, the rich red colouring of some bushes of red-leaved maples with an underplanting of the dark purple honesty.

Every year, as the arrangement becomes a little better, one sees how it may be further improved; there is no finality in gardening.

AN APRIL GARDEN

The flowers of March and early April are so precious that it is worth taking some pains to bring some of them together in a well-considered colour harmony. In my book *Colour Schemes in the Flower Garden* there is described, and illustrated by the plan below, a border for the early bulbs, such as scilla, chionodoxa, crocus and a few of the smaller narcissi, with purple fumitory, dog's-tooth violets and one or two other kinds of plants, the same border being covered later by hardy ferns that are planted between the drifts of the little bulbs, and, spreading over their places in full summer growth, completely hide the empty spaces left when they died down. But, seeing that there are several beautiful shrubby things that flower at the same early time, and that would combine delightfully for colour, I have lately planned

A plan for an April garden.

another piece of ground for them, and look forward with keen pleasure to the realization of the intended garden picture. It is at one of the points where garden joins woodland, and where there is a meeting of four grass paths. Two of these go upwards to the wood, the two others to lawn and to a quiet entrance way. The place is too good for its present overgrowth of *Gaultheria shallon*, beautiful and desirable though this fine subshrub is. Some of this will, therefore, be cleared away, plenty being left in the near neighbourhood, and the place will be planted as shown in the plan. It is a promontory jutting out from the wood, the middle part some two feet higher than the grass paths, with the ground coming down all ways to the point.

Some heavy lumps of the local Bargate stone are shown hatched across. They will come out of the ground with some feeling of stratification and (I hope) the appearance of a natural outcrop. The savin, cotoneaster and background of hollies lead to the wood there, and the larger mound to the right is fully clothed with a group of wild juniper and a thick mass of alpenrose. Here also the thick overgrowth of gaultheria will be partly cleared to allow two ranges of stones to be seen; at present it is so thick that the path is nearly closed. This narrow clearing on the side of the larger mound faces north-east, and will be a happy home for hart's-tongue ferns and a suitable place for their natural increase from self-sown spores.

The soil of the promontory is peaty sand. It will suit all the plants to be used, though possibly a little lime will be given to *Daphne mezereum* and *Hepatica transsilvanica*. It is quite remarkable that at a time of year when flowers are so few there should be so many whose colours tone so well together. The colour keynote of the main group is pinkish or purplish pink, with a little white, and it may be noted that the groups are so composed that though it is a garden for March and earliest April, it will be well clothed during the summer months; for the hardy ferns will cover the place of the departed dentaria, and the spreading summer leaf growth of the bergenia and heuchera will do the same for the purple fumitory and the dog's-tooth violet. As in all plant grouping, great value will be found in the use of what for want of a better term I know as between plants: for no masses of bloom, however well harmonized, have such a fine effect as they would have if supported and occasionally interrupted by stretches of foliage of dark or neutral quality. These between plants are here represented by the towering hollies at the back, enlivened by the shafts of the silver birches, and, nearer, by the savin, by the solid deep green of the alpine rhododendron, by the glossy, clean-leaved andromeda (*Leucothoe catesbaei*) and by the dull reddish, satin-surfaced foliage of the heuchera. The alpenrose and andromeda are out of the flower scheme because of their later season of blooming, and the heuchera because at any season the leaves are of better garden worth than the flowers. *Sedum rupestre*, also a later-blooming plant, comes into the same class, the whole growth turning a bronze red, in quality nearly matching the heuchera.

The colour changes a little on the side of the promontory facing the juniper mound, where white and pale yellow lead to the bluish hepaticas. The white vinca, next to the grass, is not one of the lesser periwinkles common in gardens, but a more tufted plant. It was collected wild in northern Italy, and is a very dainty and pretty thing [now known as *Vinca minor* 'Gertrude Jekyll'. *Corydalis cheilanthifolia* is a charming early plant. By the second week of

March the new foliage shows like fern fronds of brilliantly vivid green, to be followed by the graceful blooms of purest canary yellow. Its better-known companion, *C. ochroleuca*, has paler flowers and greyish leaves. *Lithodora diffusa* is here used as a between plant, with its sombre mass of deep green ground clothing. It is early to bloom, but not early enough to take a part in the March–April show; but it will be a point of interest throughout the summer.

Apart from the colour scheme indicated, there will be another a little further along of blue, white and palest yellow, including some early bulbs, that may form the subject of some later notes.

WALLFLOWERS IN THE SPRING GARDEN

Those who live on chalky soils should remember that they would do well to give special attention to the wallflower and all its tribe. Plants of the order *Cruciferae* will thrive in any good loam, but do specially well on chalk and are never happy or really vigorous in places where the soil is light or sandy. It is easy to remember this by thinking of the natural habitat of the wild wallflower: the joints and crevices in the masonry of old walls and ancient ruined buildings, where it is most usually found, the roots feeding on the relics of the old mortar.

Those who are on a suitable soil and who are able to give a separate place to a garden of spring flowers will have the opportunity of growing wallflowers to the very best advantage. They are splendid in long drifts as a groundwork to tulips of accompanying or contrasting colours – tulips of scarlet and deep orange with the blood-red colourings, pink tulips with ivory white, leading to white tulips rising from sheets of forget-me-not and aubrieta. Then tall yellow wallflowers, largely intergrouped with the tall doronicum, with yellow tulips in front and a bold backing of the plaited-leaved veratrum and the larger fern-like leaves of sweet cicely; and these running into clumps of Solomon's seal, with corresponding dwarf yellow wallflowers to the front. There are now splendid colourings of rich, deep orange that tone grandly into the mahogany browns, and form the finest possible setting for tulips of near colours.

Many as are the good new forms of the sweet and welcome wallflowers, there is one class of colouring that has as yet escaped the bettering of which it is undoubtedly capable at the hands of the selecting seed grower. The old purple wallflower is already a valuable plant, but the redder forms that have evidently been derived from it seem to have exclusively absorbed the energies of the grower, to the entire neglect of the really good cool purple that is so badly wanted – a purple inclining towards blue rather than towards red. We want such a purple to go with tulips 'Erguste' and 'Rev. Ewbank' and the old tall double 'Bleu Celeste'. It would also be a lovely thing in combination with white tulips and double *Narcissus poeticus*, with a ground covering of aubrieta and white primroses. Any influential seed house that would promote the growing of such a good purple wallflower would be doing a signal service to horticulture and could hardly fail of finding the just reward that awaits the production of something that is really wanted.

AUBRIETAS IN THE SPRING GARDEN

Those who make careful use of the best spring flowers have been rejoicing in some recent improvements in the aubrieta. Among these, the most valuable of those now well known is the beautiful variety 'Lavender', of good size, fully bloomed and of true aubrieta colour. In the progress of variation of a garden plant, growers are apt to overlook the best purpose or intention. The iures of size, novelty and variety are often illusive; they attract and lead into blind paths. The thing to look for is the purest beauty of which the plant is capable. In the matter of colouring in the aubrieta the very finest quality may often be picked out in a batch of seedlings of the type *A. deltoidea* var. *graeca*. It is clear, pure lavender purple rather light than deep in tone. We are grateful for the fine deep-coloured variety 'Dr Mules', but to the artist-gardener it is not a plant to use by itself in large quantity. Its value is best shown when a few plants are grouped with a larger number of a good form of the more typical colouring. Of the heavy reddish colourings, and even the deep purples inclining to reddish, as far as my own feeling and experience are concerned, they are better avoided altogether. The only colourings with anything approaching a reddish tint that seems to me desirable are the very beautiful palest pink 'Moerheimii', of Dutch origin, and a slightly darker one, bought out, I think by Messrs Barr, called 'Bridesmaid'. Both are extremely pretty plants and go well together. For the present the pure, rather light-coloured kinds resembling the fine 'Lavender' would seem to be the best. It was a pleasure last spring to receive from Mr R. Wallace of Colchester a very beautiful flower of the lavender type, but better, in that it had not so much of the pale eye that in 'Lavender' is rather too conspicuous. The absence of the white eye makes the flower much more effective in the mass. I am of opinion that the size of aubrieta bloom should not be further increased. Aubrieta the size of rocket or honesty would be a disquieting anomaly. It is not in the nature of the plant, a true alpine, to have large flowers. The mass of small blooms of good form and pure colouring is the true character of the plant and the source of its charm and attractiveness. These charming spring flowers deserve to be more widely grown, both in the rock garden and the border, than they are at present. Their cultivation is not difficult, and they are ideal for the amateur.

A SUMMER'S LEASE

A JUNE BORDER OF IRISES AND LUPINS

It is a great advantage in planning gardens, where suitable ground can be given, to allot a certain number of enclosed spaces for the flowers of a limited season only. It enables the designer to create a complete picture of flower beauty in a way that cannot be done where the bloom has to be spread over a longer time. Colour photography from nature has not yet reached such a degree of precision and accuracy as can do justice to a careful scheme of colour grouping, but the illustration [right] may serve as a suggestion of the effect of a double border, mainly of flag irises and lupins, at their fullest bloom in June.

The lupins are of three kinds: the perennial, in five distinct colourings – white, purple-blue, pale purple shading to white, pink and red-purple; then tree lupins, whites and yellow; and the good hybrid 'Somerset', which, I believe, we owe to Messrs Kelway of Langport. It is not so coarse in growth as the ordinary tree lupin, is very full of flower, and can have its lifetime prolonged for several years by severe pruning after blooming, some whole branches being cut away and the remainder shortened back. The pale purple-shaded perennial lupin is a very fine plant, differing in character from the usual kinds that are so easily grown from seed, in that its whole growth is larger and handsomer, but perfectly balanced and proportioned, with a form of rare perfection, both of leaf and flower spike. Increase of size, in plants of the same nature, often gives an impression of coarseness; but in the case of this good lupin the plant is more refined, although larger than its fellows. With me it never bears seed – all the others seed freely.

The white tree lupin is a charming plant both for such a border and for groups or single plants at shrubbery edges. As I know it, it is shorter-lived than 'Somerset', and is at its best the second year from seed. There are pink China roses in the June borders that group charmingly with it. Among the purple irises, a very useful plant is *Peltaria alliacea*, not so well known as its merit deserves. It is the white mass in the picture just this side of the tall yellow lupin; another mass of the same is further away on the right-hand side. It is a cruciferous plant, bearing spreading corymbs of soft white bloom; the individual flowers are of the sweet alyssum class, but of a warmer white and more showy. Nothing could better set off the masses of purple iris or the pink of the China rose. When the bloom is over, the lower parts of the stem have a half-woody, cabbage-stalk appearance that makes one think that the plant is done, but after the stems are cut down it spreads out at the root.

June borders devoted to iris and lupins, of which Miss Jekyll had her own strain, predating the famous Russell strain. An early colour autochrome, *circa* 1912.

The borders are arranged in colour groups, masses of purple and white, with the pink of China rose and pink lupin passing to pale and strong yellows, and then again through pale yellows to purple, white and pink. Irises of red-purple colouring have a group to themselves, with red-purple lupin and a groundwork of the red-bronze foliage of *Heuchera americana*; but they also pass through those that incline to pink, to the pure pink of the China roses, and then to white. *Olearia phlogopappa* is used for white bloom, and small bushes of golden privet among the yellows. A taller bush of golden privet looks over the yew hedge, and from some aspects joins in with the yellow. The pretty catmint (*Nepeta* x *faassenii*) and white and pink pinks come close to the path edges.

MIDSUMMER IN THE GARDEN

Although the richest and most gorgeous effects of massed flower beauty may not be had till later in the year, yet the blooms of middle summer, that is to say those of the four or five weeks of which the central point is midsummer day, 24 June, have a charm of freshness and young vigour which rewards the flower lover for his patient waiting during the many almost flowerless weeks of winter and the long spells of wet and cold of such a tardy spring as that of the present year. But we are now seeing the benefit of the copious rains of May and the early days of June, and the advantage of such conditions in the case of the tender plants put out for the summer; for they did not want a single can of water, but seemed to take hold and grow away directly they left their pots. The same good fortune attended the half-hardy annuals – planted out from frames and boxes – snapdragons, French and African marigolds, petunias, salpiglossis, ageratum and the rest. But the midsummer weeks have whole families of glorious plants of their own. Following the tulips and the hybrid irises of May come all the June-flowering flag irises, now in so many fine varieties. Modern arrangement for garden purposes has abolished the old half-botanical classification and has put them for better convenience into classes for colour. When we consult a good iris catalogue and find that there are no fewer than nine classes, and that in some of these classes there are as many as fifty named varieties, one gains some idea of the wealth of material that there is to choose from. Some of the older kinds are still indispensable, such as the free-flowering grey-white 'Florentina', the pale yellow *I. flavescens*, the deep yellow 'Aurea' and several of the other old favourites. The stately *Iris* 'pallida dalmatica' [now *I. pallida* subsp. *pallida*] is still unrivalled, with its grand presence, its large pale blue lavender bloom and its handsome and persistent foliage; this last quality makes it one of the best irises for the mixed flower border or for a prominent place in the upper regions of bold rock work, for whereas the greater number of the flag irises lose their leaves early, 'pallida dalmatica' holds them in vigorous perfection the summer through. It is well, if space admits, to have a separate piece of garden devoted to irises. If they are planted in long shaped groups diagonally to the line of the borders, with spaces between for spring-sown annuals, these would hide the withering iris foliage and give a fresh display in the same ground in the later summer months.

The peonies of the albiflora class are another noble group of midsummer plants also deserving a special garden. It is a good plan to combine roses and peonies. Nothing is more usual than for the beds or borders of a rose garden to have a thin, unclothed appearance. But if peonies and roses are intergrouped, the large, widespreading foliage of the peonies gives just the generous setting that serves to enhance the beauty of the roses. The peonies are the first to bloom, and by the time they are over the roses are coming on well.

In the early midsummer weeks there is the charming and abundant bloom of the common pink China rose, good anywhere in the garden but of special value in the narrow borders that are usual close round a house, and so pleasant to see from the rooms inside when the fresh pink blooms come up just clear of the lower panes of the window. If it is combined with bushes of rosemary and lavender and the free-flowering *Olearia phlogopappa* it will be about the best filling for this kind of place, which is too often planted with rows of summer flowers only. The low-growing busy Scotch briars will also be in place in such house borders, as well as in other parts of the garden. They are the cultivated varieties of the native *Rosa pimpinellifolia*, a desirable plant in itself, with its white bloom, the opening colour of which is a faint lemon yellow, and its large black hips that are handsome in autumn. There are many varieties of these pretty Scotch briars – double white, rosy and deeper red, and pure yellow, all pretty things and suited for half-wild planting as well as for the garden proper. They are also good seaside plants, as the type may be found in many places on our coasts where heath-bearing land comes near the sea.

The Oriental poppies are also among the joys of early midsummer, of splendid effect if boldly grouped with some background of yew or other dark foliage; the tall, upright dark red *P. orientale* var. *bracteatum* at the back and then an intergrouping of some good form of the older scarlet and the new or salmon colours; this may sound a doubtful colour mixture, but the effect is fine, not only in the garden but as cut flowers indoors.

Perennial lupins, now in many good varieties, are among the most striking of the early midsummer flowers. They may be put into three classes. The true *L. polyphyllus* in white, pink, purple and a variety of lilac shades; the tree lupin in yellow and white; and the slightly woody hybrids of these two. The yellow tree lupin is a bold-growing plant of erect habit with an efficient lifetime of two to three years; its life may be lengthened and its shape improved by hard pruning in the late summer. It is a capital thing for filling up spaces between newly planted shrubs, and when young wall shrubs have been planted with unavoidable gaps between it can be trained to the wall and makes an excellent temporary filling. The white tree lupin is a smaller thing of weaker habit. It may be held up by clever staking; but is perhaps best unsupported, when it flowers profusely, sometimes not more than a foot above ground.

Other border flowers of the time are polemoniums, of which the best is *P. caeruleum* subsp. *himalayanum*; the red valerian of gardens (the proper name of which is centranthus), anchusa, rockets purple and white, orange lilies, day lily (hemerocallis), feather hyacinth, the herbaceous *Clematis recta*, gaillardias, Spanish iris, *Oenothera fruticosa*, *Campanula persicifolia*, *Delphinium* Belladonna [Group], the early *Gladiolus colvillei* 'The Bride', the large purple cranesbill *Geranium ibericum*, the tall *Asphodelus ramosis*, St Bruno's lily (*Anthericum*), the fine scarlet *Geum* 'Mrs Bradshaw', with lower growths of London pride, thrift, the old white and other pinks, and the dwarf *Campanula garganica* and *C. portenschlagiana*. The dampest and coolest parts of the borders will suit the stately *Aruncus dioicus* and its relative, the double form of the native meadowsweet, and the purple meadow rue. In wilder ground there will be wide groups of *Rubus parviflorus* with its pure white flowers like single roses, and its handsome vine-like foliage; also the nearly related *R. odoratus*, a rather taller and more woody plant with light crimson bloom and a viscous stickiness about the buds and stem that has that excellent scent of the dying strawberry leaves. In a woodland clearing near the garden there is a goodly show of Ghent azaleas and another is of rhododendrons carefully grouped for colour. A sheltered sunny place has a collection of the hardier cistuses whose blossoming time closely follows that of the azaleas. Lilacs are nearly over, but *Kalmia latifolia* takes its place in the sequence of shrub bloom, with the graceful deutzias. That capital *Viburnum plicatum* is almost a solid mass of its white ball blossom, surpassing even the old guelder rose. The abundant but much less showy flower of the type *V. opulus* gives promise of a heavy crop of its handsome red berries in the autumn.

SUMMER FLOWERS CAREFULLY ARRANGED

It has been one of the pleasant tasks of the garden to provide for the use of the summer flowers – the tender things that were formerly called bedding plants. A space of ground of triangular shape, with a boundary of high wall on one side and of low walls on the other, is devoted to these plants. As the wide end of the triangle would have been too broad a space for good effect and convenient working, a sort of raised backbone was put up, consisting of a double low dry walling filled in with good garden soil. At the end where the triangle contracts the dry walling swings in to the path on both sides, so that the whole of the small end is of raised borders. These ends and the axial backbone are planted with yuccas, crinums and phormiums that stand well up and, with their more solid aspect, make a good background to the softer plants. These are grouped in good harmonies of colour. In the immediate foreground there is a wide drift of the pretty yellowish white *Gladiolus* 'Lily Lehmann', with yellow and white snapdragons, pale yellow cannas and variegated maize. A corner group of marguerite 'Mrs Sander', though always a beautiful thing, is but a poor substitute for the *Lilium longiflorum* – a subject of wartime abstinence – to which the place properly belongs. All this patch of white and yellow is bordered by a favourite mixture, of the useful old variegated mint *Mentha suaveolens* 'Variegata', the pure lemon yellow *Calceolaria amplexicaulis* and the golden foliage of *Tanacetum* 'Golden Feather'. These are informally mixed; the mint, which would have grown too tall, has been several times pinched, and the bloom of the calceolaria is led up into it so as best to show its bright pale yellow colouring.

Towards the further corner, nearer the arch, the colour changes, passing through palest pink of geranium, gladiolus, penstemon and snapdragon to soft reds. Further round to the right the colour deepens to fullest reds, with ruddy-leaved red cannas, scarlet lobelia, geranium, penstemon and dwarf dahlias, with accompanying foliage of deep red ricinus and iresine, the same kind of colouring with different plant arrangement being here on both sides of the path. Further on again the colouring comes back to the tender pinks, leading to yellows and whites, the whole triangle being a good mass of yuccas, with a groundwork of heliotrope, ageratum, and an interplanting of pale pink ivy-leaved geranium and sweet alyssum.

The flowering mass of *Solanum laxum* against the weather-boarding of a barn acts as a background for a double border of grey, purple, pink and white colouring. Here there are pink hollyhocks, with large groups of echinops, and *Clematis* 'Jackmannii' trained over on stout pea sticks, gypsophila, lavender, the purple larkspur (*Consolida ajacis*), ageratum, light, and dark purple China asters, with pink and purple gladiolus and white snapdragons and penstemons, the whole being intergrouped with the grey foliage of *Artemisia ludoviciana* and *A. stelleriana*. The silver grey of the old weather-boarding of the barn is a good background, and forms part of the picture. The bush of *Romneya coulteri*, shown more in detail, is in the border next to the barn, just under the white solanum. Both these and the fig on the return wall enjoy the warm, sheltered border facing a little to the south of west.

THE FLOWER BORDER

This is the simplest name for the border that is to hold and display the best of our hardy flowers with any admixture of tender plants that may be desirable. Quite commonly it is called the herbaceous border, but many of its indispensable occupants are not herbaceous; or it is called the hardy flower border, but that name, too, loses its justification when we fill up with tender plants and half-hardy annuals. Therefore it had better be simply the flower border. The border itself may be of any size or length and should be considered and treated accordingly. Sometimes it is a double border with flowers on each side of the path, and this is, in many cases, a convenient arrangement. Where a plot of ground is of small size – anything under an acre – and, as is so often the case in suburban lots, in form a parallelogram with the shorter measurement next the road, it is a good plan to set the house only a little way back and then to devote a space at the back of the house (except for the width of a road or path of access) to a lawn set round with shrubs and flowers and any small trees that may be needed for shade. Then in the middle of this space, in a line with the longer axis of the ground, to drive a straight path straight along with a flower

The main Hardy Flower Border.

The main Hardy Flower Border.

border to right and left, backed by an evergreen hedge. At the end there should be a good summerhouse and all the rest of the space behind the two hedges can be kitchen garden, well screened from view. In larger places there is more scope, and perhaps a simple flower border of ample width and length, backed by a high wall, is the way in which we may best show and enjoy our flowers. Such a border may well be one hundred and fifty feet long and something like eighteen feet from the wall to the path. This will allow for a space of four feet for shrubs trained to the wall and then for a narrow alley – not a made path, but just a way to go along – convenient for access to the wall and for getting at the plants in the back of the border. In front it is convenient to have a hard path, whether of gravel or paving, but if next to the path there is a certain amount of lawn space it is a great advantage, as it enables the whole effect of the flower border to be seen from various distances and from many different points of view.

A long life of gardening and some early training in the fine arts have taught me the supreme importance of having the flowers well arranged for colours, so that the whole border becomes a picture instead of a scattered collection of unrelated colourings. I have found it the most convenient, as well as the most effective plan, to have at the two ends plants of cool colouring and to come gradually, by a progression of related colour harmonies, to a culmination of gorgeousness in the region of the middle of the length. Thus, supposing the border to face nearly south, we begin at the western end with some good blues in bold groups – delphinium and anchusa, to be followed by the steel-blue of eryngium. There is something about flowers of pure blue colouring that seems to demand a treatment with a contrast, so that just here the rule that in general seems the safest to follow, that of harmonious sequence, is in abeyance, and though there is nothing against treating the pure blues with a progression of violet and purple they are to me more enjoyable if they are given a distinct contrast of palest yellow and white. Here we have a pure white foxglove, the tall yellow thalictrum, verbascum and *Oenothera glazioviana*. The two last are specially suited for the place I have in mind, as it is partly shaded by a high wall and a large Spanish chestnut that stand not far off, and neither of these plants are at their best in hot sunshine.

The pale yellows in the border are followed by the deeper yellow of coreopsis, helenium and some of the less weedy of the perennial sunflowers. Soon we come to the splendid deep orange of African marigolds and the rich mahogany browns of the French marigolds both tall and dwarf. Then come deep orange dahlias backing fiery clumps of kniphofia, passing on to the pure scarlet of dahlias and cannas, salvias, gladioli and bedding geraniums. The use of these grand summer plants is one reason why the border had better now be called hardy or herbaceous, for there are no hardy plants that will answer the same purpose. It is true that there are monarda and *Lobelia cardinalis* and some grand phloxes, but the border is not too dry for the two first, which are happier in almost boggy ground, and scarlet phloxes brown badly in hot sunshine – moreover it is certainly more important that the border shall be beautiful than that it should be either strictly hardy or herbaceous.

At the back of the mass of rich red is a group of towering hollyhocks, blood-red, with a few of a rich, dark claret colour. The whole of the red region has also an interplanting of the red-leaved *Atriplex hortensis,* and, nearer the front, of a French form of annual amaranthus with dull red flowers of a pleasant quality and red-tinted leaves; a much better plant than the commoner form with magenta flowers. The colouring of the border now returns to orange, then passing again to yellow and on to the cooler colours. But at the eastern end we favour purple rather than blue. The wall here has a wisteria, and in the back of the border there are some *Clematis* 'Jackmanni', to be trained forward into their proper place, and some of the September aster; in the middle spaces there are galega, erigeron and *Salvia virgata*. One large drift is of the useful old garden plant clary (*Salvia sclarea*). As it comes freely from seed and we always have plants in reserve, we dig it right up when the best of its beauty is over and drop in some hydrangeas in pots in the same place. With the purple there are also white flowers – again the pure white foxglove, the tall white daisy *Leucanthemella serotina,* the fine white garden form of *Campanula lactifolia* var. *macrantha* and a good quantity of grey foliage, rue, santolina, artemisia and *Senecio cineraria*. At this end we have no yellow – only purple, pink and white. At both extreme ends the border is a little raised, and there we have groups of yucca; the taller *Y. gloriosa* and *Y. recurvifolia* and

the shorter-growing *Y. filamentosa*, telling objects when seen from a distance or from either end. There are many other plants in the border, but only enough are mentioned to illustrate the method of colouring, and even those only as a suggestion, for you may have others that in your own gardens may do the same work better and be more easily available.

As it is not possible to have any one border full of bloom for the whole summer, we plant so that the display begins only about the middle of June and is in some sort of beauty till the end of September. There is no attempt to have all high plants at the back of the border; in fact some of the tallest are pulled right down. The effect is all the better if something tall, such as a group of hollyhocks, shoots up like a mountain peak only here and there along the length, and it is all the better if some plants of fair height such as the mulleins (verbascums) and foxgloves advance into the middle of the border; there should be no monotony of evenly graded heights. I have found the disadvantage of such monotony when a special border for September was first made. It is mainly for the early Michaelmas daisies and though they vary in height from two and a half to seven feet, yet this was not enough, and the borders, though quite satisfactorily full of flower, had a certain dullness of form. In later years this was remedied by some tall dahlias and white hollyhocks, and, best of all, by a little silvery willow that soon went up ten feet and had planted just behind it a *Clematis flammula*, which grows up through its branches and flings down a cataract of its pretty cream-white blooms among the purple daisies.

The front edge of the main flower border should also have careful consideration. The natural tendency is to plant it with small things, but in a border of considerable size, something of bold and solid appearance is helpful. Here is a chance for a good use of the broad-leaved bergenia. The best for foliage is the major form of *B. cordifolia* with grand leathery leaves that stand all through the winter. The bloom comes early in the year and is a rank magenta pink, but it is easy to cut it out. Then there are the hostas, the best being the bright green-leaved *H. plantaginea* var. *japonica* and the glaucous *H. sieboldiana*. *H. plantaginea* var. *japonica* is best placed where there is slight shade as the leaves are apt to

OPPOSITE
LEFT *Hosta sieboldiana* at Folly Farm, a garden designed by Miss Jekyll in 1906.
RIGHT The red section of the Main Hardy Flower Border, *circa* 1912.

The Grey Garden, *circa* 1912, a tapestry of subtle colouring based on a structure of grey foliage, set before a grey-green wooden barn.

burn in hot sunshine, but *H. sieboldiana* has foliage of stouter build that stands sun well. A useful front-edge plant, though not wide leaved, is the crested form of the common tansy. The multiplication of the leaf divisions seems to intensify the colour of the whole plant whose feathery masses are of a splendid deep green. But the bloom stems should be carefully cut out and the leaf tufts themselves cut back at least once in the summer, in order to keep it in good form and under a foot in height.

There are many useful ways of arranging and contriving that have come to my mind from time to time during many years' work among flowering plants – work which stimulates invention and the devising of means to meet the various needs that are constantly occurring. These I shall hope to say something about in a later article.

THE USE OF GREY FOLIAGE WITH BORDER PLANTS

There are some ranges of colouring among flowers that are certainly best set off by a setting of a good grey foliage. For many years it has been one of the pleasant problems of the garden to work out such arrangements, either at the ends of long borders or in shorter detached portions where the restricted scheme of colouring is more isolated. All flowers of purple, lilac and pink are thankful for being grouped with grey, and if to these is added a suitable quantity of white bloom, there will be its own brilliancy added to the pretty harmony of tints that in themselves range from the tenderest to the most intense colouring.

In the case of a wide flower border that has a length of some hundred and fifty feet the two ends are planted with grey foliage. At the western end the grey is the setting for blue flowers, with others of tender colouring, delphinium, anchusa, *Salvia patens* and the like, with pale pink gladiolus and white and pale pink snapdragons. The colour arrangement then passes to pale yellow, then to full yellow and through orange to an increase of strength of orange and red; then to its culmination where strongest red is grouped with dark red

August borders, a riot of rich colour preparing the eye for the subtlety of the Grey Garden into which it leads.

foliage. It then passes back through the reds and yellows, and the eye, having been saturated with the brilliant warm colouring, is all the more inclined to receive the cool effects of grey and lilac and comforting grey. This is the eastern end of the border, where, after passing along something like three-quarters of its length, it is crossed by a path leading to a gateway in the high wall at the back. Here the border is raised about a foot on each side, partly for the sake of the yuccas, which are always thankful for a slight eminence, and partly to give a little emphasis to the approach to the gateway. To take the plants as they come, here are *Stachys byzantina* and *Artemisia stelleriana*, the stachys partly in the joints of the two or three courses of dry walling that support the raised border, and some plants of a grey-leaved helianthemum. Behind these come the yuccas with their own glaucous blades of foliage and the blue-grey of bushes of rue, a valuable plant for this work. Further along by the path edge there is *Senecio cineraria*, followed by santolina. Any spaces among the grey foliage of the foreground are filled with dwarf ageratum and palest pink intermediate snapdragon. Then comes a group of a common old garden plant, often despised, perhaps because it is the double form of a native plant. But pink flowers in late summer are none too many, and the old double soapwort should be properly valued. There is a so-called improved variety with flowers of a deeper colour of bad quality that should be avoided. The group of soapwort is partly overgrown by a cloud of *Clematis flammula* which also covers the site, white *Campanula latifolia* and the white foxglove of the earlier year. Further back are white dahlias and a mass of *Clematis* 'Jackmannii' trained over pea sticks, and at the extreme end a plumy mass of *Artemisia lactiflora* with *Aster lanceolatus* subsp. *lanceolatus* partly drawn over still effective clouds of clary. The only plants not actually growing in the border are the hydrangeas, which are dropped in in pots to fill every vacant space.

I have a double border [illustrated opposite] where the flowers are white and pale yellow to right and left. The foliage and flowers of the immediate foreground is of mixed masses of variegated mint, *Lobularia maritime*, golden feather pyrethrum, the pale yellow *Calceolaria amplexicalis* and the fine striped grass *Glyceria maxima* var. *variegata*. The flowers are a good form of the useful white daisy *Leucanthemum* x *superbum*, pale yellow snapdragons, and, on the left, the grand white annual balsum sold as *Impatiens roylei*, but which is probably only a white form of the well-known *Impatiens glandulifera*. Beyond this grouping the colour changes to purple and pink with grey foliage. On the right is a bold group of clary (*Salvia sclarea*) now out of bloom, but still with a useful effect of grey-purple cloudiness. Then comes a cross path, and beyond it, just through the rose arch, a short piece of double border entirely given to an effect of grey, pink, purple and white. There are big bushes of gypsophila and important masses of *Clematis* 'Jackmannii', with the strong purple of larkspur (*Consolida ajacis*), ageratum tall and dwarf, China asters white and purple, snapdragons tall and short, white and pink, and gladioli pale pink and purple. Tall pink hollyhocks are at the back and large clumps of globe thistle. The liberal quantity of grey foliage puts it all together. In the middle and towards the back is *Artemisia ludoviciana*, from four to five feet high, allowed to flower, flower and all being a pleasant grey. But the plant is all the more useful, besides being of a capital silvery grey, in that it can be cut back to any height; a plant that shows at the edge of the path is only six inches. The mass of bloom in front is larkspur (*Consolida ajacis*) from self-sown seed. It would have shot up too tall and have bloomed too early for the rest of the border, whose time is August, but it was pinched back in good time, a treatment that made it branch into many more blooming spikes and kept the bloom back to the proper season. Above this there is a mass of flower of *Clematis* 'Jackmannii' trained over stiff pea sticks to occupy part of the back, and in one part brought forward almost to the front, where it meets and partly rests on a bush of gypsophila. In other parts of the borders the grey foliage, besides the taller artemisia, is of *A. stelleriana*, stachys and santolina. The grey weather-boarding of the barn comes into the picture and forms a specially suitable background from one point of view where the main group of pink hollyhocks is seen against it.

BEDDING OUT

We hold to the old term for putting out the summer flowers, although our gardens are no longer dependent on the tender plants alone. We use them now in quite different and more sensible ways, whether as companions and auxiliaries to the hardy perennials or in spaces by themselves. In what we may now call the bad old days the object was to make a bright show for a scant three months in the more important parts of the pleasure garden, leaving them bare for the rest of the year, or, at best, planted in autumn more or less unsatisfactorily with spring-blooming flowers. I have no desire to depreciate a bedded-out garden of the older kind when it exactly fits a need, and especially when it is done with the spirit of enlightenment of our present taste and knowledge. Many a great house has an important parterre in close connection with the design of the building, and the flowers with which it is to be filled are only wanted for display after the London season. But, in this case, by means of the better ways that we have come to know of late years of arranging masses of colour, and also by the much wider range of material provided by our growers, the careful designer has more freedom of hand and has been enabled to redeem the parterre from what it too often was – a mere garish display – to a delightful presentment of colour beauty.

Even without having a parterre of formal design there is plenty of opportunity for a good use of the tender plants if it is decided to have them in a place to themselves. In my own case there is a three-cornered piece of ground where we try for good effects. It has a kind of axial backbone about four feet wide, raised by means of a couple of courses of local stone and filled with permanent plants of solid aspect – yucca, phormium, crinum and the great *Euphorbia characias* subsp. *wulfenii*. The rest of the space is chiefly for dahlias, cannas, gladioli, penstemons, antirrhinums and geraniums. A high wall on one side is made to play its part in one of the chief effects, for here there is a long stretch of brilliant red, and it is tempered and harmonized and enhanced by an intermixture of ruddy foliage richly dark. On the wall a *Prunus cerasifera* 'Pissardii' is stretched out to cover some square yards, toning delightfully with a tall old dahlia of deepest claret colour; then come strong red dahlias grouped with more bushes of *Prunus* 'Pissardi' and *Ricinus communis* 'Gibsoni'; then dark-foliaged cannas and tall snapdragons with bloom of deepest red velvet and dark leaves; then lower scarlet dahlias leading to a front mass of scarlet geranium 'Paul Crampel'. A streak of irisine runs behind these, and among the geraniums is a French variety of love-lies-bleeding: not the usual large magenta one, but the same plant with a much lower habit and of a dusky red colour both of leaf and bloom that makes a dimly glowing ground for the more brilliant flowers.

How I wish that such a thing existed as a dahlia with reddish foliage something like that of the dark snapdragon or the red-leaved scarlet lobelia, for the green of the dahlia leaves is in itself uninteresting and is obtrusive in my colour arrangement.

After the harmony of strong reds the colour passes through paler tints to a region of white and yellow. Here at the back are dahlias, the tall single 'Victoria' with the fresh-looking green of striped maize; then some tall white and pale yellow snapdragons leading to white pompon dahlias and the pretty kind, 'Lady Primrose', a plant of weak habit that easily allows it to be trained almost flat to the ground; also cannas, pale of leaf and pure yellow of bloom, and double white marguerite; and near the path a mixture that is always satisfactory. It is a groundwork of the variegated form of *Mentha suaveolens* 'Variegata' intergrouped with *Calceolaria amplexicaulis,* the calceolaria rather thicker towards the back. Quite to the front are little patches and single plants of the formerly much misused golden feather pyrethrum [now *Tanacetum*]. Some of this is allowed to flower, for its

white bloom, yellow centred, helps the picture; in other plants the flower is nipped out the better to show the yellow foliage. The mint is tipped three or four times in the season so that it grows bushy and does not flower.

In the perennial flower borders the tender plants combine with the permanent ones and greatly help to link up and carry on the blooming season. At one end of a long border, in a region of blue, white and pale yellow, there is a general filling of white and yellow snapdragons and the primrose-coloured African marigold, while the front spaces are completed with the pretty Cape daisy (*Felicia amelloides)* and the dwarf *Lobelia* 'Cobalt Blue'. Then, where in the middle of the border's length the colouring is of orange and red, the main filling is of the splendid orange African marigold with the fiery snapdragon 'Orange King', scarlet salvia, and the rich brown and orange dwarf French marigold. At the farther end, where the colour is purple, white and pink, with grey foliage, there is tall and dwarf ageratum, tall white snapdragons, and pink ivy geraniums here and there at the border's edge.

Permanent planting in a parterre, the Great Platt, Hestercombe, Somerset, designed by Miss Jekyll and Sir Edwin Lutyens in 1904.

MISTS AND MELLOW FRUITFULNESS

PLANTING FOR AUTUMN EFFECT

There would still be time, if the work is taken in hand at once, to make some arrangements of plants that would give beautiful effects of colour combination for the late summer and autumn. Some of the most refined and effective of these tone pictures are those that are in colourings of pink, white, lavender and purple, with grey foliage. Where the work of preparation has been done in the autumn there will be lavender and China roses, with gypsophila, Japanese anemones and echinops as a solid foundation, and where these occur it is easy to add some summer flowers and annuals. But if the combination has to be made afresh, it may best be done by transplanting some autumn-divided roots of some of the September-blooming Michaelmas daisies, such as the strong-growing 'Robert Parker' for tallest, with 'F. W. Burbidge' and 'Margaret' for medium height and *Aster amellus* and *A. sedifolius* for the front. With these there may be some groups of the purple gladioli such as 'Blue Jay' and 'Baron Hulot', and for pale pink the lovely 'America'.

Within the first fortnight of May should be sown some pink and white annuals. For whites, *Gypsophila elegans*, white jacobea and white linaria; for pink, best of all *Godetia* 'Double Rose', a plant that is not only beautiful in the border, but of great value for cutting. Then among the asters of medium height nothing is better than *Lavatera trimestris* of the old pure, tender pink colouring, avoiding the so-called improved variety, whose colour, though stronger, has a suspicion of rank quality from which the older one is quite free.

Then of half-hardy annuals there will be the best of the purple and white China asters, choosing them within the ostrich plume, comet and Victoria classes, with the taller 'Mammoth', formerly known as 'Vick's White'. Heliotrope and ageratum, both tall and dwarf, will come in the front of the border, and it is well to leave places for dropping in pots of *Lilium longiflorum*. If the border is of some width hollyhocks, white and pink, should have been provided in the autumn with white dahlias planted this spring.

SEPTEMBER FLOWERS

Although there is still a wealth of flower beauty in the middle month of autumn, when dahlias are at their most gorgeous and cannas, penstemons, geraniums and snapdragons are at their full growth, yet by the middle of the month one cannot help seeing that many flowers are already over or fast failing. It is therefore the more desirable, where space allows, to have special borders for a good three weeks' display that shall begin about the second week of the month and go on into October. Such an arrangement is provided in a Surrey garden where a double border, backed by a hornbeam hedge, is devoted to this season. The earlier kinds of Michaelmas daisies form the greater part of the show, among them *Aster* 'Cloudy Blow', one of the best of the newer kinds, a mass of soft double bloom in a charming tone of soft lavender and a plant of moderate height. Another new kind, 'Lady Lloyd', short enough to come near the front, is a pleasant mass of pinkish mauve. For the rest the most notable is the splendid 'Ryecroft Purple', the finest of that colouring of the novae-angliae section, and the remarkably fine grey lilac *A. puniceus*, with a generous front planting of the always admirable *A. sedifolius*. The borders are fully exposed to the sun, and no aster, especially *A. puniceus*, which is almost a swamp plant, can endure drought; therefore, as the borders are not near water, they are surfaced with a good mulch of half-decayed leaves about the end of June.

Towards the middle of the left-hand border is a little silvery-leaved willow, yearly cut back, into which a *Clematis flammula* is trained. Just beyond it is a clump of the foam-white *Aster lanceolatus* subsp. *simplex* grouped with another *C. flammula* which nearly matches it and is trained over some slanted pea sticks to come over and down to the front close to the path, where it joins into a mass of the pink *Sedum spectabile* and the grey of stachys foliage, the same kind of cool pink being repeated by Japanese anemones at the back and end. This grand sedum, beloved of bees and butterflies, is also in large front patches on the other side. The fine white daisy *Leucanthemella serotina*, is rather freely used among the Michaelmas daisies, and here and there at the back is a group of white dahlias. The season of these borders is too late for many of the China asters, but is just right for the very fine late kind formerly known as 'Vick's White', but that is now called 'Mammoth'. Other flowers in these borders are white snapdragons, white early cosmos and the fine deep purple *Aconitum japonicum*. The front edge is largely of the woolly *Stachys byzantina*, whose blooming shoots are cut out early in June the better to encourage the growth of the carpet of silvery leaves.

As the border is of fair length, the general colouring of purple, lilac, pink and grey has an interruption near the middle, where for a few yards it changes to pale yellow and white. Here at the back are white dahlias and the tall white daisy; the middle space is of the primrose-coloured African marigold, and the front of a favourite mixture of the canary yellow *Calceolaria amplexicaulis*, with the variegated *Mentha suaveolens* 'Variegata', the handsome striped grass *Glyceria maxima* and the yellowish foliage of the dwarf *Tanacetum* 'Golden Feather'. These plants, suitably intergrouped, form a delightful mixture of harmonizing tints, and the whole change serves as a refreshing contrast to the main colouring of the borders.

September borders *circa* 1912. These double borders were set between hornbeam hedges and were designed to show off the early Michaelmas daisies with other late summer flowers such as dahlias and marigolds.

Another glory of September is the quantity of bloom on some well-established plants of *Crinum* x *powellii*. They are in a deep border of light soil facing nearly south. The grand lily-like flowers are beautiful from the middle of August till Michaelmas.

GUELDER ROSE IN AUTUMN

When shrubs are planted for effect of autumn foliage the guelder rose (*Viburnum opulus* 'Roseum') should not be forgotten. There is now a wild garden picture of, as yet, 'subdued splendour', but daily brightening to a gorgeous display where a wide mass of Ghent azaleas, now grown into large bushes, are seen against some scarlet oaks, with a beech tree forming a deep golden background. Some bushes of *Vaccinium angustifolium* var. *laevifoliumi* are near the front, their foliage almost scarlet. Had there been more room behind the azaleas, a filling of guelder rose, or, better still, the type, berried form, would have been there, with one liquidambar as the culminating point of sumptuous colouring.

MICHAELMAS DAISIES

At this time of the year, when the flower borders, if not quite done for, are at least at their last stage before final dissolution, it is a joy to come upon a well-planted border of the perennial asters, with their clear, fresh colouring all the more accentuated by contrast with the general sombre rustiness of the greater part of the neighbouring vegetation. For the extension of the time of enjoyment of hardy flowers, as well as for their own beauty,

October borders by Helen Allingham. The last of the garden areas to flower, this was conveniently close to the house and later had a view through the hedging out to the distant landscape.

it is well worthwhile to have them in a separate border in some place rather away from other gardening. If a double border can be given to them alone, it is all the better, and it will add another month to the life of the hardy flower garden. In fact, it is desirable to have two separate double borders of Michaelmas daisies in different places. There are now such large numbers of desirable kinds that the difficulty is to choose few enough, for, unless a daisy border is of unusual size or length, a better effect is gained by using not more than twelve to fifteen kinds in bold drifts than by having a larger number in lesser patches.

A limited number of good kinds having been secured, the whole effect of the borders will depend upon good arrangement and good staking. It is much best, as in all other flower border work, to do it by a plan on paper. If space can be given for a border or double border for September and another for October, both should be carefully planned; then a good range of kinds, both early and late, can be used to advantage. There are such borders in the present writer's garden. As the one for September has a greater length than the later one, some other colours and kinds of plants are introduced, though the main effects are of the early daisies. Here are *Aster sedifolius* and *A. amellus,* with low plants of whiteish or glaucous foliage, chiefly stachys and white pink, near the path, with a rather thick interplanting of ageratum; then the moderate-sized *A. lateriflorus,* the pretty, smallish 'Collerette Blanche' and some seedlings of good short habit, and, further back, the taller kinds derived mostly from novi-belgii and novae-angliae. It may be as well to remind readers that novi-belgii accounts for the greater number of the tall and medium tall kinds with smooth stems and leaves, and that novae-angliae is the parent of those, also tall and of middle height, that have the stems and leaves rough and hairy and a rather strong characteristic scent, the varieties of novi-belgii being much the more numerous.

To return to the early daisy border, among the kinds of medium height are the splendid *Aster novae-angliae* 'Ryecroft Purple' and another of the same family named 'Mitchellii'. At the back is one of the best, the grand *A. puniceus*, with its large, closely clustered heads of palest grey-lilac, and a number of the tall varieties of novi-belgii; with some groups of white dahlias and in front of these that newer *Aster* 'Mrs Tynam' about three feet high, of pinkish mauve colouring. Throughout the borders are groups of plants with grey foliage, such as *Phlomis fruiticosa*, lyme grass and *Euphorbia characias*, pleasantly breaking the flowery masses. Some groups of flowers of pink colouring are admitted in this double border – Japanese anemones, double soapwort and the large stonecrop *Sedum spectabile*, the last always covered with bees and butterflies. Near the middle of the length of the border on both sides is a break of palest yellow. Here the flowers are *Dahlia* 'Lady Primrose', pale sulphur African marigold, lemon white snapdragon and flowering golden feather feverfew at the foot.

By the time the September borders begin to look a little overrun, the ones for the later kinds are brilliant with their clear, fresh beauty. Here there are no other coloured flowers; the starworts are alone, with the sole inclusion of the great white daisy *Leucanthemella serotina*, whose time of flowering, being intermediate, serves equally in the borders of the two seasons. Here is again *A. amellus*, a rather later variety being chosen; then the low-growing pinkish 'Mme. Soynuce', a late dwarf novi-belgii seedling and a lateish *A. lateriflorus*, again with ageratum and stachys next the path. Then 'J. Dickson' and 'Archer Hind', both of moderate growth; 'Flora', a home-grown seedling of pale mauve-lilac; *A. cordifolius* 'Elegans' and its lovely variant 'Diana', raised by the late Revd C. Wolley-Dod; the fine old 'Robert Parker', 'Top Sawyer', 'Ella', and three of the late novae-angliae, namely, 'J. Bowman' (reddish purple), 'Constance' (violet/purple) and a pale pink novae-angliae 'Ruber'. There are now several varieties of this in deeper pink colourings, but there is always a danger in the reddish colouring of Michaelmas daisies; it is apt to come of a heavy quality, neither good in itself nor easily employable from the artist's point of view among the fresher lilacs and purples. The older pale pink 'Ruber' is especially beautiful with the large white daisy *Leucanthemella serotina*, and is purposely trained through and among it. *Aster thomsonii* and *A.* 'Hon. Edith Gibbs' are two beautiful kinds that should not be omitted. In addition to those, or as alternatives, some of the fine newer asters should be grown: the grand 'Climax', the double 'Beauty of Colwall'; the still more recent 'Queen', 'Magnet H. Adams', and the two novae-angliae 'Lil Fardell' and 'Ryecroft Pink'. Among shorter-growing new kinds there should be 'Lady Lloyd', 'Esther' and 'Lovely'.

In soils of a light character, and possibly in all, it is well to divide and replant the asters every year, freshly preparing and manuring the ground. If they are left for two or three years they spread considerably; then the outward overgrowth, which contains the best material for replanting, is chopped off with the spade, leaving only the less profitable part of the plant.

At the same time, some of the bolder-growing kinds and any of the white daisies that come rather forward can be pinched back to half their length. This keeps them shorter and causes them to branch without delaying the flowering season. Only varieties of cordifolius and novae-angliae are not pinched, because the graceful arching form of cordifolius would be disturbed and because novae-angliae is found to be shy of blooming after being cut back. Before any shortening, the borders should be surveyed from end to end and the pinching done where the eye requires that the plant should go back. It may be done a little more boldly than the appearance of the border actually demands in June, as the flowering sprays are apt to come forwarder than one anticipates when they are loaded with bloom and sometimes burdened with rain.

THE SURVIVORS

By the end of October, after some occasional nights of rather severe frost and violent storms of rain, one does not expect to see much remaining of the summer flowers. Even the Michaelmas daisies that should still be in beauty have been destroyed by the wet and are deplorable objects, hanging in sodden masses of tangled rags. One of the pluckiest survivors of the tender plants is *Calceolaria amplexicaulis*, which still makes a fair show of bloom, well set off by its groundwork of the good old variegated mint mixed with the golden green of feverfew. Some of the snapdragons are still also good. The fine late aconite, *A. japonicum*, remains in beauty; in colour one of the finest of the blue purples. *Clematis paniculata* is in full bloom. One wonders why this fine plant is not in every garden, for it does for us in October what *C. flammula* does in September, and does it even better, for the flower is larger and of greater substance, and the foliage is proportionally more important and is of a deeper green. Near it we have a good late golden rod. The ordinary golden rods I do not care for; in fact, I dislike them, thinking the colour bad and heavy and the cluster of bloom of a lumpy, formless shape. But this late kind – I do not know whether it is a distinct species or a garden variety – is a graceful plant, taller than the commoner ones and with an open-shaped feathery flower of a good pale yellow. That always interesting plant leycesteria has now its second season of beauty, carrying its load of claret-coloured bract and berry. *Clematis vitalba* is full of its feathery seed that puffs out so prettily when it is brought into a warm room. October chrysanthemums ought now to be in flower, but our stock was killed last winter and has not been replaced. Pot marigolds, cut back in late summer, are a mass of bloom. Laurustinus, which comes into flower at the time when all else is going, is getting fairly full of bloom, and the ever-faithful China rose is still with us.

THE BLEAKNESS OF WINTER

THE LAST WEEK OF JANUARY

Of all the winter weeks, this, the last of January, is, perhaps the barest of flowers, and yet the garden is by no means devoid of interest. Some shrubs are yet to bloom; garrya hangs out its green tassels; there is still a fair picking on chimonanthus, and in intervals of frostless weather a good show on the yellow jasmine. This is so valuable a flower for cutting that it is well worth providing a temporary shelter for one plant of it at least, and, as it is generally grown against a wall, it is not difficult to arrange to have a light board forming a lean-to roof and a curtain of scrim or some such material, to let down, or to hang up, in frosty weather. Severe frost spoils the flowers that are then open, but if it is cut in any mild interval and put in water, every bud will expand. Cut in long sprays and arranged with some little branches of gold privet, it makes a pretty and long-lasting table decoration. The same gold privet is now one of the brightest things in the garden. One of its uses is to stand in the back of the flower border in the region where the brightest yellow flowers prevail.

The rampant *Rudbeckia* 'Golden Glow' is planted at its foot and trained to run into it, making it look like a flowering bush. As it is kept cut back yearly, it makes no bloom, so that we have the benefit of its bright colour without the drawbacks of the unpleasant smell. There would have been patches of snowdrops and the small snowflake and perhaps a twinkle or two of earliest scilla, but the bank of little bulbs that in former years was by now showing some flower and promise of much more had become such a tangle of weeds during the four years of necessary neglect that last autumn it was trenched up and planted with shrubs.

Though there are next to no flowers there are a number of border plants that seem to wear their best leaf dress in winter. Nothing can look better than the neat, compact tufts of the common white pink and those of its variety, the black-centred pheasant eye. Their clean-looking blueish leafage is delightful against the warm brown of the garden mould. Other grey-leaved plants, too, are in perfect foliage; *Euphorbia characias* subsp. *wulfenii*, enthroned on a raised bank, is in company with *Yucca gloriosa* and the hardy New Zealand flax (*Phormium tenax*), the great yuccas rising statuesque on their dark trunks, the phormium with its ample sheaves of great sword blades; and at their feet the silvery masses of *Senecio cineraria* combine to make a complete picture of plant beauty, even in the depth of winter. There is also, in the same grouping, *Sisyrinchium striatum*, looking like a little iris, with foliage also at its best in winter.

Another beautiful winter plant is the Alexandrian laurel (*Danae racemosa*). The gracefully arching plume-like fronds that endure for two years, with their clear-cut polished leaflets, give

Euphorbia characias subsp. *wulfenii* in the Spring Garden, *circa* 1912.

it the air of a plant of the highest refinement and nobility. There is something of the same quality about a prosperous tangle of *Smilax aspera* that is loosely trained to a wall. It is none too hardy, but was put where it has side protection from a tall bush of choisya and overhead comfort from some old ivy that bushes out from the other side and overtops the wall. It now covers a space a yard wide and seven feet up and seems as happy as in its original home on the Mediterranean. The form of the heart-shaped or three-pointed leaf is variable; sometimes it would fit into an equal-sided triangle, but usually it is longer. The points of the leaves end in fine, weak spines slightly hooked back, and the same kind of spines, more or less developed, occur at intervals along the leaf edge. There are also little hooks on the stems themselves, all helping, with tendrils in the axils, to enable the plant to climb and hang on to the rock or bush or whatever may be near.

EARLY FEBRUARY

The warm days of early February gave a sudden stimulation to vegetation. Primroses appeared in sheltered copses, crocuses blazed out in cottage gardens, and Lent hellebores, anticipating by a good ten days an unusually early Lenten season, are already making a good show. It is not often that *Rhododendron* 'Praecox' is seen in fullest beauty, for at this time of year it is rare not to have a succession of frosty nights severe enough to damage it. But this season it has come on unchecked and shows how good a winter shrub it may be. One old bush in the edge of the wood that a year ago looked so scraggy and woebegone that it only just escaped abolition is now a sight to see. Its oldest wood is a good seven feet high, and lower branches, some of them rambling away into near brambles, are loaded with open bloom and the deeper-coloured buds, and the whole bush has managed to cover itself with blooming twigs. I had always thought of its colouring as a rather weak and washy mauve, but now, seen against the dim background of dusky woodland mystery, it is strangely and surprisingly beautiful. It is a useful example of one of the most important lessons one has to learn in pictorial gardening, that of putting the right plant in the right place – the place of its best welfare and its best appearance. The individual bloom also is good to examine in the hand; to note the pretty wavy outline of the five segments of the corolla that join in one about halfway down the flower, and the mass of pistil and stamen flung out boldly and lily-like; and something I had never observed before – the little drop of sweet-bitter nectar, looking like a careful brush-touch of varnish, that rises for a quarter of an inch from the base of the middle segment.

Near the rhododendron are some bushes of *Daphne mezereum*, of a darker shade of the same colour. Two or three of these are planted close together, for our soil is light and sandy, and whereas on the chalk or loam that they like best they make shapely and well-furnished bushes, here they are always of a straggly, open-branched habit. Covering the ground are some spreading plants of *Erica carnea* of the rather pale colouring of the type. It is well worth putting these three bushy things together, for they bloom at the same time, their respective heights form a good sequence, and their modest colouring makes a delightful harmony. On a warm grassy bank more in the open is a group of *Crocus sieberi*, perhaps the most charming of the winter-blooming species, with clear-cut, rather sharply pointed petals of a light lavender lilac, passing into deep yellow at the base, from which rise the yellow anthers, and from their centre their tufted saffrons of deepest orange.

Following the woodland path towards the garden, there are banks and borderings of *Leucothoe axillaris*. Any garden on light or peaty soil should grow this good thing in quantity. Here it is used largely both in wood and garden. Nothing is better as an edging to clumps of rhododendrons till they have filled their whole allotted space, with hardy ferns, male fern and lady fern at the back. It looks a more suitable filling than the heaths that are so commonly used; these are better by themselves in quite open places. The leucothoe seems to have more affinity of form and colouring, and, except for a week or two in the summer when the young shoots are forming and maturing, it is in a well-dressed state the whole year, and especially in winter. It is a slightly variable plant, for in one form the leaves never change colour, but in the more usual one a certain proportion of the foliage takes on some kind of winter colouring. Sometimes the whole margin is coloured red, with ruddy streaks running towards the midrib; in others the colour is in spots and splashes, or a marble-like mixture of both, and in a few cases all the leaves of a little branch are entirely red. Whether coloured or not, this graceful shrub is one of the best things to cut for use with winter flowers in the house. The firmly textured leaves, of refined shape and finely pointed, are set alternately upon the stems, and the whole form of the little branches is just what is most suitable for most kinds of cut flowers. Another beautiful marbled leaf is that of *Epimedium pinnatum*, a valuable plant for growing in quantity in any half-shaded place. The leaves are about three inches long, of a pointed heart shape on wiry eight-inch stems; three of these come together in a sort of knotty joint, from there forming one stem to the ground, so that the whole stands a foot or more high. The yellow flowers, not unlike some delicate orchid, come on arching stems in the late spring when the young leaves are growing. But all through the winter many of the mature leaves take on a handsome reddish marbling.

Of the winter foliage plants, other than shrubs, some of the most important are among the hardy ferns. The fronds of the lovely lady fern lose their strength early in the autumn; the useful male fern endures till December, and the dilated shield fern gives up at about the same time, but the common prickly shield fern is in full plumage throughout the winter. One may say 'plumage' because the whole effect of a group of this fern is that of a deep green feathery mass. Polypody too, is in perfect frondage. Nothing is more satisfactory than a mass of this native fern at the foot of a northern facing wall or in any place where there is a rough stone edging, or in the lower and rougher portions of the rock garden.

HARDY FERNS IN WINTER

There are a certain number of our hardy ferns that are not only at their best in the early winter months, but that will endure in beauty throughout the whole of the cold season. Of our larger common kinds the graceful lady fern is the first to go, and by the end of October the male fern is looking yellowish and possibly a little dishevelled, but the prickly shield fern (*Polystichum aculeatum*) holds its deep green fronds bravely right through the winter. The hart's-tongue (*Asplenium scolopendrium*) is another of the good winter ferns, for then the masses of glossy foliage are at their best. It is one of the kinds of which there are innumerable varieties in different forms of cresting and tasselling. These are interesting curiosities, but, after all, they are vagaries, if not monstrosities, and with but few exceptions are actually less beautiful than the type forms, which are all that is wanted for simple gardening.

Another of the good winter ferns is the common polypody, abundant on woody banks on sandy soils, and frequent on mossy tree trunks and moss-grown roofs. For rough dry walls in cool aspects nothing is better than these ferns. The polypody, though slow to take hold at first, increases fast when well established. The wall of a tank facing north is now well clothed with polypody and hart's-tongue, with some tufts of maidenhair spleenwort (*Asplenium trichomanes*) showing just beyond the sculptured lion's head which lets in the water.

A small space of sheltered ground might well be given as a complete hardy winter garden, of which the ferns would be the chief occupants. It would have besides some bushes of the berried pernettyas, as well as the taller-growing kind that fruits more sparingly, and it should have the good winter foliage of aucuba and skimmia, and between the ferns and green bushes groups of Christmas roses, of which the large early kind flowers in November. There would also be tufts of *Ophiopogon jaburan*, that handsome Japanese plant of which a striped variety is grown in greenhouses. But the type plant, with its handsome tufts of dark green linear leaves, is hardy, and its form and habit are in pleasant contrast to those of the ferns. Moreover, it flowers so late that its spikes of purple bloom, something like grape hyacinth, still show colour throughout November.

SOME WINTER EFFECTS OF FLOWER AND SHRUB

No garden, if thoughtfully planted, need be without an appreciable amount of bloom on hardy plant and bush during the winter months. No reasonable person expects to find flowers flourishing in actual frost; but in the milder spells that occur throughout the cold season there are a number of flowers that may be trusted to appear faithfully. Towards the end of November there is the large Christmas rose, coming into bloom a good month before others of its kind. The flowers are of large size and great substance. By the middle of December there will be the yellow winter jasmine, that will go on for some weeks; and from November onwards, in all open weather, flowers may be gathered from the charming winter iris (*I. unguicularis*). It is true that in the last few winters, since there have been rainy and comparatively sunless summers, this capital plant has been more shy of bloom. It is a native of Algeria, and it would seem probable that a vigorous bloom may depend a good deal on such a thorough ripening of the rhizome as it always receives in its natural habitat. It is therefore desirable to give it a dry and sunny place, such as on a slightly raised border against a south wall, in rather poor soil; for we find that in richer ground it produces very large leaf growth and but little bloom. There is also a beautiful white variety. Also from November onwards Czar violets should be in flower. After Christmas, snowdrops and the little yellow winter aconite make charming effects in wild ground, such as beneath trees in thin woodland; the winter aconite will even grow under beeches. Periwinkles are flowers of February, prettiest also on banks in wild ground. The same month brings the blossom of *Daphne mezereum*, whose low toned pinkish bloom, coming before the leaves, reminds one by its strong, pleasant scent of the several others of its family that are among the sweetest of the garden's flowers. The winter sweet (*Chimonanthus praecox*), with its excellent and penetrating perfume, is another shrub bloom of midwinter, though it is hardly showy enough to class among flowers of special effect. The witch hazel (*Hamamelis*) bears some resemblance to the winter sweet, in that the blossoms come closely set on the leafless shrub and have the same kind of yellow colouring. But though the petals are much narrower, and are curiously twisted, the bloom is so abundant that it has a distinct effect as a flowering shrub; moreover, it is hardier and can be planted in the open.

But, though we have all these precious winter flowers, the greater value of the garden will be in the deep, rich colouring of our best evergreens – yew, box, holly, cypress, bay and ilex, to name only some of the more important. Then, of lowlier shrubs, *Mahonia aquifolium*, in its many colourings of green, red and varying shades of ruddy bronze, is of the utmost value. There are also skimmia, leucothoe and its allies, and the beautiful Alexandrian laurel (*Danae racemosa*). Rhododendrons, especially those of the ponticum class, are in their deepest and glossiest foliage. Besides these, we have the evergreens of grey and glaucous colouring – juniper, deodar and *Picea pungens*, retinospora [dwarf forms of *Chamaecyparis*] and other. Some of these also take on a ruddy tint in winter. But there are trees and shrubs of quite other colouring: a whole range of gold-variegated varieties that can be used with excellent effect, especially if grouped rather near together. Of the trees, the golden hollies and cypresses are among the brightest, and among shrubs the golden privet is of fine colouring and has the good habit (although it is really deciduous) of holding its leaves till well after Christmas. The gold-variegated elaeagnus is also one of the handsomest of shrubs with coloured leaves. The gold-splashed euonymus is only hardy in the south; even at an hour's journey south of London it is generally spoilt by frost. The hardy bamboo *Pseudosasa japonica* is bright and cheerful through the worst of the winter.

Delightful effects of red and yellow colouring may be obtained by rather large plantings of the yellow- and scarlet-barked willows, and the red dogwood. For this kind of use the willows should be cut down every year at the end of winter, for the shoots of a year old are the brightest in colour. It should be remembered that two of our hardy ferns, namely, polypody and hart's-tongue, are at their best in early winter. At the same season, in some years, masses of berries on hawthorns, especially when wet with rain, are surprisingly bright in colour.

When, as this year, there are very few holly berries, we much miss their brilliant scarlet in the case of trees that usually bear well. Where mistletoe grows freely, as in some places where there are old lime trees, the bright yellow-green of the great bush-like masses has a strange effect by contrast with the grey stems and branches of the leafless trees; for it looks as if all the life were in the parasite only. Many people have been disappointed by trying to grow this handsome thing from the berries taken from branches cut for winter ornament; the berries are then quite unripe. They are not fit to sow till April.

THE CONSERVATORY OR WINTER GARDEN

With the increasing popularity of conservatories it may be helpful to make a few suggestions as to their better treatment. The usual plan is to bring in any tender plants that may be in bloom and to range them, dotted about singly on the stages, while any floor space holds a miscellaneous collection of larger plants, placed according to height alone, and without any consideration of the effect of colour and environment. Such a method is wasteful all around, for any beauty that might be gained from well-assorted colouring is lost; there is a confused and distracting mass of bloom, instead of something intelligible and satisfying to mind and eye, and probably there are three times too many plants brought together; whereas one-third of their number better employed might have served to make a delightful garden picture.

What is most commonly overlooked is the need for a good quantity of foliage plants as a framing to the flowers, and another usual weakness is losing sight of the need of restraint in the number of kinds presented. It is much better to show a good group of one plant at a time, or of any two that associate well, with a setting of suitable greenery, and then to pass on to another group of either allied or different colouring. This kind of restraint does not mean monotony such as one may see in many large places where there is a whole house full of nothing but coleus or cineraria or calceolaria.

A conservatory or anything of the nature of a winter garden may be made the most of, and be certainly far more enjoyable, if the fixed wooded stages are done away with altogether, and the whole place treated as a rock garden, with a stone bench and a clear paved space, according to the available area, where other chairs and a tea table may be placed.

For forming the rock work, a clever arrangement of stones will gradually rise in more or less stratified fashion to a little above the height of the pipes, so forming a kind of rugged wall in front of them. In places the stonework will pass from this to the outer wall over the pipes, which will also be enabled to give off some of their heat laterally forward, through little caves of mystery contrived here and there in the stonework, such hollowed places serving also the valuable pictorial purpose of giving dark shadowy backgrounds for plants with white or light coloured flowers. In arranging the stories, spaces are left where pots can be dropped in – spaces large enough for a good group of some one kind of plant at a time. All in between is planted with green things, such as selaginella and the small wild maidenhair fern of southern Europe; these would be near the path, with larger ferns and aspidistras further back, where the flowering plants will be of bolder character.

This kind of arrangement also admits of having a number of the more important things planted out; among climbing plants or such as may be used as climbers there are bougainvillea, lapageria, mandevillea, *Plumbago auriculata*, the lovely pink *Luculia gratissima* and *Daphne odora* – all requiring a free root run. Where there is a good space there are some of the plants of noble aspect that also thrive best when their roots are not confined, such as musa, brugmansia, hedychium and cannas; while among those that are docile to pot culture there are the very beautiful rhododendrons, hybrids of tropical and subtropical species, and the tender Indian lilies, *L. sulphurem*, *L. nepalense* and *L. neilgherrense*, with the more easily cultivated *L. longiflorum*, *L. brownii* and varieties of *L. speciosum*.

All this supposes a house of moderate temperature, but the same kind of treatment can be most satisfactorily applied to those of any of the grades known as 'stove' heat. When visiting gardens where orchids are grown, it has always been a matter of keen regret to see a collection of some of the most lovely and wonderful flowers merely placed one after another on a straight shelf or suspended from the roof in a straight row, with the ever-present consciousness of how much better they could be employed. For here also an arrangement of rocky banks and walls with a good groundwork of greenery would not only form a delightful garden picture, but would enable each kind to be seen to much greater advantage. Moreover, so many tropical orchids are epiphytal, growing on trees in dense forest, that they do not require the bright light that is essential to the well-being of so many greenhouse plants; therefore, a house that is a lean-to against a high wall would suit them well, and the rockwork could be built higher. Any space of wall that would otherwise be bare can be covered with ferns and mossy growth by fixing wire netting so that it hangs parallel with the face of the wall and about two or three inches from it. If this is packed with common moss or spagnum mixed with a little earth, and some small ferns are planted in it, it soon becomes a sheet of greenery. A house such as this would be most satisfactory with only a few of the more easily grown orchids – the noble phaius, *Coelogyne cristata*, calanthe and several varieties of *Cymbidium insigne*, with a few other tropical plants such as pancratium and hippeastrum in variety and with foliage of acalypha, *Pandanus veitchii*, caladium, croton, dracaena and *Begonia rex*.

The paths in any such house should be paved with flagstones that have natural, not rectangular, joints. The dipping tank for watering is arranged to look like a little rock pool; the usual iron tank is let into the ground and its hard edge is hidden by stones unevenly overlapping. It can be made all the more interesting if the outside gutters are so adjusted that they come to a point where the rainwater, led by a pipe through the side of the building, feeds a little rocky channel inside and comes with tiny falls and splashes into the tank.

EVERGREENS FOR DECORATION

In a well-stocked garden of fair maturity there will be a number of other shrubs that can be cut for indoor decoration besides the berberis, holly, box, yew, and laurel that are commonly in use. Notably among them is bay, precious for any decorative quality, quite unsurpassed for anything of the wreath or garland type, and so beautiful in detail that it is a pleasure to have a small spray near at hand for the enjoyment of the wonderful form of its wave-edged leaves and their perfect 'set' upon the branch. Then there will be the highly polished foliage of Japan privet, one of the handsomest of evergreens. Moreover, the bushes will be all the better for the pruning of their long summer growths. The leaves are so much like those of the orange that it is good to put them with dessert dishes of oranges and grapefruit, and also a pleasant reminder of the way oranges come to table in southern lands, picked with a spray of foliage. Branches of aucuba, whether green or variegated, and either berried or not, are finely decorative in something large, such as the great vases of Chinese porcelain that are in some old houses. On a smaller scale branches of skimmia come in for the same use, either the well-known *S. japonica* 'Oblata' or the larger *S. japonica* 'Veitchii'. It is a dioecious shrub and if the berries are desired there should be a pollen-bearings plant within the group. It is noticeable in this winter, when evergreen berrying shrubs are not fruiting well, that skimmia berries are unusually abundant.

Choisya and escallonia can be used in moderation, and those who, in some sheltered nook, have the true smilax (*S. aspera*) may cut a few sprays and enjoy them indoors as pleasant reminders of happy rambles in Mediterranean regions. Those who have had the wisdom to grow on a good quantity of that lovely plant *Danea racemosa* (the Alexandrian laurel) will have one of the finest things for indoor decoration, but it is never too abundant, for the graceful fronds take nearly two years to grow, and can only be cut in strict moderation. It is, perhaps, the more precious for this, as the gift of two or three fronds, so long-enduring in water, is of value to anyone who has a keen appreciation of beauty of form.

It is not every garden that has the peat-loving smaller shrubs in quantity, but where this is the case nothing is more useful, not only in winter, but throughout the year, for accompanying flowers of moderate size than the graceful sprays of *Leucothoe axillaris*. The hanging clusters of white bloom in June are of less account at a time when the garden is full of flowers, but in winter the value of the foliage is inestimable. Though it grows freely in light soils it is never so abundant as to become commercial winter greenery; neither can its near congener *Leucothoe catesbaei*, a kind that is much like it on a larger scale. But it is a matter for wonder why the free-growing *Gaultheria shallon* is not well known to London florists and others who deal in winter evergreens, for not only is it a handsome and well-enduring thing, but it is a grand grower in light soils. In the writer's woodland garden alone a wagonload would not be missed.

SOME IDEAS ON GARDEN PLANNING

GARDEN PLANNING: AIMS TO BE KEPT IN VIEW

The nature and area of sites vary so greatly that it is only possible to make certain general remarks on what are the most desirable aims to be kept in view. The first duty of the designer is so to treat the ground that, with due regard to utility and convenience, it shall be in accordance with the style and calibre of the house, and, above all, that it shall be beautiful and entirely enjoyable. A garden must be a place of repose and charm, with varied forms of interest, each one of which should be kept separate and thoroughly well worked out. Many a garden is spoilt by a fussy jumble of details, each one of which, if treated carefully and quite apart by itself, would be a success, whereas the attempt to display all together is only confusing and distracting, and a place which ought to be for comfort and happiness becomes a source of mental worry, perplexity and weariness. To take an example: if there is a beautiful distant view from any part of the ground it is better to approach it through a grove of quiet planting, so that it is framed by green things that are not in themselves showy or insistently attractive. If the view is seen over an elaborate parterre full of bright flowers, the full effect of both is lost. The parterre is in place near the house, overlooked from the house itself, or from a terrace immediately adjoining it; it should have its own background, also, of quiet greenery. Some of the most beautiful examples are where there are large trees and a lesser undergrowth – not so near as to rob or overshade the garden, but taking their own place as a dignified background and shutting off the flowery parterre from any other of the garden delights. The same principle holds good in the choice of shrubs and plants; the best result can only be secured by the exercise of an almost severe restraint. Each portion should have its own character and show some definite intention; although the complete garden, by the skill of the designer, is so linked together that one part follows another in orderly sequence and takes its appointed place in the co-ordination of the whole. The designer should give the place just those trees, shrubs and plants that it needs and that will best serve to make it beautiful; not one each of a great number of kinds. The different sections of a large garden will provide for the placing of a considerable number of various sorts, but if these are wanted for their own sakes in a garden of small or moderate extent, they should be in a special place and, frankly, as *a collection*.

AN OUTDOOR SITTING PLACE

A pleasant place for sitting out, close to the house and yet completely in the open air, is one of the most desirable of garden comforts, and, though our climate is so variable that even in summer it is by no means every day that one wishes to sit out, yet when a spell of moderate heat comes we long for some change from the airlessness of a house and the warmth of carpets and other indoor upholstery and desire the underfoot coolness of a stone pavement and the comparative liveliness of the open air.

An outdoor sitting space.

For such a pleasant place, the pavement, nearly level with the grass, gives a space of some eighteen feet by twelve feet, the size of a small room. The brick wall at the back is nine to ten feet high and is ornamented with niches holding sculpture and with pilasters finished at the top with baskets of fruit in carved stone. Tall trees behind the wall shut off actual sunlight and heat, and temper the light to a degree that is pleasant for reading or working, and there is comfortable space for a number of friends to gather round the tea table. In a more ambitious scheme the seats would be of stone or marble, with sculptured ends and feet, and the pavement would be a little raised and have a moulded nosing.

In the case of wooden seats, there is always the question of the colour of the paint. Usually they are sent out from the factory of a dead white colour, even if the white has not been slightly tinted with blue in order to make it appear colder. Such treatment of white is in place in the case of the daily freshness required of personal and table linen, but there are other considerations that should be regarded about our outdoor seats and tables, for in their case the dead white is apt to be painfully glaring, and it will be found advisable to modify the colour to something a little more soft and suave, putting a little umber and black in the white paint, so that it comes to something near the colour of the lightest part of a beech tree trunk. Then it will be found that table, chairs and pavement are in a much better harmony, and that the whole thing has a more sympathetic and inviting aspect. Cushions, of course, add to the comfort of all seats, and though a bare seat, whether of wood or stone, is well enough for a temporary perch, yet for a longer stay a cushion is a necessity. For the covering it is better to avoid any of the usual indoor materials, but a suitable thing may be found among the Willesden canvases, and as they are waterproof no harm will be done if the cushion is accidentally forgotten and left out at night. The choice of colour should be not among the bright light greens, but among those of a more neutral shade, a kind of faint brownish green. The properly chosen colour goes delightfully with the low-toned white paint or with the naturally weathered grey of plain oak.

There is hardly a house with garden adjoining where such a place may not be contrived. If a protecting wall does not exist or cannot be provided, there is the alternative – by no means a bad one – of a living hedge of yew, box or laurel. There has been a certain revulsion of feeling about the use of laurel of late, no doubt because it is such a long-suffering shrub and has been put to so many ignoble uses. But it may safely be said that no hardy evergreen is capable of making so handsome a hedge in so short a time, if it is properly planted and properly treated. It has the advantage over yew, box and holly that it is much less costly, for it can be planted at twice the size for about half the price, and will grow to a desired height in a quarter the time. But it should never be clipped with shears, for the large polished leaves are a sorry sight when they have been cruelly mutilated by this kind of thoughtless trimming; it must be done with care and judgment with a knife or secateur. Either of the usual kinds of laurel, the Caucasian or the broad-leaved, are good, but the broad-leaved is the more handsome. If a hedge is to be planted and still more economy is necessary, hornbeam or beech will do; though both are deciduous, they hold their brown leaves nearly the winter through, beech holding them rather the longer of the two.

An outdoor parlour would be admirably suited to some London or near suburban houses where there is but little space; many houses actually in London have gloomy, grimy places at the back that, by a little invention and ingenuity, could be converted into something very pleasant, or if there is no restriction to a moderate outlay in money, into something really beautiful. It is a matter that has been much neglected, but that if properly planned would add greatly to the utility, amenity and value of a town house.

There is another form of outdoor parlour that may easily be made in a country garden, in some place where there is no actual shade, by planting a certain number of the large-leaved weeping elm, with stems seven to eight feet high. A rough wooden framework is wanted for training the branches to form a roof, back and sides; the branches are long and lissom, and are not difficult to guide so as to cover the required space.

PLANTED BANKS AS HEDGES

There are many places within or near the pleasure grounds or on the near edges of park lands where there must be a hedge, either to mark a boundary or as a screen or shelter, either planted directly on the ground level or on a bank. Such a hedge, whether of hazel on a raised ridge, as in the usual field boundaries in the southern counties, or of holly or thorn or whatever it may be, if well planted and maintained, is always pleasant to see; but in many cases, by a little thought, something equally efficient but very much more beautiful and interesting may easily be devised.

Our common gorse, as a hedge plant, is much neglected. It is true that, after some years' growth, it becomes leggy and ragged, but then no shrub is more amenable to vigorous pruning or is more easily kept within bounds if it is only carefully watched and attended to in good time. It is a good plan to grow it from seed in a wide and not very high bank, thinning out the seedlings so that they stand from fifteen to eighteen inches apart.

The bank should have a base of from ten to twelve feet, and be about two feet six inches high in the middle. When the whole has grown to a height of four feet the plants on one side of the bank are cut to within four inches of the ground to the middle or ridge line; within the next summer they will throw up a quantity of young green growth, and can be allowed to grow on for four or five years. The other side, as yet uncut, is kept pruned back a little till the side first cut is up four feet, and then in turn is cut down; after this the cutting of the alternate sides may be done at such regular intervals as will enable the gorse, by its natural growth and without trimming, to be kept to a height of four, five or six feet, as may be desired.

A bank of broom can also be planted in the same way, but is less easily managed than one of gorse, and has not the same quality of continuous bloom; but it is a beautiful object, both

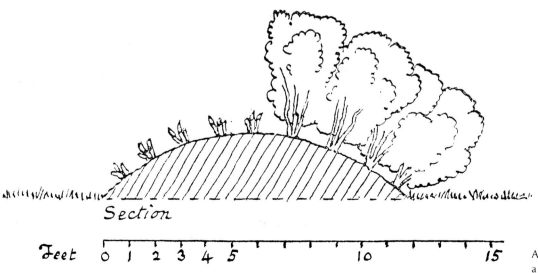

A planting plan for a planted bank.

when in flower in May and at other seasons when it shows its mass of deep, rich green. Broom cannot be cut down close, although the upper part can be pruned back while it is young; but it grows so quickly from seed sown in place that the same system of renewal of half the bank at a time can be carried out by removing the older bushes on one side and sowing afresh.

Hedge banks may also be planted in various other pleasant ways. When economy of space is not absolutely needful, a bank of earth ten feet wide at the top and about three feet high will give scope for excellent planting. There are quite a number of small trees and bushes, either native or nearly related to native kinds, that have a half wild character, for in this kind of planting it is desirable to avoid things of true garden aspect. In planting such a hedge there should be a groundwork of well-grouped holly, whitethorn and blackthorn; then there would be patches of spindle tree, with its bright green bark and lovely fruits, deep orange berries showing through and opening of rosy coats; and bushy small trees of snowy mespilus (*Amelanchier*).

At the top edge of the bank on the cooler side would be tufts of butcher's broom, and, clambering among the thorns and hollies, honeysuckles, both the wild and the early and late Dutch, and the native clematis, traveller's joy; sweet briar also, and the beautiful native *Rosa arvensis* and a garden variety of the same that has a more rambling habit, and some of the garden roses of wild character, such as the single musk rose and a recent hybrid of American origin called 'Evangeline', looking like a bigger and better dog rose. Some of the bushy roses will also be in place in the hedge – the native burnet rose, the parent of the Scotch briars; *R. pimpinellifolia* 'Grandiflora', a Russian form of the same, but rather larger; and the single pink *R. virginiana,* which grows into wide, bushy masses and bears bunches of red hips, bright in autumn, when the foliage also takes fine bronze red colouring.

Then there will be the brooms – the common yellow and its good variety andreanus (yellow and mahogany red), the white Spanish, the creamy praecox, these all flowering in May; to be followed in late summer by yellow Spanish broom, a tall-growing shrub, best planted in the middle space where it can shoot up among the thorns and hollies. Some of the better brambles will also find a place, and will give a quantity of useful fruit convenient for picking. These may be any fine selected forms of the native kinds, not forgetting the cut-leaved *Rubus laciniatus* and the large-fruited loganberry. The native brambles are such common plants that one is apt to overlook their beauty, which is scarcely less than that of vine foliage.

Bushes of flowering ivy will be well in place at the top of the bank, but we have not yet done with suitable small trees, for there is the wild guelder rose, or water elder. This bushy tree, though it is naturally a native of damp places, such as the fringes of water meadows, is most accommodating; when grown in drier places it assumes a closer, more twiggy habit, and is more fully set with the flat, white bloom, followed by the abundance of red fruit that in September, when the leaves are also turning a reddish colour, makes it one of the most ornamental of small trees.

Another bushy viburnum, the wayfaring tree, will also be well in place, for though it prefers chalk it will grow anywhere; the large, flat heads of berries, some red and some black, are conspicuous in autumn, and the broad, deeply veined leaves with mealy under sides always attract attention. The common elder will also be suitable, and if one of the rambling roses already mentioned is encouraged to grow up it, the bloom of both elder and rose will follow one another closely at midsummer and a little later. Privet should also have its place, and here, untouched by the pruning knife, it will develop, as nature intended, into a shapely little deciduous tree, closely set with white bloom, followed by neat clusters of intensely black berries.

Besides the small trees and bushes, there are a number of our native hedgerow plants that will greatly add to the big bank's beauty. Of climbing plants, besides the honeysuckle, roses and clematis already noted, there are the two bryonies – the green bryony, with its light green, vine-shaped leaves, abundance of tendrils and garlands of red berries, the only British representative of the gourd tribe; and the black bryony, of much the same way of growth, but related to the yams. This is the one of the handsomest of our hedgerow plants, with its highly polished pointed, heart-shaped leaves of deepest green, the colour in many cases deepening to a fine bronze purple, and its wide-flung wreaths of scarlet berries.

Then the bank should show, in between the bushes, other of our native flowers – the wild cow parsnip, foxgloves, black mullein, yellow toadflax, white bedstraw, great knapweed and field scabious. If the earth bank has a side distinctly shady, it may be planted with hardy ferns – polypody, male fern and dilated shield fern, with primroses for April and stitchwort for May, and *Iris foetidissima*, with its deep green, shining foliage, good at all times of the year, and its handsome pods of scarlet berries in November.

These are only a few of the plants that could be made use of, but as it is always well, and especially in this kind of wild planting, to have a good quantity of one thing at a time, they would be quite enough for the planting of some hundreds of yards; but if the space to be dealt with is still greater, anyone with some knowledge of plants and sympathy with their ways would think of others that could be as well employed.

PLANTING IN DRY WALLS

Where gardens are on hilly sites, giving opportunities for the making and planting of retaining walls, nothing is more satisfactory or encouraging than the rapidity with which they become clothed with more or less permanent vegetation. When flower borders are planted, however well and fully, there is some degree of their appearance till the plants have become established; but the conditions of wall planting are so favourable – the roots finding a cool, rambling region among the stones, the collars protected from winter cold and the heads in full air and sunlight – that they appear to establish themselves at once and more effectively. Planted a year and a half ago, and less in the case of the biennials, the wall surface, now presents a fully clothed appearance, and, although the soil is of a poor, sandy character, the plants are in full growth and vigour. Masses of the grey santolina set off the purple of catmint and the white and yellow of the tree lupins just above. In a year or two, when some plants of *Cistus* x *cyprius* are grown – a few blooms show above the second patch of santolina – the picture will be still more complete. Snapdragons are true wall plants, and should be used largely in the joints of dry walling. Besides those grown as annuals, it is well to make a second sowing about midsummer. This gives small plants to put into the wall joints towards the end of September, or at any time during the month when there has been a good rain. In many places they are too tender to survive in the open ground, but the wall joint gives so much shelter and such a comforting degree of dryness in winter that the plants do well and are in bloom from the end of May and all through June, the flowering season being taken up by plants made from cuttings and wintered in frames; these again being followed by the spring-sown plants. Foxgloves and mulleins are also grand plants in walls where these are in gardens large enough for them not to be out of scale. But even in small places one need not be afraid to plant large things in walls. Many a planted wall is monotonous in effect because its occupants are small things only.

GARDEN CRAFTSMANSHIP IN YEW AND BOX

Topiary work may either make or mar a garden. When it is rightly used, and chiefly as the living walling of an enclosed space, it is not only good in itself, but also the best possible background for the display of flowering plants. But it should be considered in close relation to the near building, for it is, in fact, or should be, a part of the architectural design. There is no material so good for this work as our native yew, with box as a good second. When yew is well planted and liberally treated it is by no means slow of growth, though to keep it close and compact the yearly shoots must be shortened. This is usually done in the autumn with the hand shears, but in the case of straight-sided hedges the trimming can be done more quickly by slashing with a sharp fag-hook at the end of May, when the young shoots are still tender and light green in colour. A wall of yew may well have a number of top enrichments, made by letting the growths rise at intervals, and forming them into square blocks, or balls, or pyramids; or the wall face may be varied with niches or projections and arched ways for passing of paths; but it should all be symmetrical and good in proportion.

There are many ways of clipping and training single yews, whether large or small, into decorative forms of bird and beast, and curious patterns looking like turned work. These should be used with great caution; they may sometimes be seen scattered about a garden for no obvious reason, and especially when they are many in number and placed without any definite design, the effect is only bizarre and perplexing. Sometimes a cottager will exercise his native wit by the shaping of a yew to his fancy, and the result, though probably whimsical, and from the point of view of design, indefensible, is yet always pleasing, and has a certain charm that is in keeping with that of his old cottage.

There can be no better guide or inspiration for those who are contemplating topiary work than this book of Mr Lloyd's [Garden Craftsmanship in Yew and Box], for the teaching of his own work and experience is brought to bear on all its practical details. The large number of excellent illustrations show, first, the work in the making, and, further, the finished form that has stood for many years in some of the best of our old and famous gardens.

THE YEW CAT

The garden is not one that is suited to the display of topiary work, and no such work was originally intended. But some yews at the end of a clump of shrubs grew into a form that suggested some kind of bold sculptural treatment, and already offered a plinth or base for some monumental figure. Hence the cat, which is best seen from some distance across the lawn.

A sketch of the topiary cat done for the gardeners to show the intended effect.

The topiary cat in the late 1920s, a picture taken by Frank Young, one of Miss Jekyll's under-gardeners.

AROUND THE HOUSE

PLANTING A CARRIAGE DRIVE

It is perhaps the better general rule in garden design that the planting just within the entrance gate, and from there to the house, should be kept green and quiet, as a more suitable introduction to a bright display of flowers in the garden proper; but no one can find fault with the feeling of gracious hospitality that prompts the planting of bright flowers as a cheering welcome to the visitor. A suggestion for such a planting in a belt on each side of the road is shown in the illustration [below]. A wide grass verge is next to the road. There must necessarily be a good proportion of evergreen shrubs, so as to secure a well-clothed appearance in the winter months. There are, therefore, close to the entrance, groups of green holly, enlivened by the silvery stems of birches. Then follow rhododendrons and common junipers, with pernettyas and andromedas (*Leucothoe*) to the front, and beyond them tamarisk, a beautiful shrub that is too much neglected in general planting. After a good stretch of groups of shrubs of green foliage, with suitable companions of deciduous habit, there comes a region where reddish colour, both of bloom and leaf, predominates. Here the foliage, if not itself red, is of that soft grey that either takes a pinkish tinge or that, by its natural tenderness, harmonizes well with pink and reddish bloom; this will be tamarisk, retinospora [dwarf forms of *Chamaecyparis*] and *Cotinus coggygria*. At the far end and on the opposite side the prospect is further varied by a glow of golden foliage and yellow bloom.

A planting plan for a carriage drive.

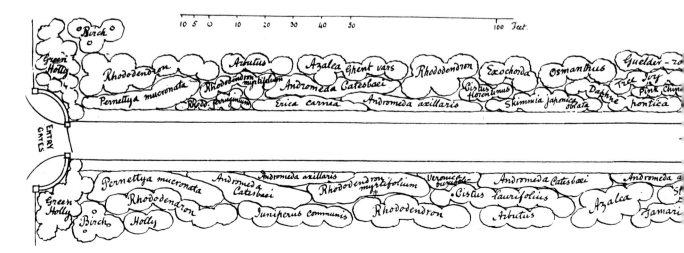

The shrubs are planted in generous masses; the long-shaped drifts are important, especially where much of the planting is viewed from a distance; it joins one group in pleasantly with the next, and avoids the meaningless, spotty appearance so often seen. The position of any of the groups of shrubs can be taken as a suggestion for a more extended planting of the same, or of shrubs of the same class, on the further or garden side; thus, the road background of rhododendron and juniper would have more of these and would form the back of a rhododendron garden; while further along arbutus, tamarisk and retinospora, also added to in number and disposition, would be an admirable background for clumps of azalea, kalmia and heaths.

THE WAY IN

A footpath from a secluded lane leads to a small West Surrey house. It arrives at a roomy stone-built porch with an arched entrance. Hollies were planted to right and left, and now meet, arching overhead. The near banks have *Leucothoe axillaris* and hardy ferns now in full growth. The path turns a little to the left a few yards away and on the right some rough stone steps lead into a space of garden that very soon turns into copse. The main intention of the modest path is to give an impression of seclusion. The longer stretch of it has a low bank on the right and a handsome young beech tree with a tall, smooth, grey trunk, also backed by hollies; and there are glimpses into the wooded ground beyond. The bank itself is clothed with turfs of whortleberry and masses of common hardy ferns – male fern, lady fern and polypody. There is a general setting of woodrush (*Luzula sylvatica*), such a useful and well-looking plant for rough places in shade. It would always seem better to keep the planting of

The porch from the garden framed by hydrangeas in tubs. The holly tunnel can just be glimpsed through the round arch.

such an entrance path, and in larger places, that of the carriage road, quiet and restful, as a better preparation for any garden glories that may be beyond.

BORDERS ROUND A HOUSE

A house is nearly always surrounded by some kind of flower border, serving for the rooting of any climbing plants that may be trained upon its walls or anything that is to show at its foot. It seems out of character with the solidity of masonry, and still more so if the building has any dignity or architectural merit, whether of a humble or an exalted character, to let the planting be of a soft or temporary kind. This consideration is often overlooked, for nothing is more usual than to see in such borders rows of wallflowers or crocuses, followed in the summer by rows of some bedding plant or half-hardy annual. Something better has been attempted in the case of my own home. On the south side there is a vine in the middle, a fig at the far end and some tall China roses reaching to a library window. These, with one white jasmine and a myrtle, lately planted, give quite as much wall covering as is needed. A box bush trimmed square is at the south-west angle, placed there to stop draughts. The four-foot wide border next the house is planted with buses of rosemary, *Olearia phlogopappa* and hydrangea. China roses show up among the rosemaries and look in at the windows with welcome effect from inside. A few back spaces are filled with *Nicotiana alata*, but with the main bushy planting the wall foot is fully clothed winter and summer, for though the hydrangeas lose their leaves this is made up for by a slight covering of fir boughs, as they are just a little tender.

The same square box bush shows at the end of the house wall that faces west. Here again

The South Terrace with a mass of rosemary by the open door from the sitting room.

there is a vine on the wall and hydrangeas at the foot with a group of pink *Crinum* x *powelli*. Any empty spaces in this border have a front filling of sweet-leaved geraniums, the charming pink 'Pretty Polly', the scarlet 'Moore's Victory' and the still sweeter-leaved radula varieties. Further along the same border is *Escallonia rubra* var. *macrantha* and Macartney rose (*R. bracteata*), another vine and more crinums.

   On the north side of the building two wings come forward enclosing a stone-paved court whose axial line cuts across the landing just beyond the tank. It is the only part of the garden where there is rigid formality of design, and is all of stone-walling, steps and pavement. The three steps and landing are repeated on the near side of the tank; other short flights of low steps lead upward to the house and downward to the garden. At the far end, just in front of the yew hedge, is a stone-walled bed with two groups of acanthus and hydrangeas between them. A later planting of a white crinum takes the place of the hydrangeas, and for the future will throw up its four-foot-high lily-like spikes of bloom that will show up finely against the dark yew background.

FROM INDOORS – LOOKING OUT

Throughout the summer and in any sunny mid-season days, the door from the sitting room to the woody side of the garden stands open. The ground rises gently to the south, and shallow steps lead to a strip of lawn from the middle of which one of the main green walks goes up through the wood. There is a long range of lead-lighted windows to the right; the middle light centres the green walk, and the view ends about two hundred yards ahead at a fine old Scots pine. There are no flowers on this side, except when the river of daffodils in the slight hollow of an ancient packhorse track, whose flow ends just to the left of the two birches is a rippling tide of horsfieldii in April, and when rhododendrons on the right of the green walk are in bloom in May, to be followed by groups of white foxglove to right and left [illustrated on page 113]. The intention was to keep everything on this side quiet and restful and a little mysterious, and nature has kindly responded to this desire.

There is a narrow border close to the house where the treatment is a little gayer, for between a general planting of rosemary there are bushes of *Olearia phlogopappa* and hydrangeas and plants of pleasant scent within easy hand reach; the rosemary itself, sweet verbena, myrtle, and that good old plant, of late much neglected and lost in many gardens, balm of Gilead (*Cedronella canariensis*), hardy here (south-west Surrey) with slight protection. But just in front of the windows there are big bushes of the old pink China rose, showing from within their bunches of lovely clear colour against the green of the little lawn, and some on taller stems still better displayed, because their background is the quiet and often misty effect of the more distant birches.

WILD THYME ON THE STEPS

A short flight of shallow steps leads from the path just in front of the house to the narrow lawn and wide wood walk on a slightly higher level. The lawn itself is quite unorthodox, for the grass in it is mostly fine native fescue, and there are a number of small native plants that should not be in a proper gardener's lawn, but that are very welcome in mine – heaths, milkwort in three colours, bedstraw, the pretty yellow tormentil, mouse-ear hawkweed and wild thyme. The thyme is in patches just above the steps, and has so freely come down and invaded them that one cannot avoid treading on it – a matter that the little carpet does not at all resent, but only the more readily gives off its sweet scent. Some seedling rosemary has come at the right-hand end of the steps and is also welcome.

GREY FOLIAGE ON A LOW WALL

A dwarf, dry wall retains a border and path on the west side of the house. The house wall is partly clothed with a grape vine, and some of the lower part with the deep glossy green of *Escallonia rubra* var. *macrantha*. The grey foliage of phlomis, lavender, santolina and stachys shows well against the full, clear green of the vine and deep green of the escallonia. Nearer the front is a big bush of *Fuchsia magellanica* var. *gracilis* in full autumn flower; its warm glow tells well against the further grey, which is taken up again in quieter tones by the dusky grey-green of rosemary.

THE COURT AND ITS PLANTING

Close to the house, and in fact a part of its design, is a small paved court between two projecting wings. The upper storey overhangs it at the end by a few feet, and this overhang is carried by a great oak beam which is supported by curved oak braces coming forward and at the two ends by one brace of the same in a line with the beam. This forms a six-foot-wide space of shady overhang, a pleasant place for summer sitting and for preparation work of home industries, such as the picking over of roses and various sweet things for pot-pourri and other such half-outdoor matters. The paving of this wide step swings round on the same level for about three yards and then meets the box edging, a few inches lower, that encloses a bed which has some large plants of male fern at the back, the rest of the bed, as well as the one opposite, being filled with three kinds of red and white fuchsia, the tall-growing 'Mme Cornelison' towards the back, and in front 'Cannell's Delight' and the double 'Ballet Girl'. After this the space is occupied by a little green on either side with a paved path between, leading to one of the sets of steps and landings that are on the right and left sides of the ten-foot-square tank. Where the paving next the house swings round to join the box-edged beds there is on each side a good wide space for the placing of plants in pots for the summer. The intention is to have a groundwork of good greenery with some flowering plants between. The foliage plants in pots remain all the summer; the groups of flowering things are renewed as may be required. The front edge of greenery is all of *Hosta plantaginea* var. *japonica*, whose pale green leaves are a good setting for the flowering plants. Then there are pots of hart's-tongue fern and the beautiful dilated shield fern, with a few male ferns for a solid background. The flowering plants are young pink hydrangeas, followed later by lilies, of which some of the best are *L. speciosum* in white and pink colourings and the Japanese *L. longiflorum*; but anything choice in white and pink is welcome and seems to suit the quiet court better than more brightly coloured flowers. Some groups of *Francoa ramosa* are welcome, as the foliage is good and the long arching sprays of bloom come well with the fresh greenery of the hostas and ferns.

Lilium auratum near the North Court.

The North Court festooned with *Clematis montana*.

PLANTS IN STEPS AND PAVEMENTS

It was the example of natural growth of small plants in the joints of steps and at the edge of pavements that led to their being so planted intentionally, and in very careful hands it is a charming way of gardening. What nature does in this way is full of surprises, for it sometimes happens that what one would have considered a most unlikely plant places itself in dry wall or pavement and justifies its intrusion by a distinct success. But though plants will of their own accord do well in most unlikely places, when they are intentionally placed it should be with the fullest sympathy with what is known of their needs. It is also important that it should be done in strict moderation, for there are gardens that should be taken as warnings where the plants in pavements are so much in excess that it becomes impossible to use the paving for its original purpose as a place to walk on, and there are steps so much crowded with vegetation that no one can go up or down without some crushing or bruising of pretty plants. Some rough sandstone steps lead up to a loft over a stable. They have a partial coating of moss, but where they join the wall an accumulation of dust and various small debris have formed a little deposit of soil in which erinus thrives and this year is accompanied by the pretty wild herb robert (*Geranium robertianum*). Higher up in the same flight of steps a bush of rosemary has come, also from self-sown seed, and has thrived so well that it has been necessary to cut back all the front branches to allow of free passage.

ROSEMARY GROWING IN MASONRY

When a plant gets its seeds into the joints of stonework it is interesting to see how little it seems to need to give adequate sustenance. A rosemary, no doubt from seeds from a bush at the foot of the steps, is flourishing in the mortared joints where a rough stone stair, giving access to an outside door of a loft, meets the back of a stable building. The original mortar may have partly come out of the joints, but no soil other than natural dust, and perhaps a little dried and decayed moss, is there to sustain the seedling rosemaries, which have already grown to a height of four feet six inches and are making good young shoots at the top. They are growing more or less flat against the wall as if conscious that they must not encroach on the space required by those who pass up and down the steps. A rock pink and a tuft of alyssum are also growing well, apparently in nothing. In Italy rosemary is sometimes used, trained close, to cover low walls. It should more often be grown in this way at home in places where a good wall covering up to a height of about five feet, and in a fairly warm aspect, is wanted. The common pink China rose trained just over and among the rosemary would make a still more enjoyable wall veiling.

Some other examples of shrubs and even trees, rooting apparently in nothing, have occurred in the same garden. The tall, shrubby *Sorbaria tomentosa* is growing in the apparently sound joints of brickwork. About the year 1913 a seed of Scots pine lodged in the top of a cottage chimney; it grew and made steady, short-jointed increase for eight years, and had become a bushy little tree over two feet high, when it was killed by the long drought of 1921. Another chimney on the same cottage has now on its top a thriving little birch tree, whose ultimate fate is as yet unknown.

PLANTS IN STEPS

In some gardens the placing of plants in joints of paving has been much overdone, but a moderate amount is pretty and interesting. It is best of all when the plants come of their own will, as on some steps in a part of my garden. Here there is a moderate growth of asarum and the tiny *Thalictrum minus*, the maidenhair meadow rue. No plants could be more suitable or look so well in such a place. There are also some tufts of *Corydalis ochroleuca*, the one that, for form and growth, is almost identical with the native *C. lutea*, but that has a quite different effect, one of charming refinement, because of the pale green of the stems and foliage and the tender white and pale yellow colouring of the flowers.

PLANTS IN POTS

It is not quite easy to find suitable plants for pots that have to be stood in prominent positions. Zonal pelargoniums are always satisfactory, and there are now so many varieties that it is easy to make a choice for habit, marking and colouring. Of other plants, fuchsias are among the most useful, and of these the red-and-white-coloured kinds have the liveliest and prettiest effect. Four Italian pots stand on paving above a rectangular tank close to the house. On each side of the tank is a square landing, with steps up to the pavement and down to the garden. The wall of the tank is well clothed with hart's-tongue fern. The water comes in by a lion mask of Portland stone that spouts into a sculptured shell of the same, and so makes a little pleasant splashing before it reaches the water level. The four pots above form a part of this decorative furnishing. This year the two outer pots held geraniums, a good old sort named 'Mme Lemoine', of a soft deep pink colour and with a handsomely zoned leaf. Next year it will be fuchsias, for though the geraniums make most show, it is the fuchsias that are really the prettiest and the most suitable. The kind is 'Ballet Girl', with scarlet sepals and a wide filling of the white petals. It is in the same category with the taller and always delightful 'Mme Cornellison' and its smaller variety, 'Delight', all with scarlet and white flowers. The hanging blooms tend to a graceful bending of the branches, a feature all the more noticeable in 'Ballet Girl', because the doubling of the petals makes the flowers heavier and the branches therefore more bending.

A decorative arrangement of pots in the North Court.

SOME THOUGHTS ABOUT COLOUR

COLOUR IN THE FLOWER GARDEN

One of the first things which all who care for gardens should learn is the difference between true and delicate and ugly colour, between the showy dyes and much glaring colour seen in gardens and the beauties and harmonies of natural colour. There are, apart from beautiful flowers, many lessons and no fees: oak woods in winter, even the roads and paths and rocks and hedgerows; leaves in many hues of life and death; the stems of trees; many birds are lovely studies in harmony and delicate gradation of colour; the clouds (eternal mine of divinest colour) in many aspects of light, and the varied and infinite beauty of colour of the air itself as it comes between us and the distant view.

Nature is a good colourist, and if we trust to her guidance we never find wrong colour in wood, meadow, or on mountain. 'Laws' have been laid down by chemists and decorators about colours which artists laugh at, and to consider them is a waste of time. If we have to make coloured cottons, or to 'garden' in coloured gravels, then it is well to think what ugly things will shock us least; but dealing with living plants in their infinitely varied hues, and with their beautiful flowers, is a different thing! If we grow well plants of good colour, all will be right in the end, but often raisers of flowers work against us by the raising of flowers of bad colour. The complicated pattern beds so often seen in flower gardens should be given up in favour of simpler beds, of the shapes best suiting the ground, and among various reasons for this is to get true colour. When we have little pincushion beds where the whole 'pattern' is seen at once through the use of dwarf plants, the desire comes to bring in colour in patterns and in ugly ways. For this purpose the wretched alternanthera and other pinched plant rubbish are grown – plants not worth growing at all.

When dwarf flowers are associated with bushes like roses, and with plants like carnations and tall irises, having pointed and graceful foliage, the colours are relieved against the delicate foliage of the plants and by having the beds large enough we relieve the dwarfer flowers with taller plants behind. In a shrubbery, too, groups of flowers are nearly always right, and we can follow our desire in flowers without much thought of arranging for colour. But as the roots of the shrubs rob the flowers, the best way is to put near and around shrubberies free-running plants that do not want much cultivation, like Solomon's seal and woodruff, and other plants that grow naturally in woods and copses, while with flowers like pansies, carnations, roses, that depend for their beauty on good soil, the best way is to keep them in the open garden, away from hungry tree roots.

A purple border by Mien Ruys at Dadamsvarrt in the Netherlands. Mien Ruys' father was an old friend of Miss Jekyll's and Mien learnt much from Miss Jekyll on the use of colour in gardens.

By having large simple beds we relieve the flowers, and enjoy their beauty of colour and the forms of the plants without 'pattern' of any kind. Instead of 'dotting' the plants, it is better to group them naturally, letting the groups run into each other, and varying them here and there with taller plants. A flower garden of any size could be planted in this way, without the geometry of the ordinary flower garden, and the poor effect of the 'botanical' 'dotty' mixed border. As, however, all may not be ready to follow this plan, the following notes on colour, by a flower gardener who has given much thought to the subject, will be useful:

One of the most important points in the arrangement of a garden is the placing of the flowers with regard to their colour effect. Too often a garden is an assemblage of plants placed together haphazardly, or if any intention be perceptible, as is commonly the case with the bedding system, it is to obtain as great a number as possible of the most violent contrasts; and the result is a hard, garish vulgarity. Then, in mixed borders, one usually sees lines or evenly distributed spots of colour, wearying and annoying to the eye, and proving how poor an effect can be got by the misuse of the best materials. Should it not be remembered that in setting a garden we are painting a picture – a picture of hundreds of feet or yards instead of so many inches, painted with living flowers and seen by open daylight so that to paint it rightly is a debt we owe to the beauty of the flowers and to the light of the sun; that the colours should be placed with careful forethought and deliberation, as a painter employs them on his picture, and not dropped down in lifeless dabs.

HARMONY RATHER THAN CONTRAST Splendid harmonies of rich and brilliant colour, and proper sequences of such harmonies, should be the rule; there should be large effects, each well studied and well placed, varying in different portions of the garden scheme. One very common fault is a want of simplicity of intention; another, an absence of any definite plan of colouring. Many people have not given any attention to colour harmony, or have not by nature the gift of perceiving it. Let them learn it by observing some natural examples of happily related colouring, taking separate families of plants whose members are variously coloured. Some of the best to study would be American azaleas, wallflowers, German and Spanish iris, alpine auriculas, polyanthus and alstroemerias.

BREADTH OF MASS AND INTERGROUPING It is important to notice that the mass of each colour should be large enough to have a certain dignity, but never so large as to be wearisome; a certain breadth in the masses is also wanted to counteract the effect of fore-shortening when the border is seen from end to end. When a definite plan of colouring is decided on, it will save trouble if the plants whose flowers are approximately the same in colour are grouped together to follow each other in season of blooming. Thus, in a part of the border assigned to red, Oriental poppies might be planted among or next to kniphofias, with scarlet gladioli between both, so that there should be a succession of scarlet flowers, the places occupied by the gladioli being filled previously with red wallflowers.

WARM COLOURS are not difficult to place: scarlet, crimson, pink, orange, yellow and warm white are easily arranged so as to pass agreeably from one to the other.

PURPLE and LILAC group well together, but are best kept well away from red and pink; they do well with the colder whites, and are seen at their best when surrounded and carpeted with grey-white foliage, like that of *Cerastium tomentosum* or *Senecio cineraria*; but if it be desired to pass from a group of warm colour to purple and lilac, a good breadth of pale yellow or warm white may be interposed.

WHITE FLOWERS Care must be taken in placing very cold white flowers such as *Iberis sempervirens*, which are best used as quite a highlight, led up to by whites of a softer character. Frequent repetitions of white patches catch the eye unpleasantly; it will generally be found that one mass or group of white will be enough in any piece of border or garden arrangement that can be seen from any one point of view.

BLUE requires rather special treatment, and is best approached by delicate contrasts of warm whites and pale yellows, such as the colours of double meadowsweet, and *Oenothera glazioviana*, but rather avoiding the direct opposition of strong blue and full yellow. Blue flowers are also very beautiful when completely isolated and seen alone among rich dark foliage.

A PROGRESSION OF COLOUR in a mixed border might begin with strong blues, light and dark, grouped with white and pale yellow, passing on to pink; then to rose colour, crimson and the strongest scarlet, leading to orange and bright yellow. A paler yellow followed by white would distantly connect the warm colours with the lilacs and purples, and a colder white would combine them pleasantly with low-growing plants with cool-coloured leaves.

SILVERY-LEAVED PLANTS are valuable as edgings and carpets to purple flowers, and bear the same kind of relation to them as the warm-coloured foliage of some plants does to their strong red flowers, as in the case of the cardinal flower and double crimson sweet William. The bright clear blue of forget-me-not goes best with fresh pale green, and pink flowers are beautiful with pale foliage striped with creamy white, such as the variegated forms of Jacob's-ladder or *Iris pseudacorus*. A useful carpeting plant, *Acaena microphylla* assumes in spring a rich bronze between brown and green which is valuable with wallflowers of the brown and orange colours. These few examples, out of many that will come under the notice of any careful observer, are enough to indicate what should be looked for in the way of accompanying foliage – such foliage, if well chosen and well placed, may have the same value to the flowering plant that a worthy and appropriate setting has to a jewel.

A flower border plan, from *The English Flower Garden.*

IN SUNNY PLACES warm colours should preponderate; the yellow colour of sunlight brings them together and adds to their glowing effect.

SPRING.—The names of flowers prevailing at this season are printed in plan.

SUMMER.—State of the same border with the names of flowers in full bloom at that season.

AUTUMN.—State of the same border with the names of the autumnal blooming plants.

Plan showing the principal groups in a border of hardy flowers; the plants placed to form masses of harmonious colouring, and their progression simply, but carefully, arranged to produce a fine colour-effect. Many groups of small plants and bulbs, that could not be shown on the plan, are planted between and among the larger masses, their colour always agreeing with that of the surrounding flowers.

The white borders at York Gate, Adel, Leeds. Unlike many white gardens these borders were not formal gardens but borders laid out in a style drawing on Miss Jekyll's ideas.

A SHADY BORDER, on the other hand, seems best suited for the cooler and more delicate colours. A beautiful scheme of cool colouring might be arranged for a retired spot, out of sight of other brightly coloured flowers, such as a border near the shady side of any shrubbery or wood that would afford a good background of dark foliage. Here would be the best opportunity for using blue, cool white, palest yellow and fresh green. A few typical plants are the great larkspurs, monkshoods and columbines, anemones (such as *A. japonica, A. sylvestris, A. apennina, A. hepatica,* and the single and double forms of *A. nemorosa*), white lilies, trilliums, pyrolas, habenarias, primroses, white and yellow, double and single, daffodils, white cyclamen, ferns and mossy saxifrages, lily-of-the-valley, and woodruff. The most appropriate background to such flowers would be shrubs and trees, an effect of rich sombre masses of dusky shadow rather than a positive green colour, such as bay, osmanthus, box, yew and evergreen oak. Such a harmony of cool colouring, in a quiet shady place, would present a delightful piece of gardening.

BEDDED-OUT PLANTS, in such parts of a garden as may require them, may be arranged on the same general principle of related, rather than of violently opposed, masses of colour. As an example, a fine effect was obtained with half-hardy annuals, mostly kinds of marigold, chrysanthemum and nasturtium, of all shades of yellow, orange and brown. This was in a finely designed formal garden before the principal front of one of the stateliest of the great houses of England. It was a fine lesson in temperance, this employment of a simple scheme of restricted colouring, yet it left nothing to be desired in the way of richness and brilliancy, and well served its purpose as a dignified ornament, and worthy accompaniment to the fine old house.

CONTRASTS – HOW TO BE USED The greater effects being secured, some carefully arranged contrasts may be used to strike the eye when passing; for opposite colours in close companionship are not telling at a distance, and are still less so if interspersed, their tendency then being to neutralize each other. Here and there a charming effect may be produced by a bold contrast, such as a mass of orange lilies against delphiniums or gentians against alpine wallflowers; but these violent contrasts should be used sparingly and as brilliant accessories rather than trustworthy principals.

CLIMBERS ON WALLS There is often a question about the suitability of variously coloured creepers on house or garden walls. The same principle of harmonious colouring is the best guide. A warm-coloured wall, one of Bath stone or buff bricks for instance, is easily dealt with. On this all the red-flowered, leaved or berried plants look well – Japan quince, red and pink roses, Virginian creeper, pyracantha, and the more delicate harmonies of honeysuckle, banksian roses, and *Clematis montana*, and *C. flammula*, while *C.* 'Jackmanii' and other purple and lilac kinds are suitable as occasional contrasts. The large purple and white clematises harmonize perfectly with the cool grey of Portland stone; and so do dark-leaved climbers, such as white jasmine, passion flower and green ivy. Red brickwork, especially when new, is not a happy ground colour; perhaps it is best treated with large-leaved climbers, magnolias, vines, aristolochia – to counteract the fidgety look of the bricks and white joints. When brickwork is old and overgrown with grey lichens, there can be no more beautiful around for all colours of flowers from the brightest to the tenderest – none seems to come amiss.

COLOUR IN BEDDING OUT We must here put out of mind nearly all the higher sense of the enjoyment of flowers; the delight in their beauty individually or in natural masses; the pleasure derived from a personal knowledge of their varied characters, appearances and ways, which gives them so much of human interest and lovableness and must regard them merely as so much colouring matter, to fill such and such spaces for a few months. We are restricted to a kind of gardening not far removed from that in which the spaces of the design are filled in with pounded brick, slate or shells. The best rule in the arrangement of a bedded garden to keep the scheme of colouring as simple as possible. The truth of this is easily perceived by an ordinary observer when shown a good example, and is obvious without any showing to one who has studied colour effects; and yet the very opposite intention is most commonly seen, to wit, a garish display of the greatest number of crudely contrasting colour. How often do we see combinations of scarlet geranium, calceolaria and blue lobelia – three subjects that have excellent qualities as bedding plants if used in separate colour schemes, but which in combination can hardly fail to look bad ? In this kind of gardening, as in any other, let us by all means have our colours in a brilliant blaze, but never in a discordant blare. One or two colours, used temperately and with careful judgment, will produce nobler and richer results than many colours purposely contrasted, or wantonly jumbled. The formal garden that is an architectural adjunct to an imposing building demands a dignified unity of colouring instead of the petty and frivolous effects so commonly obtained by the misuse of many colours. As practical examples of simple harmonics, let us take a scheme of red for summer bedding. It may range from palest pink to nearly black, the flowers being pelargoniums in many shades of pink, rose, salmon and scarlet; verbenas, red and pink; and judicious mixtures of iresine, alternanthera, amaranthus, the dark ajuga and red-foliaged oxalis. Still finer is a colour scheme of yellow and orange, worked out with some eight varieties of marigold, zinnias, calceolarias, and nasturtiums – a long range of bright rich colour, from the palest buff and primrose to the deepest mahogany. Such examples of strong warm colouring are admirably suited for large spaces of bedded garden. Where a small space has to be dealt with it is better to have arrangements of blue, with white and the palest yellow, or of purple and lilac, with grey foliate. A satisfactory example of the latter could be worked out with beds of purple and lilac clematis, trained over a carpet of *Senecio cineraria*, or one of the white-foliaged centaureas, and heliotropes and purple verbenas, with silvery foliage of cerastium, antennaria or *Stachys byzantina*. These are some simple examples easily carried out. The principle once seen and understood (and the operator having a perception of colour), modifications will suggest themselves, and a correct working with two or more colours will be practicable; but the simpler ways are the best, and will always give the noblest results. There is a peculiar form of harmony to be got even in varied colours by putting together those of nearly the same strength or depth. As an example in spring bedding, *Myosotis sylvatica*, *Silene pendula* (not the deepest shade), and double yellow Primrose or yellow polyanthus, though distinctly red, blue and yellow, yet are of such tender and equal depth of colouring, that they work together charmingly, especially if they are further connected with the grey-white foliage of cerastium.

COLOUR IN THE FLOWER GARDEN I

There are now many among those who desire to do the best for their gardens, and especially among those who have also some knowledge and appreciation of fine art, who wish to arrange their flower borders as an artist considers and treats a picture, by the employment of flowers in masses of well-related harmony of colouring. The study of this is so interesting and the result so surprisingly repaying that no one who has once given it careful attention will again neglect it. As a branch of gardening it is like the discovery of a new country, with a wealth of natural riches awaiting industrious exploitation. But, as with all ways of gardening that are redeemed from the most commonplace, it needs care and thought. There is no greater mistake than to think that a garden once started will go by itself. Besides the simple duty of good cultivation, it requires, first of all, thoughtful planning, and then constant watching and unremitting care. The giving of this necessary attention is the test of the love of a garden, showing whether it is genuine or whether it is only an affectation, or, at best, a matter of only half-hearted interest.

If the planning of different parts of a garden can be so arranged that each portion represents the best that can be done at a certain season, the result will be all the better. No one space of planted ground can be at its best for the whole summer; it can only be patchy

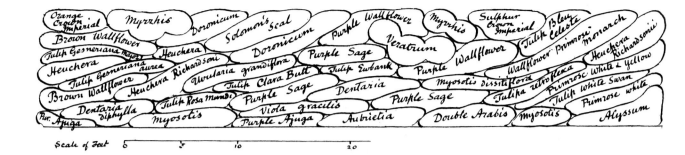

- never a garden picture. But by having the various portions severally devoted to about one or two months at a time, living pictures can be made, such as will show the very best that we can do with our flowers.

A planting plan for spring flowers.

In the following diagrams and descriptions such colour groupings are suggested. Any one of these, faithfully worked out, would indicate the principle, and would be an encouragement to further effort and invention. The space of each, diagram only admits of a certain number of the plants of the season being shown; any of the same time and colouring could equally be used. The intention of the plan is to show someone a simple way of getting a good colour effect; the identity of the actual plants used does not so much matter. In the plans following the one for the spring flowers [above], the choice of plants is, more or less, for one month only, the later flowers being of larger growth. If borders for a longer season are desired, the plants shown for any two neighbouring months could be intergrouped with those that are of the same or near colouring.

To make anything satisfactory of a border or garden of spring flowers it should be in a place of its own, preferably detached from the summer garden. When spring flowers have to give place to summer plants, the garden cannot have the permanent things of large foliage upon which so much of its good effect depends. These are such as the large-growing veratrum, with its handsome, pleated leaves; myrrhis, Solomon's seal and others of smaller growth, such as heuchera and purple sage. There are also a number of the plants that must be replaced in early summer, and tulips, to be taken up in June and replanted in November. What may be called the groundwork plants — heuchera, ajuga, asarum and purple sage — are of great value. A border may be brilliant with bright-coloured flowers alone; but if it is to be a picture, it wants some of its brightness to be relieved by something quiet, in good harmony, but comparatively neutral. Blood red wallflower and red and orange tulips have twice their value when rising from a setting of the reddish satin leaf (*Heuchera americana*), and flowers of purple and pink are made more beautiful by the nearness of the ruddy grey-purple of the sage.

The general colour arrangement — beginning on the right — is of palest yellow with white and blue, the blue giving way to pale purple and pink, followed by deeper purple and red-brown, with orange and strong reds as the left-hand end is reached.

Flower borders arranged for June will have flag-leaved irises, peonies of the albiflora kinds, China roses and lupins, both of the perennial and tree classes; the flowers latest to bloom

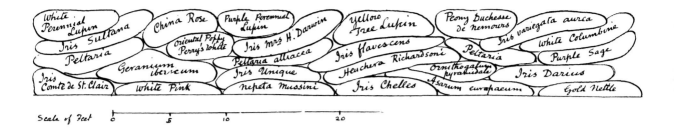

White Perennial Lupin
Iris Sultana
Peltaria
Iris Comte de St. Clair
Geranium ibericum
White Pink
China Rose
Oriental Poppy Perry's white
Iris mrs H. Darwin
Peltaria alliacea
Iris Unique
nepeta mussini
Purple Perennial Lupin
Iris Chelles
Yellow Tree Lupin
Iris flavescens
Heuchera Richardsoni
Peony Duchesse de nemours
Iris variegata aurea
Peltaria
Ornithogalum pyramidale
Asarum europaeum
White Columbine
Purple Sage
Iris Darius
Gold Nettle

Scale of Feet   0   5   10   20

A planting plan for a border of June flowers.

being some of the earlier delphiniums. The plan [above], being a section of a flower border only, cannot include all the available material; it only shows the more important. But among the groups shown, a useful and little-known plant, *Peltaria alliacea*, is included. It is one of the crucifers, about eighteen inches high, with wide corymbs of cream or white bloom. It may well be used even more freely than is shown on the plan – always with good effect. It is easily raised from seed. The purple sage, advised for the earlier borders, will also be useful here, and may be planted more largely with advantage. There are so many of the beautiful forms of flag-leaved iris and of the June-flowering peonies that a much larger length of border, or of double borders, will be wanted, or, indeed, a whole garden may be made with them without there being any sense of monotony or undue repetition.

By judiciously ringing the changes, and by having in mind one general colour harmony at a time, the plants will fall into delightful pictures. In one part there would be a preponderance of yellow and white; in another of pink and white; then of pink, white and lavender; then of light and dark purples, and so on, each living picture preparing the eye for the fuller enjoyment of the one that is to follow.

The next plan [opposite] shows an arrangement for a section of a flower border for July. *Salvia sclaria* is the old garden clary, a rather large branching biennial, four feet high. It bears a quantity of bloom of a pale bluish colour, with large reddish mauve bracts, the mixture of tints forming a very charming effect of cloudy, soft colouring. It is apt to deteriorate, both flowers and bracts becoming paler; it is therefore well to note good-coloured plants and to secure seed from these alone. Those who wish to grow this good plant should be on their guard, because in some of the seed lists the name clary is wrongly given to another plant, *Salvia viridis* var. *comata*. It should be made clear that *Salvia sclaria* is the one required.

Of the remaining plants shown on the plan, the only others that call for special remark are *Isatis glauca* and the crested tansy. The isatis has rather wide, glaucous leaves and large, loose racemes of bright yellow flowers, with a delightfully soft, refined effect, probably caused by the individual blooms being small, so that there is some play of light and shade between them. The stems are two to three feet high and rather weak, so that they require careful support. Next to it on the plan is a front group of crested tansy, whose splendid richness of green sets off the yellow bloom of the isatis. It is all the better if they are more definitely grouped together and partly intergrouped. But it should be noted that the tansy requires careful control. In common with the type it is a plant of strong growth, and, though the variety with the richly crested foliage is not so rank and tall a grower, yet it is

Salvia Sclarea — White Pea — Campanula macrocarpa — Yucca recurva — Camp. hederacea white var. — Yucca recurva — Yucca glauca — Yucca recurva — Phlox Avalanche — Clematis Flammula — Delphinium — Clematis recta

Salvia nemorosa virgata — Camp. macrantha alba — Purple Galega — Eryngium oliverianum — Yucca filamentosa — Delphinium Intermediate — tall yellow — white Galega — Lilium croceum

Purple Sage — Erigeron speciosum — Chrysanthemum maximum — Eryngium giganteum — Delphinium Belladonna — Antirrhinum — Helenium pumilum — Glyceria aquatica — Delphinium grandiflorum

Ageratum mexicanum — Statice latifolia — Lilium candidum — Tradescantia virginica — Dwarf Ageratum — Anthirrhinum yellow Intermediate — Isatis glauca — Oenothera missouriensis — Crested Tansy — Golden Feather — Calceolaria amplexicaulis — Variegated mint

Scale of Feet   0   5   10   20

A planting plan for a border of purple, yellow and blue flowers for July.

too tall for the front edge of the flower border. Early in June the shoots that would develop bloom are cut about two-thirds down, and as the plant will persist in trying to make blooming shoots, they should be watched and pinched, so as to keep the mass of beautiful greenery to the height of a foot or fifteen inches.

COLOUR IN THE FLOWER GARDEN II

The plan for the portion of a border for August [on page 76] shows a quite restricted range of colouring of white and pink, lavender and purple, with a good deal of grey foliage. At the back are groups of a beautiful pink hollyhock and of echinops (globe thistle), with *Clematis* 'Jackmanni'. As the clematis grows, it is trained to cover a stiff, branching spray, which is arranged to come partly over and partly through the echinops. The groups of *Lilium longiflorum* can be planted in place, but they are better brought on in pots and put out when the buds are formed. *Artemisia ludoviciana* is a tall, silvery-leaved wormwood that bears pinching to any height. Normally it throws up flower stems four feet high, the whole being of a pleasant grey colour; but when the grey foliage only is wanted, it can be cut back to any height down to a foot. It is a strong-growing plant, running freely at the root, and should be replanted every two years. The clear pink of *Gladiolus* 'America' is delightful in such a grouping as the plan shows.

This one group is given as one of several that may be arranged for July and August, when there is such a quantity to choose from. In another place, or in another section of such a border, there might be a large group of white and yellow, with a front planting of golden feather feverfew, *Calceolaria amplexicaulis* and variegated *Mentha suaveolens* 'Variegata'. This, with the addition of some long patches of annual sweet alyssum (*Lobularia maritima*), and with the components differently massed and grouped, will be enough for quite a long stretch of edging. With it, the handsome striped grass *Glyceria maxima* var. *variegata*, so much better than the older striped grass, will come well at the back of the front edging, also running back among other flowers such as yellow and white intermediate snapdragons. Then would come dwarf yellow canna and double marguerite 'Mrs Sander', then *Lilium longiflorum* and taller yellow cannas, and yellow and white snapdragons backed by variegated maize and white and yellow dahlias. Further, there would be a group of a splendid colouring of rich and various tones of red, with a front planting of *Salvia splendens* and orange red snapdragon, and a very careful selection of bedding geraniums. Then

Plan labels (back to front): Echinops · Pink Hollyhock · Clematis Jackmanni / Echinops · Pink Hollyhock · Clematis Jackmanni / Echinops · Pink Hollyhock; White Phlox · Gypsophila paniculata, Gladiolus Baron Hulot, Antirrhinum tall white · Artemisia ludoviciana · China Aster Comet tall white · Gypsophila paniculata · Antirrhinum tall white · Penstemon white; Gladiolus America · China Aster Victoria white · China Aster Victoria Blue, Lilium Longiflorum · Delphinium consolida purple · China Aster Comet Blue · Godetia double rose · China Aster Victoria white · Gladiolus America · Lilium Longiflorum; Antennaria Stelleriana · Heliotrope · Dwarf Ageratum · Stachys lanata · Dwarf Ageratum · Heliotrope · Stachys

Scale of Feet 0 5 10 20

A planting plan for a border designed for purple, white, pink and grey colourings for August.

penstemons and taller snapdragons and scarlet gladioli with red-leaved cannas and the smaller red ficinus; and grouped with these the richness of the tall velvet-like dark crimson snapdragon and scarlet pompon dahlias, with others of the older decorative dahlias of strong and splendid colouring; and all brought together by a middle underplanting of the richly coloured garden variety of *Sedum telephium* [Miss Jekyll's own strain, *Sedum telephium* 'Munstead Red'] and of iresine. If one long border is in question, all these three schemes of colour could be used, keeping the pink-purple-grey one at one end, then passing to the pale yellow and white, and from that, through stronger yellow and orange, reaching the red grouping last described. Anyone who has not yet seen flowers arranged in some such manner has never known what delight of eye can be given by such a thoughtfully arranged grouping of colour.

For a special colour arrangement for September it will be well to make use of the earlier Michaelmas daisies, in some such way as that suggested by the plan [opposite]. Here, at the back, there will be white spring-planted hollyhocks, with white and palest yellow dahlias. The plan represents the right-hand half of the September border. The colouring is mainly purple and white, with a group or two of the pink *Sedum spectabile*; but in the middle of the length there is a break of palest yellow and white. This is edged to the front with the same mixture of golden foliage and yellow bloom that was recommended for the yellow region of the July border. The golden feather feverfew is not all deprived of its bloom as was usual when it was used in rigid bedding arrangements, but a little is cut off here and there close to the edge, and, for the rest, the bloom remains and joins in pleasantly with the variegated mint. The mint should be cut back several times during the summer to prevent the blooming branches from rising and to keep it close and bushy. Some care is needed to obtain the primrose African marigold of the true, soft primrose colour; it should not be the so-called lemon colour, which is too full and harsh to make the right harmony, and is the one commonly sent when primrose is ordered.

Aconitum japonicum is a fine plant commonly neglected; the colour is a splendid violet purple, with the large blooms handsomely set on a strong stem about two feet high. From its season of blooming it is often confounded with *A. carmichaelii* Wilson Group, not so good a plant, considerably taller, and weaker both in growth, bloom and colour. Towards the back of the border there is a small silvery-leaved willow, with a clear stem about five feet six inches high. Close to it a *Clematis flammula* is planted and is guided into the willow, so that the tree is half filled with the pretty clematis bloom; some of it tumbles out from among the silvery leaves, in foaming cascades, into the large grey-lilac bloom of the fine

FEET
0   10   20   30   40   50

Aster punicens with delightful effect. It should be remembered that this grand aster is almost a swamp plant, so that it should never be allowed to suffer from drought.

It is also desirable to have a special border for October, but it would be so much on the lines of the September border that a separate plan is not given. Here the later Michaelmas daisies will be the chief plants, and the colouring will be of purple and white with a little pink only. The front planting would be of stachys and ageratum. Stachys, whenever it is used as an edging, has the bloom cut out towards the end of May, when it spreads at the base to form its beautiful silvery carpet. The ageratum, both dwarf and tall, is kept cut back till the beginning of September to retard the bloom. The tall white daisy *Leucanthemella serotina* is of great use both here and in the September border, as its blooming time is common to both. A specially good effect is gained by intergrouping it with one of the paler

A planting plan for borders devoted to September flowers.

BELOW LEFT
The September borders, framed by an arch of laburnum.

BELOW RIGHT
The September borders, looking back towards the house.

pink forms of the tall *Aster novae-angliae* 'Ruber'. Anyone whose eye is trained to sensibility in the matter of colour will recognize that the deeper colourings of the reddish asters are nearly always less satisfying than the paler, and less suitable for accompanying the excellent purple colourings, pure and strong in the deeper, and pure and tender in the lighter of the type-coloured asters. The pink colourings nearly always show an unpleasant, rank quality; even the paler are not altogether free from it, but in their case, as it is less pronounced, it is more tolerable. In arranging a border one looks for the other asters whose lilac or grey-lilac has a warm quality, such as 'Coombe Fishacre' and *A. cordifolius* 'Elegans', to lead pleasantly from the pinks to the purples.

THE BLUE BORDER

Failing the more ample space that would enable me to do full justice to flowers of the purest blue, I have to be content with a bed four to five feet wide and about eighteen feet long. But as other garden lovers may have more space and may wish to do a satisfactory bit of blue gardening, I may offer these suggestions. One hears of blue borders being planted in which there must be nothing but blue, but I venture to say that to confine oneself to this is to obey an uncomfortable, self-imposed restriction in order to keep within the strict meaning of a word. It is injuring a garden for the sake of a word. Surely it is better that a border should be beautiful rather than that it should be rigidly and exclusively blue? I have always found that a mass of pure blue calls for the accompaniment of something white, cream white or palest yellow. And though in general garden practice I am for putting together plants whose colours form a gradual sequence of harmony, such as a progression of strong yellow merging into orange and passing gradually from that to red, I think that blues, on the contrary, prefer a contrast; and though it is quite possible to design harmonious arrangements of pure blue leading to violet and then to other purples, yet the company of warm white or palest yellow seems better to content a trained colour eye.

   The display of the blue border begins in June with some bold masses of *Delphinium* 'Belladonna' accompanied by the early *Gladiolus* 'Colvillei', *G.* 'The Bride'; also anchusa, of which the best variety is the pale dropmore form named 'Opal'. With these are the tall feathery spikes of *Aruncus dioicus*, the great meadowsweet of the borders of alpine torrents, and *Filipendula ulmaria*, the double form of the meadowsweet of English streamsides. *Penstemon heterophyllus* is a new garden plant, with numerous many-flowered spikes about a foot high. The colour is variable, but as it may be anything from a reddish purple to a pure blue, it is included in the suggestion for a blue border [opposite] in the hope that a good blue form may soon be fixed and generally available. *Clematis recta* soon follows with its masses of cream white bloom so delightful with anything blue. It is a herbaceous, non-climbing kind, forming shapely bushes of bluish foliage of much the same colour as rue, and masses of foam-coloured bloom. When this is over and carefully cut away the foliage is still of good effect in the border. The groups marked 'L.C.' are the white Madonna lily (*L. candidum*), six to nine bulbs in a patch planted rather close together. 'L.L.' stands for *Lilium*

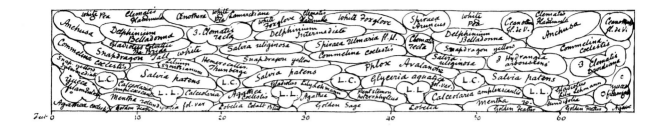

longiflorum. These are best brought on in pots, three bulbs in a pot, and the group shows three pots sunk in the ground close together. Towards the end of July the felicia and lobelia in the front edge will be making a show, also the snapdragons.

A planting plan for a blue border.

The front patches of *Mentha suaveolens* form the groundwork of a favourite mixture which every year gives me greater satisfaction. It is an old garden plant that has of late most undeservedly fallen into disuse, a native plant in the typical form, but with this variety that has clear variegation of yellowish white patches. It has to be stopped two or three times during the season to prevent the formation of the flower stem, and then makes a delightful setting for the pure pale yellow of *Calceolaria amplexicaulis*, an excellent old plant that goes on flowering till the end of September. At the extreme edge, notched in to the mentha, some patches of golden feather pyrethrum [now *Tanacetum*]come well; some of it is allowed to flower and in some the bloom is pinched out the better to show the golden foliage. When there is space enough to widen this warm yellow white bordering we plant at the back *Glycerin maxima* var. *variegata*, a handsome grass, warm white striped, a great improvement on the older striped grass. As this is at its best before the normal time of flowering, we give it a check by lifting and replanting in spring. The blue flowers of the later summer are *Commelina tuberosa* Coelestris Group, of purest, deepest blue, whose only fault is that of closing in the early afternoon, and the always beautiful *Salvia patens* put out from pots for the summer. *Plumbago auriculata* is not shown on the plan [above], but is another tender plant useful to drop in with the pot.

Hydrangea arborescens will be found of much use. It forms a neat shrub about three feet high, covered with cream white flowers that have the merit of being long lasting. *Ceanothus* 'Gloire de Versailles' is not a pure blue, but a grey blue that is quite admissible, giving a mass of bloom in middle summer if suitably grown and pruned. *Salvia uliginosa* is rather new to garden and a precious plant in the late summer; it grows tall and straight, up to five feet with flowers at the top of a pure and brilliant blue.

The plan [above] shows at the back some plants of *Clematis flammula* and white everlasting pea. They are deep-rooting things that take some years to come to their best. Their purpose here is not only their own beauty, but that when grown they serve to cover other earlier flowering plants that are out of bloom. When the delphiniums are over and the flower stems are cut, the pea or the clematis is trained over and, supported by the delphinium, give their own bloom from July to September.

COLOUR NAMES AND DESCRIPTIONS

There have been lately a number of articles on the description of colour in flowers. Some are in favour of a colour chart, which may possibly be of use to those who have but little aptitude for the perceptions of colour distinctions. But without such a means of reference, there are quite enough ordinary examples in natural objects and substances and flowers with an obviously typical colouring to serve as a basis for an accurate description of the colour of a flower. Some colour words have been so long misused that they have passed into the language with their unblushing error. Such a word is golden. We read in plant lists 'brilliant golden yellow', meaning a bright yellow such as in buttercups. The colour gold is not brilliant yellow; it is hardly yellow at all. I lay a piece of gold on a sandy path and it just matches. If it was rightly used it might fit some straws, or some of the indefinite shades of rather dull yellow in annual arctotis, calendula, and helichrysum. Bright yellow or brilliant yellow anyone can understand without any reference to gold.

Another misused word is flame. In plant lists it is meant for a brilliant red or scarlet, such as in some bedding geraniums, in nasturtiumms, and in *Tropaeolum speciosum*, whose popular name is flame flower. But the colour of flame is not red at all; it is a rather indefinite yellow, with occasional flares of a dull bluish tint. It is the incandescent coals that are a red or reddish, but are never of so perfect a scarlet as *Tropaeolum speciosum*. Why not say scarlet at once? There are various degrees of scarlet, some deeper than what we may consider the type, and some inclining to orange, but a useful central range of type may be accepted from the colour of some well-known objects, such as a postal pillar box or a guardsman's tunic. Blood-red is a fine word, and stands for a grand colour, such as is well shown in some dahlias and hollyhocks. Magenta is a kind of purplish-red, capable of unpleasant violence, which is offensive to many a trained colour eye. In view of the fine reds existing, it may safely be excluded from gardens. As the name is derived from a sanguinary battle, it ought to have stood for a good blood-red; it corresponds to some forms of the French *amaranthe,* where in foreign plant lists it serves as a useful warning. One of the most oddly misused words is amethystine, and it seems to have been accepted even by learned botanists. It is common to find in plant lists such a plant as a delphinium described as a brilliant amethystine-blue. No amethyst is blue, or anything the least like blue; it is reddish-purple; in all but the best examples a washy reddish-purple. I can only suppose that when the word was first used in connection with the colour of flowers, the careless giver of the name muddled up amethyst and sapphire, and said amethyst when he meant sapphire, which is a gem of a pure blue colour. It is pleasantly noticeable that in some recent catalogues the word amethyst is properly used. Messrs Cheal have a dahlia named 'Amethyst' quite rightly named. They have also a fine deeper purple one named 'Porthos', not so obviously named for colour unless it is in reference to the 'purple' patches in the musketeer's adventurous career!

The various names mauve, lilac, lavender, purple and violet are much confused, but are all useful if properly used. Mauve especially is commonly used too loosely; it actually means the rather feeble reddish-purple of the common wild mallow (*Malva sylvestris*) – mauve in French. Lilac should stand for the same kind of colouring, but deeper, that of the slightly reddish-purple of the old garden lilac. Lavender speaks for itself, for though there are good forms of lavender whose colouring may be a shade lighter or darker, it has always the same quality of colour.

The word blue is grossly misused, commonly serving to cover a number of purple and purplish flowers, such as campanulas and China asters, that are not blue at all. The word should be kept for the pure blues, such as the deep colour of commelina and *Salvia patens*, of cornflower and gentian, the medium blues of nemophila and phacelia, and the tenderer blues of forget-me-not, *Felicia amelloides*, *Cynoglossum amabile* and *Plumbago auriculata*. There are vague words in common use denoting blue that are difficult to define. I do not know what is meant by azure, except that it is some kind of palish blue; azurea in botanical wording seems always to mean a pure blue, but azure is so vaguely used that it is perhaps better excluded from plant lists and left to the poets.

One of the most trustworthy colour words is sulphur, because the substance is so nearly invariable in colour that if a flower is described as sulphur one knows exactly what is meant. Primrose is also useful to denote a shade of pale yellow near sulphur, but a slight shade of green. Salmon is also a good colour word for a whole range of pink or pale rosy shades with a warming yellowish inclination. Orange is a fine colour word, and needs no explanation. Lemon is also a good word, for though it may have shades deeper or lighter, the quality of the colour is invariable. The word citron may be usefully employed for shades of colour lighter and tenderer than lemon; of this class the now popular grapefruit is a good representative, as its colour varies so little.

Descriptive words for foliage are also plentiful. Grass green usually stands for a full, bright green. Apple green I am never sure of, but think it means the colour of some unripe apples. Bottle green for the deepest polished foliage describes itself, and so does sage green, a quite useful word. Glaucous is a fine word for the many plants whose foliage is of a grey colour inclining to blue, such as that of the common pink, eryngiums, many of the cabbages and notably seakale. Silvery grey is also permissible, for though it is not really like silver it may well stand for the colour of the artichoke, *Stachys byzantina*, several of the artemisias, and other plants that make such a beautiful setting to flowers of pink and purple colourings. Thus it appears to an old student of colour that it is pleasanter and quite as effective to describe a flower as, say, primrose yellow than as Pl.XVI., S.24.

# ROSES

SOME GARDEN ROSES AND THEIR USES

The grandly grown roses that we see on the show benches are brought prominently before the public, and quite rightly, for all must wish to see the highest degree of beauty and culture of which the best of flowers is capable. But there are whole classes of roses that are not seen at shows and yet are the ones that give us the most real happiness. These are what we know as garden roses – the intimate and well-loved friends of every day – roses that cost us no anxious watching to see if a bloom is up to a certain standard at a fixed date, no trouble or expense of packing, conveying or setting up, no heart-burnings as to whether the exhibit will receive recognition or be passed over. Our garden roses give us happiness and true satisfaction only – 'sweet solace', in the delightful phrase of our garden lovers of three hundred years ago. They are so many that we have their bloom from May to late November, and so various of kind and habit that there is no place, from the ordered terrace and fully dressed parterre to the wild waste and woodland, for which there are not roses ready.

Some of the oldest are still among the best; no rose scent equals that of the old cabbage rose (*R.* x *centifolia*) and its variety the moss rose. Then, in full young summer come the damasks, of bushy growth, some red, some parti-coloured; and the charming white with red picotee edge, known by either of two names – 'Reine Blanche' or 'Hebe's Lip'. Besides these, there is the velvet rose, a double damask of very dark colour, and other doubles of pale pink colouring. These damasks come very near the gallicas, old garden roses that were in great favour in the early years of the nineteenth century, and many were the varieties that were catalogued in rose lists of the time. Until lately, we knew these gallicas as the Provins roses, and the cabbage roses and its relatives as the Provence. But recent botanical authority has taught us to reverse these names, and that the gallicas are rightly named Provence and the centifolias Provins. The name York and Lancaster, so commonly given to the striped and splashed damask, really belongs to a gallica; the parti-coloured damask is 'Rosa Mundi' or cottage maid (*R. gallica* 'Versicolor').

There is much charm in the old cinnamon rose, now rarely seen; but its flat-shaped rosy bloom and neat foliage make it too good a thing to deserve neglect. There is nothing much sweeter than the early foliage of the native sweet briar (*R. rubiginosa*) some warm day in May. It may be found in some districts as a woodland shrub, but is none the less wanted in the home garden. We are grateful to the late Lord Penzance for his work in crossing it with other roses and so producing larger and better-coloured blooms, while retaining the scented

LEFT
The garland rose in the Hut Garden.

ABOVE RIGHT
The rose and peony beds at Upton Grey, a garden designed by Miss Jekyll in 1908.

foliage. But for wild planting the type is good enough, with its pretty pink bloom and brightly coloured hips.

There is a whole range of pretty things among the Scotch briars, derived from the native *R. pimpinellifolia*, that is found as a low-growing bush in many heathy places near the sea. The single lemon-white flower of the wild plant has broken into doubles of a number of colourings – white, pale and deep pink, deep rose and yellow; one double pink with unusual sweet scent and dark leaves that I remember as a child and have sought for all my life has come to me at last, to my great joy.

The old cottage white rose, half double, with broad, flat, bluish leaves, known as *Rosa* x *alba*, but not considered a true species, is a prime garden favourite, with its pink varieties, 'Maiden's Blush' and the still more delightful 'Celeste', one of the best of all roses in the half-opened bud state. These make big bushes, easily kept in shape by judicious pruning, or they may be made to climb high enough to cover a cottage porch.

The old China or monthly rose, best of all in its ordinary pink colouring, is always one of our prized garden roses, full of bloom in early June and again in September, and never without a good show of flower all the summer; the best of all roses to have near a window. The dwarfer form, with brilliant red colouring, 'Cramoisie Supérieure', is a charming rose, and the still smaller 'Lawranciana' is a gem for the rock garden.

A warm wall is the place for the Macartney rose (*R. bracteata*), with its large, solid white bloom of almost magnolia texture, and handsome tuft of deep yellow stamens and deep green, polished leaves. That wonderful Chinese rose 'Fortune's Yellow' is only happy on a wall in our warmest south-west or the Isle of Wight, but where it does well its flaming masses of flower are a sight to see. Another rose that is thankful for a warm wall is the double *R. roxburghii* f. *normalis*, a bush that has a remarkably well-dressed appearance with its dainty leaves and widespread bloom, shading from tenderest pink to a full crimson centre, and its large round buds covered with stiff green bristles.

The American *Rosa virginiana* is useful as a wide-spreading bush, both in garden and half-wild thickets. It bears shade better than any other rose; in fact, the pink flowers burn badly in full sun; but it seems to be proof against all Rose ills and rose enemies, for I never remember to have seen on it any blight, defect or injury. The highly polished leaves turn a brilliant orange colour, sometimes actually scarlet, in the late autumn, making it a plant of notable use in combination with others of fine autumnal colouring. There seems to be two distinct forms, one being larger and altogether more free than the other. The charming double variety, one of the most lovely of roses in the half-opened bud, must belong to the smaller-growing kind, as it forms compact bushes.

For garden roses of yellow colouring we have the rather tender Persian rose, with its double variety, and the Austrian briar. The name Austrian is misleading, as they are both Asiatic in origin, and appear to be nearly related. The so-called 'Austrian Copper', the only rose of vivid scarlet colouring, is a sport from the yellow; both colours have been known on the same bush; the red is a thin film laid over the yellow. The old yellow cabbage (*R. hemisphaerica*), formerly a favourite in gardens, is now almost out of cultivation. A valuable addition to yellow garden roses has lately been made in *R. xanthina* f. *hugonis* from middle Eastern Asia, a briar in general appearance. Another new rose species, though not yellow, that is a welcome garden rose is *R. moyesii*, in colour a deep red with a kind of dusty-looking surface.

The Japanese *R. rugosa* is useful both in the garden and in wilder places. It is best to avoid the type colouring, a rather pronounced magenta, but is better pink, and the white is always good. The large fruits are very handsome. It is a capital plant for rough banks or for making a prickly hedge, for all its kind are fiercely armed. The beautiful double form 'Blanche Double de Coubert' should not be forgotten. It makes a large solid bush of fine deep green foliage and abundance of milk-white bloom. After a few years' growth all the rugosas are the better for a drastic pruning, cutting away everything to within nine inches of the ground.

Of climbing roses for any kind of garden use there is an ample choice, even considering the numerous good modern ramblers derived from *R. multiflora* and *R. wichurana*. Rose 'Ruga' is a grand old thing, 'Dundee Rambler' and the 'Garland' rose, both nearly white, and 'Flora', pink (a favourite rose of the old flower painters) and one or two others of these old ramblers, hybrids of *R. sempervirens* and *R. arvensis*, are as good as anything that has followed. The varieties of *R. moschata* are also full of beauty and should be oftener grown. Their power of climbing seems to be without limit. I have an old rose, whose actual origin is unknown to me, but from whose appearance I should guess to be a hybrid of *R. moschata* and *R. arvensis*. It has rushed up into a tall birch, and must be full fifty feet high and is still growing. Such a rose is beautiful in rough ground, where there are natural brakes of holly, thorn and bramble, with rough grass and bracken in the open spaces between; for it has a habit and character that look absolutely wild, and yet it gives a greater quantity of bloom than any actually wild rose.

The old climbing roses derived from *R. pendulina*, that we know as boursaults, should not be forgotten, though the one best known, the 'Crimson Boursault', the easiest to grow and the most free of bloom, is one rather to be avoided, for it is of a harsh crimson colour. The variety 'Morlettii' is much better, and also the one named 'Mme Sancy de Pavabere', but, best of all is *R*. 'Blush Boursault', one of the loveliest and cleanest-coloured of all roses; it has the outer petals of a tender white of singularly pure quality, deepening to a delicate pink in the middle.

Many of the modern hybrids, the roses within the usual classification of Hybrid Perpetual, Tea and Hybrid Tea, that are not of show quality, but are of strong constitution and good bushy habit, prove to be good garden roses, but, as a rule, it is difficult to specify many of these as their behaviour varies much in different gardens. But a word may safely be said of the supreme importance, both as a bold bush, or semi-climber or pillar, of the French 'Rose Zéphirine Drouhin', free and hardy, of a good rose colour that never turns purple, and of sweetest scent. It is long lasting when cut, pleasant to handle because almost without prickles, flowers all the summer through, and culminates in excellence as the flower year comes to an end. It was known to me on the Continent many years before it was to be had in England; repeated enquiries for it in the home nurseries only brought the answer that there was no demand for it. Happily it has at length received recognition; it is a rose that should be in every garden.

Many old roses may still be found in out-of-the-way gardens; good things without name, some of them of the kind of value of the old 'Mme Plantier', that charming rose of large bushy habit with masses of white bloom in long-stemmed clusters, of whose origin I know nothing.

SOME OF THE SWEETEST ROSES

It may be assumed that all who are acquainted with the old garden roses will agree that none excels, or even equals, the old cabbage rose (*R. x centifolia*) in charm of fragrance. In its variety the moss rose, with its curiously crested calyx, a close, mossy growth with a viscous exudation that has its own special sweetness – a scent that recalls both that of the dying strawberry leaf and of the young foliage of sweet briar – this amalgamates delightfully with the perfume of the flower. There is another rose which has distinctly that wonderful and mysterious scent of the dying strawberry leaf, an old kind called 'Glorie des Rosomanes'. It is only half double and of a good deep red colour, and of rather thin straggly growth. The foliage points to its being near a China. There is an old tea rose, 'Goubault', that should not be lost sight of for the sake of its remarkable and delicious scent, which is like that of a ripe nectarine. I have not had an opportunity of meeting with any of the roses that have been lately in competition for scent, but their fragrance must, indeed, be remarkable if it is any better than that of 'Rose à Parfum de l'Haÿ', a large loosely double rose, whose colour, alas, is such a pronounced magenta that it is purposely planted where it is not much seen. But the scent is wonderful, strong and of the purest Otto of Rose. It is a hybrid of rugosa, the dark green, polished, plaited leaves showing its nearness to that species. From what other parent it can have derived its unfortunate colour and its incomparable scent I do not know. The flower of sweet briar is less distinctly fragrant than the leaves, and these are at their sweetest when quite young in May. At that time of year one cannot pass near a bush of sweet briar without being aware of its welcome greeting. Of modern, well-scented roses the merit of 'Zéphirine Drouhin' should be remembered. It is a rose that should be in every garden. It does well in any soil, the flower is a fair size and well shaped, the colour is a good full rose that does not turn purple, it is pleasant to handle as it has very few prickles, its scent is one of the sweetest, and it seems to bloom better and better as the season advances. It does well as a pillar, or pegged, or growing free among shrubs. In the garden where this note is written it is trained to bamboo rods that are fastened horizontally on to short stumps about two feet high, a convenient device both for seeing and cutting.

SOME TEA ROSES

With the multitude of beautiful roses in modern lists one is apt to overlook the merits of some of the older tea roses, especially as the hybrid teas have of late years so largely taken their place. And as there are other who are better qualified for writing about the later and exhibition kinds, these few remarks about some of the older favourites may not be out of place. One of the earliest of the old teas to bloom is the pink 'Homère'. Near a warm wall it may be had as early as the last days of May, and it is quickly followed by 'Mme Falcot', of deepest apricot. 'Souvenir d'um Ami' and 'Catherine Mermet' remain in remembrance as two of the loveliest of pink roses, with 'Bridesmaid', a deeper form of 'Catherine Mermet'. 'Anna Oliver', yellowish flesh colour with pink-backed petals, is always welcome, and of the same class of colour is 'Souvenir d'Elise Vardon'. Other old favourites are 'Docteur Grill', copper yellow; 'G. Nabonnand', pale rose, shaded yellow; 'Safrano', yellow and copper orange; 'Deoniensis', a splendid great yellow white, and its climbing form; 'Maman Cochet', rose, and its white variety; 'Princesse de Sagan', a splendid deep red of small growth; 'Madame Lombard', ever faithful and always in bloom; and 'Goubault', coppery red, with a wonderful scent like a ripe nectarine. The Dijon group can never be forgotten – the original 'Gloire de Dijon', the one most free of bloom, and its derivatives 'Bouquet d'Or' and 'Madame Berard'. A south wall is usually too hot a place for all but the tenderest roses, but it is the place for the glorious Chinese 'Fortune's Yellow'; it also suits 'Adam', a fine old pink rose, and the warm white 'Triomphe de Rennes', one of the roses of loveliest form, and 'Lamarque', which flowers in clusters of large bloom nearly white and has the unusual merit of retaining the flowers in good order for several days. These and others of that rather vague class called noisette, which may well be considered with the teas, comprises also other old favourites, such as 'Alister Stella Gray', yellow shaded, a very charming rose of climbing habit with clusters of bloom that go on into late autumn; 'William Allen Richardson', also climbing and one of the earliest to bloom; 'Rêve d'Or', the pretty pale 'Céline Forestier', and the old 'Ophelia', yellow and salmon. All of these are climbers.

GOOD CLIMBING ROSES

The spring work of pruning, tying up and training the plants that clothe wall, fence and pergola sets one thinking about climbing and rambling plants, and all their various ways and wants, and of how best to use them. One of my boundaries to a road is a fence about nine feet high, wall below and close oak paling above. It is planted with free-growing roses of several types – 'Aimée Vibert', 'Madame Alfred Carrière', 'Reine Olga de Wurtemburg', and 'Bouquet d'Or', the strongest of the Dijon teas. Then comes a space of *Clematis montana* and *C. flammula*, and then more roses – 'Madame Plantier', 'Emelie Plantier' (a delightful rose to cut), and some of the grand sweet briars raised by Lord Penzance. From midsummer onwards these roses are continually cut for flower, and yield an abundance of quite the most ornamental class of bloom. I like to have cut roses arranged in a large, free way, with whole branches three or four feet long, easy to have from these free-growing kinds, that throw out branches fifteen feet long in one season, even on our poor, sandy soil that contains no particle of that rich loam that roses love. I think this same 'Reine Olga de Wurtemburg', the grand grower from which have come our longest and largest prunings, must be quite the best evergreen rose, for it holds its full clothing of handsome dark green leaves right through the winter. It seems to like hard pruning. I have one on a part of the pergola, but have no

An effective use of *Rosa filipes* in the White Garden, Sissinghurst Castle, Kent.

pleasure from it, as it has rushed up to the top, and nothing shows but a few naked stems. One has to find out how to use all these different roses. How often one sees the wrong roses used as climbers on the walls of a house. I have seen 'Gloire de Dijon' covering the side of a house with a profitless reticulation of bare stem, and a few leaves and flowers looking into the gutter just under the edge of the roof. What are generally recommended as climbing roses are too ready to ramp away, leaving bare, leggy growth where wall clothing is desired. One of the best is climbing 'Aimée Vibert', for with very little pruning it keeps well furnished nearly to the ground, and with its graceful clusters of white bloom and healthy-looking, polished leaves is always one of the prettiest of roses. Its only fault is that it does not shed its dead petals, but retains the whole bloom in dead brown clusters. But if a rose wishes to climb it should be accommodated with a suitable place. That excellent old rose the 'Dundee Rambler', or the still prettier 'The Garland' rose, will find a way up a holly tree, and fling out its long wreaths of tenderly tinted bloom; and there can be no better way of using the lovely Himalayan *Rosa brunonii*, with its long, almost blue leaves and wealth of milk-white flowers. A common sweet briar will also push up among the branches of some dark evergreen, yew or holly, and throw out aloft its scented branches and rosy bloom, and look its very best. Some of these same free roses, however, are best of all if left a clear space to grow exactly as they will, without any kind of support or training. So placed, they grow into large rounded groups. Every year, just after the young laterals on the last year's branches have flowered, they throw out vigorous young rods that arch over as they complete their growth, and will be the flower bearers of the year to come.

Two kinds of roses of rambling growth that are rather tender, but indispensable for beauty, are 'Fortune's Yellow' and the banksians. Pruning the free roses is always rough work for the hands and clothes, but of all roses I know, the worst to handle is 'Fortune's Yellow'. The prickles are hooked back in a way that no care or ingenuity can escape, and whether it is their shape and power of cruel grip, or whether they have anything of a poisonous quality, I do not know; but, whereas hands scratched and torn by roses in general heal quickly, the wounds made by 'Fortune's Yellow' are much more painful and much slower to get well. The flowering season of 'Fortune's Yellow' is a very short one, but it comes so early, and the flowers have such incomparable beauty, and are so little like those of any other rose, that its value is quite without doubt. Some of the tea roses approach it in its pink and copper colouring, but the loose, open, rather flaunting form of the flower and the twisted set of the petals display the colour better than is possible in any of the more regularly shaped roses. It is a good plan to grow it through some other wall shrub, as it soon gets bare below, and the early maturing flowering tips are glad to be a little sheltered by the near neighbourhood of other foliage. I do not think that there is any other rose that has just the same rich butter colour as the yellow banksian, and this unusual colouring is the more distinct because each little rose in the cluster is nearly evenly coloured all over, besides being in such dense bunches. The season of bloom is very short, but the neat, polished foliage is always pleasant to see throughout the year. The white kind and the larger white are both lovely as to the individual bloom, but they flower so much more shyly that the yellow is much the better garden plant.

OTHER CLIMBING PLANTS But the best of all climbing or rambling plants, whether for wall or arbour or pergola, is undoubtedly the grape vine. Even when trimly pruned and trained for fruit bearing on an outer wall it is an admirable picture of leafage and fruit cluster; but to have it in fullest beauty it must ramp at will, for it is only when the fast-growing branches are thrown out far and wide that it fairly displays its graceful vigour and the generous magnificence of its incomparable foliage. The hardy chasselas, known in England by the rather misleading name *Vitis vinifera* 'Royal Muscadine', is one of the best both for fruit and foliage. The colour of the leaves is a fresh, lively green, and in autumn they are prettily marbled with yellow. Where a very large-leaved vine is wanted, nothing is handsomer than the North American *Vitis labrusca* or the Asiatic *V. coignetiae*, whose autumn leaves are gorgeously coloured. For a place that demands more delicate foliage there is the parsley vine, that has a delightful look of refinement, and another that should not be forgotten is the claret vine, with autumnal colouring of almost scarlet and purple, and an abundance of tightly clustered black fruit, nearly blue with a heavy bloom. Many an old house and garden can show the far-rambling power of the beautiful *Wisteria sinensis*, and of the large-leaved *Aristolochia microphylla*, one of the best plants for covering a pergola, and of the varieties of ampelopsis, near relations of the grape vine.

The limit of these notes only admits of mention of some of the more important climbers, but among these the ever-delightful white jasmine must have a place. It will ramble far and fast if it has its own way, but then gives little flower; but by close winter pruning it can be kept full of bloom and leaf nearly to the ground. The woods and hedges have also their beautiful climbing plants. Honeysuckle in suitable conditions will ramble to great heights; in some districts most noticeable in tall hollies and junipers as well as in high hedges. The wild clematis is most frequent on the chalk, where it laces together whole hedges and rushes up trees, clothing them in July with long wreaths of delicate bloom, and in September with still more conspicuous feathery seed. For rapid growth perhaps no English plant outstrips the hop, growing afresh from the root every year, and almost equalling the vine in beauty of leaf. The two kinds of wild bryony are also herbaceous climbers of rapid growth, and among the most beautiful of our hedge plants. The wild roses run up to great heights in hedge and thicket, and never look so well as when among the tangles of mixed growth of wild forest land or clambering through some old gnarled thorn tree. The common brambles are also best seen in these forest groups; these again in form of leaf show somewhat of a vine-like beauty.

THE JOYS OF OBSERVATION

It is hardly possible to walk round even one's own familiar garden without seeing something fresh that had not been noticed before, either in form, habit or colour, where plants are grown, not only in borders and shrub edges, but also in generous reserve batches. And I can hardly think of a more interesting pursuit than the growing of good garden plants in still larger quantity, the better to have opportunity of observing and noting slight distinctions in a good direction. This wider field of observation being denied me, I have to be content with my own restricted area, and find that even within this there is much to be observed. For if one has some knowledge of plants and has a desire to see them at their very best, the mind forms a concept of what that best may possibly be, and as the years pass and painstaking is not spared, both in cultivation and observation, in the elimination of the less good and the fostering of the better, it is a joy to see how the flower gradually approaches and finally arrives at the desired goal.

But such is the possible variation of natural structure that a plant may spring at once into some form of beauty without the long process of guidance and selection. Such a joy awaited me recently, when, looking at a trial patch of old garden roses, the eye was arrested by something strange and quite beautiful. It is just a damask rose of the usual slightly doubled form, but it was the colour, a delightful paleish rosy red, that drew attention. The colour is very near that of 'Zéphirine Drouhin', but from the different and slighter texture of petal it has a hint of semi-transparency, with that backward and forward and translucent play of colour, light and shade that results in an extraordinary richness of effect. How it came there I know not, for though this class of colouring in the damask rose may be quite well known, I had never before had it in my garden, and it is growing in the middle of a patch of *Rosa x centifolia* (cabbage rose). It seems also to have some slight affinity with *R. x centifolia*, because the sweet-smelling glandular viscosity at the back of the flower and upper part of the flower stalk, though always present in the damask in a slight degree, much more pronounced in *R. x centifolia* and so highly accentuated in the mossy variety, seemed to be in a stage midway between the two. The charming colour of my new-found damask has also just that shade of warmth that makes it all the more harmonious with the generous bunch of golden stamens in the centre. If such a variety is fairly well known one wonders why it has not before been warmly praised; is it that we are only now waking up to a reasonable consciousness of colour refinement?

It brings to mind the general neglect of the better coloured of the old boursault roses, good old garden flowers that, among the numbers of the modern ramblers, have been almost forgotten. But if any boursault rose is in a garden it is pretty sure to be the crimson one, of a rather rank colour, while the varieties named 'Morletti' and 'Madame Saucy de Parabere' are of thoroughly desirable shades of rosy red, and the still better 'Blush Boursault' is without any rival among roses, for its charming colouring of pure milk white shading to a centre of shell rose.

SCOTCH BRIARS

Early in the rose season comes the welcome bloom of the Scotch briars. They are the garden forms of the native *Rosa pimpinellifolia*, found wild in some heathy lands near the sea. Their presence in such places points to their value for gardens where the soil is naturally poor and sandy, and especially for bare banks fully exposed to sun and air. The type plant, with its single blooms of a lemon white colour when first opened, is well worth garden use, but the one most often seen is the double white; this also appears to be the most vigorous. There are other varieties, in several shades of pink, rose and crimson, and some, generally of weaker

Scotch briar roses flanking the
Main Terrace and South Lawn
at Munstead.

growth, with yellow flowers. There is one specially desirable kind which I remember as a child, but have since lost sight of. It has unusually globular flowers of a pale pink colour which never open wide. The colour is quite even all over, and the scent extremely sweet. The foliage is bluish and dusky in tone. The species *R. pimpinellifolia* 'Grandiflora' may be described as identical, only of a larger size.

THE ROSE 'ZÉPHIRINE DROUHIN'

In the seventies of the last century the writer of this note first knew and admired this useful rose in the mountain home of friends in Switzerland. It was so evidently a rose for every garden that it was a matter of wonder that it seemed to be unknown in England. Enquiries among friends in the trade, to whom it was evidently not known, only brought the answer: 'We have no demand for it', and it was only by repeated assurances of its merits, stressing them by saying that if it was known it would become the most popular rose in English gardens, that some impression was made, and that it crept into the catalogues of our nurseries. It may safely be said that it is everybody's rose, for it is one of the most easily grown. It appears to do well in all soils, it is of a good rosy-red colour that never turns purple, is of sweetest scent, very free of bloom and pleasant to cut and carry as it has next to no prickles. It is a continuous bloomer, in the middle season coming in great terminal clusters and going on all through September and into October. It is an admirable pillar rose, but the way we find best is to have it pegged down or, rather, tied down to about eighteen inches or two feet above ground. We have three such long beds, the highest three feet, but the prettiest is the lowest. For this we put in little posts two inches thick and eighteen inches out of the ground, at suitable distances apart, and run long bamboo rods from post to post, fixing them with iron staples, with a few of the same running in long diagonals across the bed, just enough to secure some of the long growths in such a way as to cover the bed suitably.

WILD AND WOODLAND GARDENING

WILD GARDENING

It is only within the last forty years that we have become aware of the possibility of extending our gardening into the wild, and it seems strange that it should be so, because already in Tudor times it was foreshadowed as a regular garden practice. Thus, we read in Bacon's essays, in his ordering of a stately garden of some thirty acres, there is first the quiet green forecourt leading to the house, then the main garden, and lastly the 'Heath or Desart in the going forth'. And though in this 'heath', some of his planting, of standard roses and shaped evergreens, is such as we should now reject, yet we cannot improve upon his counsel to have thickets of sweet briars and honeysuckle and on the ground thyme for its sweetness when crushed underfoot.

It must not be supposed that wild gardening is easy; I am inclined to think that to do it worthily needs more knowledge of the ways of plants than is wanted for any other kind of garden work. But if one may attempt to formulate something in the way of rules, one of the first of these should certainly be to observe the necessity of moderation and restraint. The sentiment to be created and fostered is the charm of a succession of gentle surprises of delight, rather than a series of rude shocks of astonishment. This is where we are so greatly helped by the indications of nature, for our best conception of our subject is engendered by what we have seen in the wild. One at a time some lovely effect is noted – of a dog rose clambering through a thorn; of a stretch of woodland rosy with its flowering willow; of a copse floor blue with bluebells or closely studded with bosses of primrose; of quiet stretches of purple-grey or ruddy heathland. In these and in many other examples of nature's gardening we see one thing at a time thoroughly well done – it is all large and simple. The plants may be only a few or they may be in tens of thousands, but they are absolutely rightly placed and in their proper environment.

The character of the ground to be dealt with must needs govern the choice of plants. It may be a dry upland field, requiring some preliminary planting of trees and bushes, or it may be a cool meadow or even a bit of boggy ground; or a rocky hillside or an old quarry all demanding special treatment. Perhaps the most favourable state of things is where a garden joins some half-open woodland, when the planting can go forward, changing its character almost imperceptibly from home to wild.

It should be observed that the plants that by long association with the home garden are fixed in the mind as garden plants are among the least suitable for putting out in the wild, and it so happens that, in the case of some kinds, the rule is just reversed in our two countries. Thus, the perennial asters, commonly known as the Michaelmas daisies, being wild plants in the States, are there suitable for the wild garden, while with us they are exclusively garden plants for, except for one species, common in the salt marshes but of a horticultural value, the genus is not represented in our island. The same may be said of the perennial sunflowers. But there is no reason why the better kinds of the aster may not come into the wild garden in the States; best of all some of the large-bloomed, free-branching kinds derived from *A. novi-belgii.* But here will come in the need for restraint, for the numbers of good kinds are now so many that it may be difficult to make a choice. One kind in fair number, or two related kinds, to be seen at the same time, will be best. On the other hand we have in England vast stretches of moorland on poor, sandy soil – thousands of acres at a time even in the home counties – while in the north it covers square miles without end. Therefore there is nothing more suitable, in our lighter soils, than a wild heath garden, where the native species form a groundwork for the Mediterranean, Spanish and Alpine kinds.

As all of the possible phases of wild gardening cannot be dealt with within the compass of one article, let us take an example of a garden that extends to the edge of partly wooded ground, and consider how it may be treated, taking separately one or two different paths from home garden to woodland, on a soil inclining to light. One of the paths passes through a plantation of rhododendrons and the other through azaleas, and though botanists now put rhododendrons and azaleas together, yet for garden purposes it is well to retain the separate names so as to keep them distinct; for, though they flower nearly at the same time, their habit – and in some way their uses – are very dissimilar. For one thing rhododendrons form a delightful winter shelter, and a seat somewhere among them may form an enjoyable winter sun trap, while the azaleas are quite bare of leaves. Then their colours do not always agree. Even among the rhododendrons alone there has to be a careful selection for colour. It will be found best to keep the true purple, kinds that are near the type ponticum, away from the hybrids of *R. catawbiense,* and these *R. ponticum* being of large growth should be nearest the wild garden side. They also do well and look best in the near neighbourhood and partial shade of trees and their foliage is the finest in winter. Birches accompany them well, the silvery stems showing up finely among the dusk leaf masses. If the place is suitable for undershrubs there are *Gaultheria shallon* and *Leucothoe fontanesiana* and some of the vacciniums and the candleberry gale (*Myrica cerifera*). This delightful sweet-leaved shrub should occur often near the paths, so that a leaf or two may be readily picked and crushed in the hand for the sake of enjoying its incomparable scent. And, it may well be planted on each side of some very narrow secondary path where the passerby must necessarily brush up against it.

With the birches there should be some common green hollies, and by this time we are quite in the wild land. Soon the hollies and birches give place to oaks and hazels but

Munstead
Wood from the
wood in 2003.

between them is a space of fairly open ground; here is a chance to plant some daffodils of the yellow or bicolour trumpet kinds. We try to place them as nature plants and for a general rule this may be described as first a nucleus, where the bulbs are fairly close together, with others more singly streaming away; but it may be easily shown by a diagram. Where there is a fair space or nothing growing on the floor of the wood but its own thin grasses and mosses and other lowly plants, it has a good effect if the groups are in a series of nearly parallel drifts, preferably running north and south; for then in low evening sunlight, when yellow daffodils look their best and the whole garden picture is mellowed with golden light, the level lines of nodding bloom are surprisingly beautiful.

Where the trees give place to little thickets of something between bush and small tree we plant in with it some rambling rose with single bloom – best of all the free-growing 'Evangeline', whose flowers are much like the wild dog rose in character, but are larger and of greater substance and borne in more generous clusters. It is a perfect rose for the wild garden though the Himalayan musk rose (*R. moschata*) runs it very close. Other thickets would have honeysuckle; such free-growing kinds as what are known as the early and late Dutch honeysuckle *(Lonicera periclymenium* 'Belgica' and 'Serotina') or some of the type clematis such as *C. montana* and *C. flammula* or the wild grape vines *Vitis thunbergi* and *V. coignetiae.* The thickets themselves – in England usually of whitethorn or blackthorn, with or without holly – may be of any handsome fruiting bushes, such as *Euonymus europaeus* (spindle tree), the Siberian crabs (*Malus baccata* and *M. prunifolia*), the scarlet-fruited thorn (*Crataegus coccinea*) and the Indian *Cotoneaster frigidus.* Pretty small trees such as *Amelanchier canadensis* are also delightful things in the wild ground.

The other path from the home garden that also leads to the woodland passes first through ground where a natural growth of birch and holly comes next to the garden. The path lies in a slight hollow with easy banks on each side and, here and there, a cool bay level with the path or even a little below it. On the banks are large groups of common hardy ferns and there is a natural background of bracken (*Peridium aquilinum*). The level and sunk bogs are deeply prepared with leaf mould; in one is the wood lily (*Trillium*), in another bloodroot (*Sanguinaria*) and in the deepest and coolest the royal fern (*Osmunda regalis*). At the back there are wide-spreading patches of Solomon's seal (*Polygonatum multiflorum*), a true wood plant, and standing up in the bracken background large groups of pure white foxglove. The walk goes gently uphill and presently comes to an open clearing some sixty feet across and a hundred and fifty long. The path now takes an easy winding line and here and there are the azaleas. They are in sunlight more or less for the greater part of the day, but the surrounding trees shift the sunny places so that none is subject to a whole day's burning heat. They stand well apart, eight feet or more from plant to plant, so that they have space to develop well and to grow into their small tree form. They are the hardy Ghent kind and, though no azaleas actually clash for colour, they are planted so that those of tender tinting are at the two ends, with a gorgeous mass of the reds and yellows towards the middle of the length. Planted with them is again the sweet candleberry gale, and the vacciniums that turn so fine a red in autumn when the azalea leaves are also richly

The Fern Walk, a masterpiece of natural planting.

The main Woodland Walk, looking towards
the sitting-room window. Partly planted
with rhododendrons, it had an old Scots pine
as a focal point.

coloured. Treated in this manner almost by themselves in ground of a wild character, these beautiful azaleas are much more effective than in tamer garden use.

The many bulbous plants, besides the daffodils, that flower in the early year, are more enjoyable and show their truest beauty to much greater advantage in the wilder ground than in the restricted garden. The fine Dutch crocuses, as well as several species, are at their best in their turf; Snowdrops are happiest under trees in any strong soil; the summer snowflake (*Leucojum aestivium*) revels in moist ground. Spanish squills (*Hyacinthoides hispanica*) are lovely with pale primroses under trees, and the smaller scillas and chionodoxas in sunny banks. Then, besides the bulbous plants there are many that are better in the wild ground than in the garden, such as the blue Italian *Anemone apennina*, the deeper blue Greek *A. blanda* and all varieties of the wood anemone (*A. nemorosa*). Delightful though the home garden may be there will be found in this kind of wild planting a whole new range of interest and perception of beauty in the ways of growing and flowering things.

A SELF-SOWN WOOD

It is often cited as a matter for wonder, or at least some degree of surprise, that when a wood of one kind of tree is cut down, quite other kinds of trees soon appear as seedlings.

But country folk, who are familiar with the ways of woodland, know that such changes are only in the ordinary course of events. The ground under trees is full of various nuts and seeds, brought by birds and squirrels as well as wind-blown. While it is covered with woody growth and there is but little light and sun warmth reaching the earth, the state of things is not favourable to development, so that the seed, after lying dormant for some time, either decays or germinates feebly and throws up a weak, leggy growth that is of no account. Many seeds, after lying for some time, perish in this way, but some retain the possibility of vitality for a number of years, and meanwhile the supply is continually renewed. As soon as the wood is cut down, the conditions at the earth surface are changed. The sun warms the ground and the combined action of heat, light and moisture stimulates the seeds. The same occurs with the lower plants in copses of underwood. These copses are usually allowed to grow for seven years. For the last three years before cutting, when the leafy branches meet and mingle overhead, there is hardly any wild growth below. One pushes through with some difficulty, finding only the carpet of dead leaves under foot. But as soon as the copse is cut, the seed stored in the ground comes to life. By the second year there are masses of primroses and campions, and, in some places, a perfect turf of seedling foxgloves, while the bulbs of the bluebells and the creeping roots of the wood anemones take heart again and flower and flourish.

A small wood of ten acres adjoins my garden. Formerly it was a wood of Scots pine of some seventy years' growth. Under the close-growing trees the ground was bare but for a scant sprinkling of whortleberry, heath and bracken at the lighter edges. Thirty-five years ago the pines were cut and the ground left bare. Soon it became covered with heath, ling and short bracken, and, on one side especially, a stronger growth of whortleberry. Then, year by year, tree seedlings of many kinds came up in considerable quantity, so that there was not a yard of ground without one or more. This went on for some nine or ten years before the land came into my hands, and by then the seedlings were, in many places, so thick that it was impossible to get between them. From that time onwards the problem was how best to thin them, also to cut out a few paths on the easiest lines to serve the future laying out of the ground where house and garden were to be.

What is most remarkable about these few acres of seedling growth is the large number of trees and shrubs of native species that are present. The larger trees are represented by beech, oak, ash, Spanish chestnut, lime, birch and Scotch fir. I believe I may say that every British conifer and evergreen is among them, except box; for, besides the seedlings that one would expect from the original pines, there is a spontaneous growth of spruce, larch, yew and juniper, also holly in abundance. Ivy and honeysuckle, both of woody growth, though hardly classed as trees, are in plenty; the latter in large quantity – in many places covering the floor of the wood with a treacherous knee-high tangle that makes walking difficult. Of the apple tribe there are no fewer than six, namely, mountain ash, white beam, wild cherry, crab, whitethorn and blackthorn. There are a few saplings of ash and sycamore, and though it is at the top of a dry hill, several plants of willow, evidently from wind blowing of the feathered seeds. There are also hazel and elder, broom and gorse. Of less common shrubs,

Rhododendron 'Multimaculatum' amongst silver birch at the woodland edge.

though fairly frequent in the neighbourhood, there is one example of alder buckthorn (*Rhamnus frangula*), a bush that always arrests me with a sense of interest. I cannot say why, as it is not conspicuous or specially beautiful; perhaps it is because one only comes upon it now and then, and because it is one of the woodland things that no one seems to know the name of. There is one example in a wood not far off that has assumed the shape of a tree, with a single tall trunk about five inches thick.

Those mentioned account for twenty-five of our native trees and hard-wooded shrubs, not counting ivy and honeysuckle. I can only think of fourteen others that are not represented. These are elm, wych elm, poplar, field maple, alder, horse chestnut, walnut and hornbeam among trees; and of shrubs, dogwood, *Viburnum opulus* and *V. lantana*, common buckthorn, spindle tree and privet.

RHODODENDRONS GROUPED FOR COLOUR

How seldom one sees, even where care has been taken to secure the best kinds, that any attention has been paid to grouping rhododendrons with a view to good colour effect. Unlike azaleas, whose varied colourings are always harmonious, rhododendrons want separating into at least three groupings, that is to say, if they are to do all they can for us in the way of colour beauty. It is much to be recommended that the delicate pinks be kept away from the purples, and the comparatively few that have salmon shades from the purplish

Rhododendrons
in the woodland
where paths
converge.

reds, and all these away from each other. It may help others whose eyes are also offended by the usual colour-jumbling of these grand shrubs to give the names of a few that are found to go happily together. Of course the many beautiful white-coloured ones go well with all the groups. For a grouping of pink, white and red the following have a good effect:

PINKS
'Aclandianum'
'Bianca'
'Blandyanum'
'Broughtoni'
'Concessum'
'Congestum roseum'
'Cynthia'
'Fair Rosamond'
'Ingrami'
'Kate Waterer'
'Mrs Penn'
'Papilionacea'
'Titian'

REDS
'Baron Schroeder'
'John Waterer'
'James Marshall Brooks'
'Paxtoni'
'Pelipodas'

WHITES
'Album elegans'
'Album grandiflorum'
'Cunningham's White'
'Delicatissimum'
'Mme Carvalho'
'Minnie'
'The Queen'

For a grouping of colours of shades approaching lilac and violet-purples with suitable whites, purples and lilacs,

WHITES	PURPLES AND LILACS
'Album grandiflorum'	'Contortum'
'Baroness Schroeder'	'Cyaneum'
'Candidum'	'Everestianum'
'Fair Ellen'	'Fastuosum Flore Pleno'
'Mme Masson'	'Lady Normanton'
'Nivaticum'	'Reine Hortense'
'Perspicuum'	
'Purity'	
'Sappho'	

give a grouping of very charming appearance. The old ponticum does best with this group.

Those of salmon colouring, such as 'Mrs R.S. Holford', 'Lady Eleanor Cathcart' and 'Mrs F. Hankey', should be kept by themselves with a few warm whites. The many splendid flowers of the strong crimson colourings with those approaching magenta should form a separate group.

It is easy in laying out a piece of ground for rhododendrons to throw the masses into such groupings that only one of such schemes of colouring is seen at the same time, and the double benefit is gained of showing the plants to their highest advantage and of gaining the impression of a much wider range of good colouring than can be obtained in the old mixed style of planting.

THE AZALEA GARDEN

Those who live and garden on soils that are sandy or peaty, although they may be debarred from much that may be done on those that are of loam or lime, yet have one distinct compensation in that they can do well with *Ericaceae*, that large family of shrubs that includes rhododendron and azalea, andromeda (*Leucothoe*), erica, vaccinium, kalmia, gaultheria and others of this delightful order. It is well to devote quite a large space to azaleas, either alone or in company with some of the vacciniums, for, long after their blooming time, when the leaves of the azaleas have taken on their ruddy tinting, the vacciniums, especially *V. angustifolium*, will form points of still more brilliant colouring, the leaves turning almost scarlet.

My azalea garden is a clearing in natural woodland of oak, birch and Spanish chestnut. It is on hilly land and by nature drier than is desirable, for azaleas are thankful for ground that is fairly moist, though they cannot endure any place that is actually waterlogged. The surrounding trees are not near enough to rob them at the root but their height gives passing shade in the middle of the day. A very slightly winding path passes upwards for nearly a hundred yards, coming out at the top into a further clearing planted as a heath garden. The azaleas are carefully grouped for colour. At the lower end they begin with some of fairly strong colour, soon passing to the most brilliant deep orange and red, then following through yellows to white; these, again, leading to stronger colouring. Their size when of mature growth was considered at the time of planting; they should stand about eight feet apart, not evenly; but sometimes a group of the same may be a little closer, showing as a connected mass.

Now, after some eighteen years, they have grown in their natural form, varying from those that are dense and bushy to the more free-growing kinds that take a graceful small tree form. All those in the middle and lower parts of the ground are of the Ghent varieties, but at the upper end there is a large group of the common *R. luteum*; a welcome forerunner, in the middle of May, of the later kinds. Between these and the Ghents is a group of *R. occidentale*, a Californian species perhaps the most beautiful and sweetly scented of any. Why this lovely thing is not more commonly planted it is impossible to say but it certainly should be in every garden where it is possible to grow azaleas. It is later than the Ghents, flowering early in July; the leaves have more polished surface than in other kinds, and the flowers, in various tintings of white, tinge or inclining to palest pink, are of the most refined form and distinguished appearance.

The main groups are in bloom during the last day of May and the first fortnight of June their scent is delicious and carries far; it has often been noticed by passersby in a wooded lane more than a hundred yards away.

In order that the azalea ground may have some later interest, there are groups of cistuses – many them; the hardy, bushy *C. laurifolius* and the larger and more graceful *C. x cyprius*, with some bushes of *C. x florentinus*, all white-flowered; and, lower still, the half-trailing yellow *Halimium lasianthum* subsp. *formosum*.

The paths are of the natural fine-leaved grasses of the heathy uplands – mostly *Deschampsia flexuosa*; when this grass grows naturally it comes in dark green tufts with graceful, feathery bloom, but when kept down by mowing or treading it makes a close, fine sward.

The azaleas were planted in peat; in their earlier years and when dry seasons occurred later they were watered when needful. They may even need some screening protection above ground in droughty seasons. In a former garden a number were lost from actual sun dry-ing; they were not succoured in time, the leaves dried up, crackling and crumbling when touched, and the plants could not be saved. Every year, or at the very least every two years, the stems of the azaleas are well cleared of grassy invasions and they are given a mulch of something manorial, preferably stuff from a shoeing forge; this contains a good proportion of hoof parings, which are rich in ammonia and decay very slowly.

For named kinds of Ghent azaleas these may be recommended. For white, 'Viscocephala' and 'Davidii', the latter, best of all, but yellowish. For pale yellow the double 'Narcissiflorum' and 'Pontica globosa'; for fuller yellow, 'Nancy Waterer', a grand kind with large bloom, and

Ghent hybrid azaleas mixed with common yellow azaleas massed at Munstead Wood.

'Ellen Cuthbert'. For orange, 'Princeps', with red tube, and 'Gloria Mundi', a glowing, intense deep orange. For reds, 'Pallas', 'Grandeur Triomphante' and, brightest of all, 'Sang de Gentbrugge'.

WHITE FLOWERS IN THE WOODLAND

When a garden adjoins woodland, or any kind of copse where the soil is cool or even damp, many will be the opportunities for beautiful wild gardening. There are so many plants suitable for such places that the difficulty will be to make a choice, for in this kind of planting, where it is desirable above all things to preserve those characters of tranquillity and mystery that are the chief charms of woodland, these may easily be destroyed, or at least disturbed, by the presence of such a number of flowering plants as would be bewildering by constant attraction of attention. It will be enough in such a space as an acre of ground if there are something like three main plantings of fairly large growths, and that even these should not all be in flower at the same time. It is just this restraint as to numbers of kinds that is so restful and enjoyable in the actual wild, whether it is the wood of primroses of April or the bluebell wood of May or the shaded hillside of foxglove of June, or the wide stretches of autumn-flowering grey-purple ling. So also it will be if, in some one acre of the woodland, we plant goodly stretches of white foxglove, and, to follow it, bold drifts of one of the tall campanulas of the alpine woods, either a good white variety of *C. persicifolia* or one of the handsome white forms of *C. latifolia*. The purple forms of either are also good, but the white are better, and it is the white to which these notes chiefly refer. Then there is the graceful native plant *Chamerion angustifolium*. The rosy colour of the natural plant is excellent on the outskirts of some wood of Scots pine, but it is the white that is the best in summer leafing woodland. It is not quite so rampant as the type plant, just a shade more refined in growth and whole aspect. It is also a valuable plant to have in the reserve garden to cut for the house.

Wide grass paths, anything from seven to twelve feet in width, pass through the wood, sometimes straight leading up to a fine tree from which other such paths radiate, while others, again, move in easy, sweeping lines, so that a certain length only is visible, and a slight turn displays a different picture. It is in relation to these especially that the groups of tall white flowers are planted. Along the path edges are good masses of common hardy ferns of the bolder kinds – male fern, dilated shield fern, and, in the moister places, lady fern, royal fern (*Osmunda*) and other free-growing genera with an undergrowth of water forget-me-not. There is no end to the delightful inventions that may be made in such ground, to be varied or amended from year to year as conditions change and as new ideas present themselves. There is no doubt that, in time, new introductions from China and elsewhere will prove themselves invaluable for woodland treatment, where they may prove to be more at home than in the garden.

WHITE FOXGLOVES IN WOODLAND

The foxgloves made a good show in the recent summer. Their places had been chosen with some care, and so that there should always be some kind of dark or dusky background to the flowering groups. This care has been amply rewarded. But in any woody ground it is not difficult to find proper places for bold foxglove masses. Perhaps a group of holly or yew may provide a fitting background, or there may be some place where there is a more distant tangle of tree or bush growth, with a mystery of bluish-grey colouring. For woodland offers any keen gardener who strives for pictorial effects endless opportunities – many more than are available in the more crowded conditions of the flower border. For it gives precious suggestions for doing one good thing at a time, of making living pictures in those simple ways that are always the most satisfactory. The foxgloves are those of our own special strain;

White foxgloves amongst the bracken in the Woodland.

pure white, without even the dim yellowish little blotches usual in white ones. Where the soil is, either naturally or by proper preparation, of rather deep leaf mould they grow luxuriantly. Some of them are of a surprising height. We had examples this year up to eight feet, with as many as 127 blooms, counting the few unopened blooms at the top of the spike. They can still be planted, but it is well when putting out those that are to bloom next year to interplant with some smaller to follow the next season.

LILIES IN WOODLAND EDGES

A place where the soil is thin and sandy, and whose natural growth is of heath, bracken and whortleberry, is one of the least promising for the growing of lilies in general, but with a little consideration and a good deal of careful cultivation, there are some kinds that will do well. *Lilium auratum*, in deep preparation of leaf mould and some enrichment, can be grown to perfection. Next to this, one of the most satisfactory classes of lilies is that of the umbellatum group: grand things with upstanding flowers in varying shades of bright orange. Some stand six feet high, others three to four feet and of various intermediate heights. We have them in a sunny clearing at the edge of the copse that is given to the hardier kinds of cistus. *C. laurifolius* delights in the sandy ground and forms quite large bushes. *C.* x *cyprius*, with its long, arching branches, stretches them abroad and covers wide spaces. Between them the groups of tall orange lilies shoot up; those of a lower habit nearer the front, where they meet some well-grown tufts of alpine rhododendrons, berrying pernettias and heaths.

Ferns and lilies at the Shrubbery edge.

A HEATH GARDEN IN WEST SURREY

The poor soil of the southern Surrey hills, originally covered with a natural growth of gorse and heath, is obviously a condition in which a planting of heaths could be trusted to do well. A piece of young woodland, where, after the cutting down of a wood of Scotch fir, there had come up seedlings of the same, with holly, birch and scrub oak, with an undergrowth of bracken, wild heaths and whortleberries, was partly cleared some years ago for a planting of azaleas and this clearing was recently extended for a heath garden. The ground was not entirely laid bare, for when the trees had been removed, the lines of the paths staked out and the general space marked where the heaths should be, it was not dug all over, but some strips of natural heath and whortleberry were left untouched, the better to combine the planted with the wild. Now, when it has been three years planted and all has grown together, the appearance is as if the heaths had all grown there naturally.

The taller heaths were planted some few yards back from the main path. The first dark mass is a group of the fine early blooming *Erica lusitanica*. It is followed on the left by *E. australis,* the best blooming heath of May. Others of the larger kinds are *E. arborea* var. *alpina* and *E. x veitchii*, a beautiful hybrid of *E. lusitanica* and *E. arborea*, but slightly tender and apt to be broken down by snow. Then there is the upright-growing *E. terminalis* and some of the taller callunas that run up to nearly three feet. A little lower, but showing up in several bold masses, is the Cornish heath (*E. vagans*) in three rather distinct colourings. The front spaces next the paths are largely planted with the Irish heath (*Daboecia*) that carries an abundance of its large bells from middle summer to late autumn. The white is on one side, the type colour, red-purple, on the other, but the white is so good a thing that it is repeated in other portions. Other front places have the pretty pink-flowered *E. ciliaris* and its stronger Portuguese form, *E. ciliaris* 'Maweana', with larger, deeper coloured bells and a more tufted habit, and the native, *E. tetralix*. The ground is too dry for *E. tetralix* to come naturally, but it does well when planted. On the sunnier sides the heaths are backed by groups of cistus; the quite hardy *C. laurifolius*, which grows into large bushes seven feet high, and the equally large growing, though more loose habited, *C.* x *cyprius*, the kind commonly sold as *C. ladanifer*, with its large white flowers dark blotched at the base of each petal, and the delicious resinous fragrance that is freely given off even in winter. Other bushes that are in the back parts of the heath garden are *Vaccinium corymbosum*, a round bush of close, twiggy habit with berries like large whortleberries, and *V. angustifolium* var. *laevifoliumi*, whose leaves turn a splendid colour in autumn. There are also some of the choicer brooms: *Cytisus* x *praecox*, whose early pale yellow bloom comes at the same time as the bright young green foliage of the whortleberry and harmonizes with it in a charming way, and the pink-flowered hybrid 'Dallimorei'. In the region where the azalea ground joins the heath garden there are also some bushes of candleberry gale (*Myrica cerifera*) purposely put near the path so that in passing a leaf or two may be picked and crushed in order to get the best of the delicious scent. The paths through the heaths are like naturally worn footpaths in wild, heathy places.

WOODLAND ROSES

When considering what will be the best roses for woodland planting the first thought that comes to mind is that such severe restraint as to kinds will have to be practised that suitable roses will be but few; and yet, on further thought, they seem to be almost too many. The greater number of our familiar garden roses will be out of place, for good wild gardening must never look like laboured horticulture, just as a path in wild woodland must never look like a garden path, but must be just as easy a way to go among the trees and bushes, taking the most natural line between the tangled places and leading on to further mysteries and pleasant surprises. But the surprise must not be that of finding a garden rose in woodland; it must be the feeling that here is a beautiful woodland rose that has come of its own will and is completely at home.

The best place for roses is where, for a time, the trees give place to half-open ground, with brakes and tangles of such things as thorn, holly, scrub oak and bramble. And first among the roses to be planted will be our native sweet briar, for it is just in such places that it naturally occurs. It may be planted in generous quantity, and near the path the better to have its delicious scent, whether freely given off or induced by being rubbed against in passing. If the woodland should have here and there a quite open spot, and especially if the soil is poor and sandy or peaty, with patches of heath, there will be the place for the burnet rose (*R. pimpinellifolia*), the parent of the Scotch briars of gardens; with the native burnet rose there may be the Russian species (*R. pimpinellifolia* 'Grandiflora'), closely allied and in appearance almost identical, but a size larger in its whole growth and in its white, lemon-tinted bloom. They both blossom early, from the end of May for some three weeks onward, and both have another season of beauty in autumn with their large black hips and bronzed foliage.

Any single rose of climbing habit, except perhaps those of brightest red, will do in the wild brakes. One of the best is the musk rose, with its clusters of milk-white bloom and free climbing ways. In some of these roses there seems to be no limit to their power of climbing; I have a rose with a flower in small clusters much like that of the native *R. arvensis* and a leaf resembling a *R. moschata*, that has climbed full fifty feet into a birch tree, but is equally happy rambling about among trees and bushes of lower growth. The type *R. multiflora* is delightful in the wild. Once well planted it forms great brakes by itself; the long rods of two -year-old wood arch over and produce quantities of short side-shoots loaded with pyramidal clusters of close-set bloom about the size of bramble flowers. It is one of the few roses that gives off its scent, but it does it most generously, loading the air with a delicious fragrance for a distance of many yards. There is also a capital rose for wild use in a large form of *R. multiflora* var. *cathayensis*; it is a hybrid of *R. multiflora* and *R. moschata*, with warm white flowers as large as those of the musk rose and the clambering habit that is common to both parents.

Some of the single-bloomed hybrids and varieties of *R. wichurana* are also in place in wild ground, but best of all, the unusually free-growing *R.* 'Evangeline', with flowers in large, loose clusters and in great abundance. The individual bloom is much like our dog rose, but glorified both in size and substance. The hybrid *R. rugosa* 'Lady Curzon', with very large pale pink single flowers, will be well in place; not too near the path, for it is one of the most fiercely armed of all roses, and if one of its wide-flung branches catches in one's clothing it is no pleasant task to get free with bare hands. Many of the type roses of lesser growth will come well near the path, such as the white 'Macrantha' and the pink 'Andersoni'. If there is a dampish place it will suit the American *R. virginiana*, a rose of bushy habit, spreading freely at the root. It likes a little shade, as the pink flowers burn in full sunlight; the leaves turn a brilliant colour in October – a gorgeous harmony of orange, red and red-bronze.

It is needless to enumerate the many other rose species and varieties that can be used in wild ground, for those named are among the easiest to be obtained and are already more than enough for a large stretch of woodland.

BULBOUS PLANTS AND THEIR USES

GROUPING OF HARDY BULBS

It will be the daffodils that come first to mind when it is a question of arranging and grouping hardy bulbous plants. For these there is no better place than a stretch of thin woodland, where they can be seen both far and near. For the manner of the planting, on which much of the success of the display depends, it may be confidently recommended that they should be placed in long drifts, more or less parallel, and that these should also be more or less parallel with the path from which they will be seen. A pattern something like long-shaped fish is advised, all going in one direction in a thin, open shoal, and the actual bulbs clustered or scattered within the fish-like outline.

When ample space has to be dealt with, there may be three or four of these drifts of the same kind, and it is interesting and instructive, as well as good to see, to have the whole arrangement of kinds in a proper sequence as to species and hybrids. [The following are the old classifications of *Narcissus* and have been retained so readers might better understand Miss Jekyll's basic ideas.] Thus, at one end of the plantation there would be *N. poeticus*, single and double, followed by the older hybrids of *poeticus* – the barrii group; then *N. x incomparablis* and some of its varieties, and lastly the trumpets. For these large plantings, as to the *poeticus* hybrids and *incomparabilis*, the best for landscape effect are the paler kinds rather than those that have the more brightly coloured eyes; for instance, I would plant in quantity the cheap and always good old early 'Stella' rather than 'J. C. Backhouse', although the latter is the handsomer flower.

When it comes to the trumpets, the grouping would begin with the finest of the older bicolors, 'Horsfieldi' or 'Empress', and would then pass on to the full yellows, such as 'Emperor'. The Pyrennean *N. pallidiflorus* should not be forgotten, for, though from its very early blooming it is not an actual companion to the later kinds, yet it delights in wild planting. It may be the experience of others, besides that of the present writer, that whereas this charming daffodil dwindles and dies out in garden cultivation, when planted in woodland it thrives and increases, not only at the root, but by a multitude of self-sown seedlings. It is pale in colour and would come best at the place where the incomparabilis hybrids join hands with the trumpets.

If in the wood there are any spots of damp ground, there would be place for the tall snowflake (*Leucojum aestivum*), a plant that groups well with the daffodils. Nearly all the ordinary narcissi will succeed in a variety of soils, but where the ground is distinctly chalky, *poeticus* and its hybrids will thrive amazingly for the type is a native of the limestone alpine pastures. These might well be intergrouped with *Colchicum autumnale,* a plant that belongs to the same soil and region. It cannot, of course, be regarded as a companion to the daffodils, for its flowering season is September, but meanwhile the great tufts of large polished leaves are handsome objects, and the bold, crocus-like mauve-pink flowers are a joy in the late summer. In obtaining them, the type plant should be asked for; there are garden varieties of deeper colour named *C. speciosum* and other, but the paler, purer tint of the old plant is much the best for planting in the wild.

Besides the daffodils, there are one or two classes of bulbs that are better suited for growing in quantity by themselves than in lesser numbers in combination with other plants. The Dutch crocuses, now so cheap and plentiful, are seen at their best in a half-wild place, such as where garden gives place either to open or to thinly wooded parkland, and where they are beyond the influence of the mowing machine, for they need the full growth of the foliage that goes on after the bloom is over. Moreover, they are so bright and showy that they would outshine and overpower others of the smaller bulbs that flower at the same time, and therefore, as a main rule, they are better kept apart.

In the case of crocuses it is best that they should be planted in drifts of one kind, or at least of one colour at a time and preferably in the way described for daffodils. Many a good place has been spoilt by an unwary planting of a quantity of cheap bulbs in mixture. Like all else in good gardening, there should be a definite intention towards some aspect of pictorial beauty. Thus the purple crocuses might come first, followed by, or at one end intergrouped with, the white. If crocus space is limited, the yellows could follow, but they would be better apart, in a generous planting by themselves.

The common snowdrop, in the heavy or chalky soils that they prefer, are also good in large sheets or groups by themselves. In such places they increase and spread and form such lovely pictures of plant beauty that one does not wish to add anything that would distract the attention from the one complete and simple effect. It should be remembered, in establishing a plantation of snowdrops, that they are thankful for deep planting.

But there are other of the smaller early bulbs that may be brought together with delightful effect. Thus, the early scillas, *S. sibirica* and *S. bifolia,* and the chionodoxas, *C. lucilliae* and *C. sardensis,* with their slightly varying shades of blue, are all beautiful with the pure white of *Leucojum vernum,* that looks like a handsome snowdrop, and with some of the best of the true snowdrop species such as *Galanthus elwesi, G.* x *allenii* and the broad-leaved *G. plicatus.* With these there should be some of the anemones, which, though not bulbous, come naturally as garden companions and may well be noted here. The first to bloom, with the earliest of the little squills, will be the hepaticus soon to be followed by *Anemone coronaria,* whose fine white variety 'The Bride' is a fitting companion to the early bulbs. But as its flower and whole habit is larger and more robust than that of the squills, it should be kept well to the back, with some drifts of *A. appenina*, a beautiful species that is not nearly enough seen in gardens. Its blue is not pure enough, though lovely in itself to go well with the scillas, but they do not clash as its season is just a little later. It is a capital thing in strong soils increasing and spreading into wholesome-looking sheets in half-shady places under the edge of shrubs. It pleasantly recalls some springtime rides of many years ago in the Roman *campagna*, where its blue stars are sure to be seen among the herbage at the foot of thin bushy brakes – such spots in England would be the places to look for the earliest wild white violets.

There are others of the spring bulbs that may be used in happy colour combination, with some of the earliest shrub plants. Dog's-tooth violets (*Erythronium dens-canis*) and *Corydalis solida*, the latter a favourite in old cottage gardens are happy in combination. The corydalis has solid little round yellowish tubers that go down a good depth. The flowers of both these plants are of colours nearly alike and that merge pleasantly one into the other; a low-toned purplish pink, very near that of *Daphne mezereum* which with *Rhododendron* 'Praecox', may well stand in the background. The picture may be made complete by the addition of some of the Lent hellebores that have the same kind of purple-pink colouring – hybrids of *H. orientalis*. There are other beautiful erythroniums that are best treated separately, such as the tall *E. oregonum* from California and Vancouver Island. This capital plant is at its happiest in the half shade of this woodland, where, when a wide patch is well established, it is a sight worth seeing in April. The pale yellow flowers on stems a foot high look like little turncap lilies; they are not only beautiful when seen in the mass, but they well repay close examination for the delicate pencillings and markings of the underpart of the flower. The leaves also are handsome with a whitish marbling on a quiet green.

It is with such variations of plants and colour that the floor of the wild garden is most suitably covered. It is not enough to say that in a wild garden anything looks well, even indiscriminate planting. Successful planning and grouping of varieties and colour forms will turn even a dull stretch of woodland into a place of beauty.

HARDY CRINUMS

Of the behaviour of *Crinum x powellii* in heavier soils I have no experience, but in a light sandy soil that is always well drained, it thrives amazingly. Some clumps that had stood for a number of years were lifted last November. The closely compacted masses of great bulbs were something like two feet through and so heavy that after digging all round and loosening them, it was a two-man job to roll them out of their holes. Their main place, a border facing south backed by a seven-foot wall, was freshly prepared and some of the bulbs replanted. Now, after nine months, they are well in flower. Formerly I thought they were tender and gave them a winter covering of dried bracken, but this has proved to be unnecessary. The bulbs, planted at a good spade depth, go down, so that when lifted they have a white neck a foot or more long. They are wonderfully tenacious of life. A heap of damaged bulbs, some of them chopped in half in dividing the clumps, were thrown aside, on to an open border in the kitchen garden. Within three months they were all trying to grow. Roots were pushing, wounds had closed and looked perfectly healthy, and, where a bulb had been badly gashed, a quantity of young growth was forming, that looked as if it would become a cluster of small bulbs, just as a hyacinth does when slashed across.

These splendid plants should be more widely grown. They want space, for the glossy leaves are five to six feet in length. A sloping bank in deep sandy soil they seem thoroughly to enjoy, though in any warm soil they do well on the flat. They are in bloom throughout August and till late in September. No flower is of finer effect for cutting and they last as long as in water as on the plant. For arranging them indoors it is worthwhile growing a patch of one of the maize-like sorghums, such as the French 'Sorgho á bolai'; the foliage is not so large as that of maize and it is also of use in the same way with dahlias or any of the border flowers of late summer.

CRINUM X POWELLII 'ALBUM'

The white form of this fine flower of late summer is one of the best things of July and August. It may not be so successful in the colder Midlands, but in all light soils in the latitude of London and southward it may be trusted to do well. It is a grand thing for large effects on some sunny bank, grouped with yuccas, phormium, and the larger euphorbias. The pink forms in several shades of colour, from a faint blush to a good deep pink, are also lovely flowers, but do not give the same impression of purity and even majesty as the white, whose individual flowers are the largest.

It is also a noble flower for indoor decoration and lasts well in water. It demands the accompaniment of some bold foliage. We find the right thing in small branches of the broad-leaved laurel, whose stiff stems in the lower part of the jar also serve usefully for the support and right placing of the heavy masses of stalk and bloom.

BULBOUS PLANTS IN GRASS AND WOODLAND

Now that the bulb catalogues are coming in, there may be many who are contemplating some free planting of bulbous plants in the outskirts of the garden, in grassland and in woody places. It is one of the most delightful ways of enjoying these plants, but from want of knowledge of the best ways of arranging the bulb, many a place that might be made wonderfully beautiful has been more or less muddled and spoilt, or, if not actually harmed, the good effect that might have been obtained has been altogether missed. The following suggestions may be helpful. Supposing a rather important planting of daffodils is desired, and the site is an orchard or a stretch of thin woodland, the first thing to avoid is the temptation to buy cheap lots of mixed kinds. The only use for these is to plant them in a reserve garden to provide cut flowers for the house; not that it is well to mix up the kinds

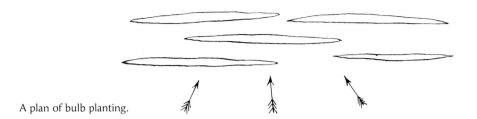

A plan of bulb planting.

when cutting, but enough of a kind or of one or two near kinds can be gathered at a time.

   If the space for planting is not large, it would be well to provide a few hundreds of two or three kinds only, such as the fine trumpets 'Horsfieldii', 'Emperoe' and 'Rugilobus'. But if the space is large, extending over some acres, there is an opportunity for planting in a proper sequence of many kinds, each kind in fair quantity. Thus, beginning at one end, one would begin by planting the trumpets, then would follow the fine 'Sir Watkin', then the incomparabilis and their hybrids the leedsii and barrii varieties; the arrangement would then pass from these onward to poeticus, both double and single. Some of the cheapest kinds are among the most effective; in the case of incomparabilis, the higher-priced kinds with the strong coloured cups, many of which are the finest in the hand, are actually less beautiful in the mass. It is better to look for the more even colour of cup and perianth, so as not to interfere with breadth of effect.

   The manner of the actual planting is of importance. Instead of planting in roundish patches, it is much better in the case of all bulbs for wild gardening to plant in long-shaped drifts, as shown in the sketch [above], the drifts all running in one direction, and being so placed in relation to paths or the more obvious points of view that they are seen from any of the ways indicated by the arrows. The advantage of such planting in pictorial effect is quite incontestable, and in the case of daffodils, seen under the low yellow sunlight of a spring afternoon, an harmonious quality of the highest artistic value is obtained. The same rule of planting applies equally to the smaller spring bulbs – crocuses, winter aconites, snowdrops, dog's-tooth violets, scillas and chionodoxas. Snowdrops and winter aconites are beautiful in groves of large trees where the ground is bare beneath. Winter aconites succeed almost anywhere, even under beeches, and increase quickly by self-sown seed. Snowdrops do best in soils that are either loamy or calcareous. Grape hyacinths (*Muscari*) flower with the later daffodils. The fine form of *M. armeniacum* called 'Heavenly Blue' is easily naturalized, and has a fine effect when in good quantity. By the second week of May there are trilliums, beautiful by themselves in cool woodland and rejoicing in deep beds of leaf mould. At the same season there should be, in damp turf in the open, two of the most beautiful of our native plants, the tall summer snowflake (*Leucojum aestivum*) and the snake's-head fritillary. If there is a stretch of grass that is almost boggy, these two plants will be seen at their best, the snowflake revelling in the wettest part.

   For later in the year there are still some beautiful bulbous plants for wild gardening. First the autumn colchicum, best in chalky soils, but good anywhere except the poorest sand. It should be planted in quantity. There are garden varieties of larger size and deeper colour, and also a superb pure white of great size and substance; but it is the type *Colchicum autumnale* that is the most desirable in meadowland, and it is in grass that it not only thrives best, but also receives the support to the weak-stemmed bloom – not a true stem, but an elongated tube – that is necessary to keep it upright. In drier ground, in short, fine turf, should be planted the beautiful *Crocus speciosus*, like colchicum, blooming in September and October, and increasing fast by self-sown seed. For the same season, in thin grass at the foot of trees and in the edges of woodland, there should be tufts of hardy cyclamens.

A RIVER OF DAFFODILS

A hundred years ago, when smuggling was rife along the Sussex coast, the site of my garden and copse, with a wide tract of the adjoining lands, was wild moorland, deep in heath and bracken, gorse and tall junipers. The place was convenient as a temporary deposit for spoils brought up at night from Shoreham, over the downs and then by rough forest ways to the heath. It was also a handy place for distribution, with one small old country town only one and a half miles distant, three miles from Guildford, and with several villages within easy reach. There are still, on my ground, evidences of old pack-horse tracks all leading to a certain point which must have been the place of hiding. One of the shallowest of these comes down to within a few yards of the garden front of my house. It seemed a tempting place for some

Old cart tracks used for daffodils to give the effect of a 'river' running out of the woodland on to the lawn.

daffodils, and a number of *N.* 'Horsfieldii' was planted. This was about sixteen years ago. They did well for several years, at first increasing only very slowly, as they do in unmanured ground, but after a time they showed signs of going back, and it was evident that they must be replanted. When lifted, the bulbs were in closely clustered masses, very small, but without sign of disease. The ground was dug up and a little leaf mould added, the shallow trough shape being retained, and a proportion of the bulbs was replanted. They have taken three years to gain size and strength, but are now flowering well, and I am again enjoying the pretty river of bloom that flows down from the copse to the garden.

CARPETING BULB BEDS

As in other departments of the garden, so in this will success or failure depend on knowledge and experience; but those who are capable of keenly enjoying the many lovely little garden pictures that may be made by assorting suitable bulbous and carpeting plants will certainly try to make more. It is not to be denied that there are close-growing plants so dense and discouraging that they may spoil and even kill delicate bulbs; but, on the other hand, there are undoubtedly combinations where the plants grown together seem to nurse and cherish each other. The nature and habit of individual plants are so different that one cannot generalize either way, or say that all bulbs are the better or the worse for all carpets; but I venture to say, from several years' experience, that many are none the worse, and are certainly infinitely more beautiful for the companionship. It may be regarded as one of the highest developments or refinements of gardening needing knowledge and careful thought in the making, and rewarding the good gardener by the sight of lovely jewels in appropriate settings. As examples that have certainly succeeded, I may quote the following: a spreading group of *Scilla siberica* was planted in 1881 and carpeted with *Sedum lydium*; neither have been replanted. The squill yearly increases in strength; the stonecrop is ragged, from blackbirds having been scratching among it, but will easily be put right. *Iris reticulata* was planted in 1882 at the junction of three carpets – of *Thymus pseudolanuginosus*, *Potentilla brauniana*, and mossy saxifrage respectively. The iris now [1885] wants division, and the saxifrage needs replanting, having grown into thick, deep tufts. *Scilla siberica* var. *taurica*, planted in 1882, comes up yearly under its covering of *Arenaria balearica*; neither as yet need alteration. The dwarf daffodils of the rush-leaved section increase and flourish under *Veronica repens*, *V. prostrata* and *V. fruticans*, *Coronilla orientalis*, and even the very close-growing *Antennaria dioica* var. *hyperborea*. *Narcissus minor* and *N. obvallaris* are not daunted by their close, rather woody counterpane of *Dryas octopetala*. Some of the crocus species are under a wide carpet of *Hypericum olympicum* f. *minus*. Some do well; others have their tops yearly nibbled off by mice, so that one cannot judge them fairly. *Brimeura amethystina* and its white variety are happy among white thyme and *Frankenia laevis*. None of the bulbs mentioned was planted later than 1882, and their carpeting plants have not been renewed except where stated. Later, a stretch of *Sedum hispanicum* has been planted with *Chionodoxa luciliae* and spring snowflake, which are doing well. A grand failure was in the case of some imported unripened *Leucojum autumnale*, planted under *Acaena novae-zelandiae*, but this was a case of gross ignorance in every way: first, the acaena is a very close-rooting, ground-robbing plant, only suitable, if at all, for covering some very robust bulb, and then the leucojum, one of the most dainty of bulbs, should have had at least a year's rest and the most encouraging treatment to regain strength.

The question may be in some cases one of soil and situation. In the examples quoted above, the soil is peaty sand over rock, standing high in a southern county. Some bulbs are impatient of drought and would certainly in such soils be the better for a living protection. Some clumps of fritillaries, nearly all dead, as I believe, from the heat and drought of the last two summers, I think might have escaped had they been comforted with a cool green covering. To venture on a generalization, probably nine out of every ten kinds of bulbs and plants would be the better for transplanting once in four years, and a considerable proportion of these, excluding the bulbs, for yearly renewal. This, at any rate, is the experience taught by a very poor sandy soil, in which bulbs increase fast and ripen well, but which is wasteful of water and fertilizing matters. Those who are planting bulb carpets should notice that there are many trailing plants that cover a large space without rooting as they trail, or rooting very slightly, so as to form only a feeble anchorage for the extending growths; these need not in any way rob the roots of the bulbs, and serve a useful purpose in summer as a living mulching to preserve moisture. As examples may be mentioned *Hypericum olympicum* f. *minus*, the alpine gypsophilas, petrorhagia, saxifrage, aubrietas, and the pinks of the grantianopolitanus, deltoides, and petraeus class, and their many hybrids. Also for the more delicate bulbs a carpeting plant should be chosen that has not a very strong roothold, such as the stonecrops named above, viz., *Sedum lydium* and *S. hispanicum*, thus keeping in mind, with due regard to appearance, the relative vigour of the bulb and its destined carpet.

In alpine gardening especially this association of bulbous-rooted and creeping plants is one of the most delightful of studies and pleasures. The failures and half-failures are only so many instructive steps to knowledge, and need not dishearten anyone, for, as says one of the ancient Fathers, I think St Augustine: 'By our sins' (repented of, of course, understood), 'as by a ladder, we climb to Heaven.'

SOME HARDY PLANTS

THE TALLER CAMPANULAS

In considering the best of the bell flowers it is convenient to take separately the tall kinds that are good in flower borders and the shorter growing ones for rock gardening and edgings. Of the taller, the first that comes to mind is the stately *C. latifolia* var. *macrantha*, a garden form of the native *C. latifolia*; the type has purple flowers, but the white variety is rather the better garden plant. A fine form is known as *C. latifolia* 'Eriocarpa'. Its height is from four to five feet; the shapely spire of bloom, with its sharply cut and pointed segments, and the regular foliage, make it one of the best plants of early summer. Not only is it first rate in the flower border, but as, in common with the greater number of the family, it has no objection to shade, it is one of the finest plants for such a place as where garden joins woodland, or in shrubbery edges, it will stand several years, growing stronger year by year. It produces an abundance of seed, sows itself freely and is best grown from seedling plants. Another campanula of bold growth and with equally large flowers is *C. macrocarpa*, with great bells of a reddish purple colour, also fine both in border and wild. [There is some confusion over exactly what plant Miss Jekyll was referring to. It may have been a form of *C. glomerata*.]

C. persicifolia has long been a garden favourite, and is one of the best of the June flowers, with its graceful habit and many blooms of white or purple. There are double forms, but it is doubtful whether the doubling, when, as is usually the case, it takes the form of a flattened rosette, is to the advantage of beauty; the best form of duplication is where the bell is neither flattened nor crowded, but has a distinct cup and saucer arrangement. In this, which is known as coronata, the flower loses nothing of its grace and distinctly gains in point of interest. It is not as common a plant as one would wish. To keep *C. persicifolia* in good order it is best to divide and replant yearly, as soon as the bloom is over. There is no need to cut the old flower stem; a sharp vertical pull brings them away, and with them anything that is of no further use to the plant. There will remain several prosperous rooted offsets that should be put out separately and will make good flowering plants for the next year.

A good border plant is *C. lactiflora*. A quarter of a century ago it had almost been forgotten, but later years have restored it to favour. It is five or more feet high, with a spreading pyramid of bloom at the top, in colour a washed-out purple inclining to white. Its best use is where a pale, cloudy effect of bloom is wanted as a setting to something of strong colour, such as *Clematis* 'Jackmannii'. There is a pure white variety and another of rather smaller habit in which the flowers are deeper purple. There can be no doubt about its merits as a garden plant, but it requires very careful and clever staking or to be so placed that it is among other plants that will support it just under the head of bloom; for the whole head is apt to be broken down by weighty of rain or of blustering wind. No doubt the increase of size and weight of the flower head in cultivation has put too much strain on the upper part of the stem which has not strengthened itself in proportion. The plant lasts for several years; seedlings self-sown often appear, perhaps too far forward in the border. When this happens, the flowering growth can be cut back when fairly forward, an experiment which has proved successful with many other plants and the season of blooming is not retarded.

Another persistent plant among the bell flowers is *Campanula alliariifolia*, with a central spike about two feet high and a quantity of blooming laterals; the numerous white bells have a drooping habit. It is perhaps a better plant for the wood edge than for the border. When established it is no further trouble, for the older plants endure for some years and are sure to self-sow with a sufficient though moderate number of successors. *C. pyramidalis*, so grandly grown as a biennial in pots by all good gardeners, is apt to be overlooked as an outdoor plant. Its best place is a joint in a cool wall where it becomes a perennial and will probably seed itself. It is best to sow the seed in a limy compost in a joint low down and await the result.

Canterbury bells have long been with us as indispensable biennials, and nothing can be finer in the late summer, especially in soils that are rich with either loam or chalk; for though good bell flowers may be grown in almost any garden, it is in these rich soils that the whole family chiefly delights. But, remembering the *C. medium* is a native of rocky places in southern Europe, it also might be tried in walls.

SOME OF THE LESSER CAMPANULAS

Of the lower-growing campanulas the one that is of the greatest general utility is *C. carpatica*, for it is large enough to be a useful plant in the front of the flower border and is too large for the bolder parts of the rock garden. Moreover, it is most accommodating, for it will do well in almost any soil, aspect or situation. The form turbinate has flowers of a deeper cup shape, while other garden varieties are more starry; but all are welcome, and when once established give no further trouble; the same plant or group will go on for years, and if a renewed or extended planting is desired it is easily raised from seed. The colouring is everything between pure white and a fairly deep purple. It is variable as to seedlings, for the produce of a purple plant may give some whites, and that of a white one is likely to throw back to purple.

There are many species of campanula native to the middle European Alps, but among them a few stand out as the most desirable in a garden. *C. portenschlagiana* is a brilliant little June flower, the neat tufts of foliage almost covered by the abundant bloom of a rich purple colour. Still more delightful is the dainty little *C. garganica*, flowering later in the summer. There is a perfect finish about the whole plant, with its charming bloom of light purple shading to white, and its exquisitely neat foliage, like tiny leaves of ivy, sharply cut at every point. Both of these little bell flowers are seen at their best in the joints of dry walling, or in any steep places in the rock garden that come near the same conditions. Another of the favourites for wall or rock joint is *C. cochleariifolia*, blooming in late summer. It is in white and purple colourings; a charming pale purple kind was raised by Miss Willmott and is now well known. It is pretty to see any variety of this little plant running at the foot or sides of rock garden steps.

It is well to remember that all these little bell flowers are happiest in limy soil, a preference that is common to nearly all their kind. Those who have been fortunate enough to have had botanical rambles in southern Italy will remember the beauty of *C. fragilis* hanging out of narrow rifts in sheer limestone cliffs. It may not be generally known that this tender plant and the nearly related *C. isophylla*, which in England are usually grown as indoor pot ornaments, may be acclimatized in a sunny wall, where the crown of the plant, set well back between the stones, is protected from winter wet, and where no frost reaches the root. If they are provided with a good compost of lime and loam, or with the natural rich topsoil of chalky places, they thrive amazingly and make larger plants than are usually seen in their native haunts.

There are some species of campanula that are not commonly grown in gardens, but that are well worthy of attention. *C. sarmatica* is a charming plant of late summer, from one foot to fifteen inches high with a profusion of light purple bells and a generally downy appearance. It is good for a place in rough rockwork with a cool exposure. *C. punctata* from the Far East – China and Japan – has drooping, whitish flowers tinged with purple and spotted, and elongated heart-shaped leaves pointed and boldly toothed. These bell flowers would be lost in the mixed flower border, where plants of a showier nature are wanted; their place is somewhere between garden and wild where a group of either, seen by itself, can be thoroughly enjoyed. I have had them on a raised bank among wild grasses and ferns, where they flourished and appeared to be just rightly placed.

HOW TO GROW HOLLYHOCKS

There are many who are deterred from growing these grand plants by the prevalence of the disease, or, more properly, the fungoid pest, that is likely to infest them, the same pest attacking more or less all the members of the mallow family, of which hollyhocks are the most important of the garden representatives. But one may say that hollyhocks are indispensable in the late summer and autumn, and they cannot be let go lightly. In strong soils they are nearly always healthy, a plant lasting for several years, throwing up several grand spikes and being well clothed with foliage to the ground. The difficulty arises in the lighter soils, for the hollyhock is what gardeners call a gross feeder, rejoicing in a soil either of loam or lime, in any case rich and deep and also well manured. There can hardly be a place whose conditions are worse for hollyhocks than the present writer's garden – on a sandy upland, which naturally produces only heath and gorse. Here all flower borders have to be artificially made; but where hollyhocks are to grow it is made deeper still, the sand taken out to a depth of three feet and the place filled with the best stuff we can get together, with the ashes of the fire heap plentifully admixed and some good manure from one foot to eighteen inches down. It is true that the plants always lose their lower leaves and are not free from disease (*Puccinia malvacea*); but as they are necessarily near the back of the border, it is a simple matter to make sure that some group of plants, of close habit or strong foliage, shall be just in front. The well-fed hollyhocks will send up fine spikes and the defect of bareness of the lower stem will not be apparent. The flowers will be so good that their absence would be a grievous loss to the garden, although they must not be expected to be so vigorous as they would be on a soil of a stronger nature. The pest can be kept in check, though not absolutely abolished, by frequent syringing with a weak solution of permanganate of potash as soon as the leaves have made some growth, or with any of the anti-fungoid preparations.

For flowering the same year, hollyhock seed may be sown in heat as early as the first days of January; but it may be sown a month or six weeks later if the plants are pushed on as quickly as may be. There is a good deal in getting a strain of seed that will give the right-shaped flower. The florists' hollyhock, so fully double that the whole flower is the same rounded shape all over and is equally tightly packed with crowded petals, is not the best for the garden; in fact, instead of being a beautiful flower it is rather an ugly thing. The best kind has a distant guard petal or outer petticoat, and the rising centre is only moderately filled. In this case the colour also is much enhanced by the play and transmitted glow of light and tint within and between the inner petals. All this is lost in the round, tight flower, where the light can only play upon the outer surface.

Iris unguicularis.

There is much beauty of tender colouring among some of the single hollyhocks, but of these the ones that are earliest to grow and are the most generally useful are the varieties of *Alcea ficifolia*, the fig-like shape of the leaf accounting for the specific name. The best are those of sulphur and white colourings, which should be secured if possible, or there will probably be a preponderance of flowers of a poor, washy, purplish pink. But if mixed seed is sown, some will be sure to be yellow and white, and seed for further use can be kept from these.

IRIS UNGUICULARIS IN ALGIERS

There has been some mention of late about this useful winter-blooming iris. A few notes from an early grower may be of interest. In the winter of 1872–3 I had the good fortune to be the guest of an intimate friend, Mme. Bodichon, a regular half-yearly resident, with her husband, Dr Eugene Bodichon, who in his earlier years had done some fine work during a devastating epidemic of cholera, and who later was responsible for the planting of eucalyptus in some of the fever-ridden districts. They lived in an old Arab house in the very simplest way, but with everything necessary for ordinary comfort. It was at the extreme end of the northern suburb of Mustapha Superieur, on the highest ground, looking over the old town far below. The outer gate in the garden wall gave on to a country road, and beyond it there was only a rough field of Dr Bodichon's with some scattered fig trees and little treasures of orchid and narcissus in the thin grass, then another small property and a convent. Beyond this was all wild ground, thinly sprinkled with the usual Mediterranean scrub. But the delight of it was the occurrence of *Iris unguicularis* and, rather more sparingly, of *I. planifolia*. They never grew in strong tufts, but almost in single roots, generally against one of the many knobs of rocky stone that rose up through the reddish soil. *I. unguicularis* stood up bravely, but *I. planifolia*, of tenderer texture, was always battered by being blown about by wind. The Revd Edwyn Arkwright, one of the few permanent English residents and a keen horticulturist, when riding with his sisters in some of the more distant wild ground, came upon the white variety and wisely secured it; the only one that had ever been found and, I believe, the parent of those that are now offered in nurseries. On leaving Algiers I commissioned M. Durando, a resident French botanist and a very good friend, to have a hundred roots of *I. unguicularis* collected for me. When they were received at home they were planted in several patches, but always in a warm aspect, either south or west. One patch was inadvertently planted against a greenhouse wall just over some *Alstromeria chilensis*. This group did best of all and flowered faithfully for several years. It should never be planted in rich soil or it will go all to large foliage and no bloom. My best flowering patch has been in its place undisturbed for quite fifteen years, but a part of it will be broken up this year in April and be put in a sheltered, sunny place against a west wall in a compost of small, sharp gravel of our local Bargate stone, broken to walnut size and less, a little old mortar rubbish, and two-thirds of our ordinary sandy soil. A recent correspondent regretted that it never seeded. This may be an oversight, because nothing like a seed pod comes near the flower, but seeds may often be found by feeling about near the root, a reminder that the long white stem is not a stalk but a style. It is much to be regretted that the well-descriptive name of *stylosa* has been altered to *unguicularis*, which says nothing to the ordinary observer.

THAT BLUE PEA

Hardly a season passes without someone writing to the horticultural papers about a wonderful blue pea. In some cases the inquiry is associated with the information that it came from Egypt and is the progeny of a pea found in a mummy case, and that it is known as the mummy pea. Almost invariably it proves to be the well-known *Lathyrus sativus* (the chickling vetch), a south European plant whose normal colour is white, sometimes faintly tinged with blue. It has been grown into a good garden plant by the bluish tinge being encouraged till it is now a pretty pea with really good blue flowers. If any such pea is brought from Egypt under the pretence that it was originally found in a mummy it may be readily understood how easy it will have been for imposters to obtain the seed from Europe, propagate them in Egypt, and sell them as mummy peas. The imposition is the more glaring as it is well known among horticulturists that no pea will germinate that is more than four or five years old. The same pretty flower is often erroneously called 'Lord Anson's Pea', a name that belongs to *Lathyrus nervosus*, a good garden plant not too common, but quite different from any variety of the annual *L. sativus*, for it is a perennial, and the flowers, instead of being solitary on slender stalks from axils, are in a cluster on the flower stalk as in the everlasting pea. There is another blue-flowered lathyrus, a perennial, that is very desirable, namely *L. pubescens*. It is seldom seen in gardens, probably because it is tender and requires a place on a warm wall or, at any rate, some kind of winter protection.

MULLEINS PULLED DOWN

A useful lesson was taught me accidentally last year by a strong plant of one of the best of the mulleins, *Verbascum phlomoides*, that was blown over by wind. It was not broken, only laid flat, and as it was in an outlying place where it did not matter, it was left lying down. When it came to flowering time I was surprised to see, besides the main spike which stood upright at the end, a whole quantity of secondary spikes rising all along the stem, all in strong bloom. There is nothing remarkable in there being these secondary spikes, for a self-sown plant always has them, though in those that are transplanted there is usually one spike alone. But in the case of this laid-down plant the axillary spikes were much more numerous and more full of bloom; also, instead of being restricted to the upper part of the spike, they ran much further down. What was still more noticeable was that the whole thing remained in flower for quite a month longer than is usual. It is a puzzle to account for this persistence; I can only suppose that the stem, lying on the ground, received some comforting and sustaining moisture.

The long mass of spikes rising from a foot to fifteen inches suggested useful ways of employing the plant in the flower border. Some strong ones were transplanted in the autumn and are being trained down in anticipation of their covering something of earlier bloom and in the hope that, although they were transplanted, the pulling down will have the effect of inducing the side growths, which otherwise might not have been developed, to appear and bloom well. The earlier hybrid mullein with the deep yellow flowers and velvet-brown centres is equally amenable to this treatment and forms a gorgeous mass in the border for early June.

The Grey Garden at Hestercombe, designed by Miss Jekyll in 1904.

SOME USES OF GREY PLANTS

Othonna cheirifolia is a plant that must always attract attention. The rather large, fleshy leaves are almost spoon-shaped; they run straight down into the stem without stalks and are of a bluish, glaucous colour that goes well with others of the grey-leaved plants that are of such value in the arrangement of cool colour effects. The beauty of the plant is in its handsome foliage, for the yellow, daisy-shaped flowers look almost incongruous; even if one has patience with them and allows them to remain, one is glad when their season is past and the plant is again all blue grey. It stands our winters well, though it is native of North Africa. The popular name is barbary ragwort. It is a plant for bold rockwork or the rock wall in full sun. Placed at the top of a wall, it forms deep, hanging sheets; on a wall four feet six inches high it comes down to the ground; on a higher wall it may possibly do the same. Besides its place on the wall, we have it at the rocky end of a raised bed backed by yuccas, with other grey plants showing beyond on another rocky mound. Near by are more yuccas and a young plant of the great *Euphorbia characias* subsp. *wulfenii*, with a groundwork of *Artemisia stelleriana* and the white-bloomed sweet alyssum (*Lobularia maritima*). With this grey setting is a planting of pink ivy geranium 'Mme Crousse' and pink carnations. Across the path is a continuation of raised border with a background of the large yuccas, the hardy form of *Phormium tenax* and euphorbia and some bushes of the beautiful grey-leaved *Brachyglottis* (Dunedin Group) 'Sunshine' [formerly *Senecio greyii*]. This shrubby groundsel is one of the most valuable of the grey-leaved small shrubs. As with othonnopsis, the yellow bloom of middle summer, though it is profuse and showy

Clary in the Main Hardy Flower Border at Munstead, *circa* 1912.

in its season, is of less value than the good grey of the foliage. The underside of the leaf is almost white with a close, downy covering; this just comes up over the margin, showing as a silver edging to the next, roundish leaves. In front of this solid background of rather large form, all of grey or greyish colouring, there is a planting of drifts of one of the large stonecrops, *Sedum telephium* var. *borderei*; the bloom is a purplish pink of low tone, and it is used not so much for its own merit as for a harmonious setting to purple and pink and white flowers. These are *Platycodon grandiflorus* 'Mariesii', both white and purple; heliotrope, that good variety 'President Garfield', of full purple colouring and sweetest scent; *Campanula carpatica* and, again, ivy geranium 'Mme Crousse', with a continued lower planting of *Artemisia stelleriana* and the little sweet alyssum, which sows itself afresh year by year. These special plantings of grey and glaucous foliage with flowers of pink, white and purple colouring are not only delightful in themselves, but most refreshing to the eye after passing large groupings of strong, warm colourings.

SOME OF THE HARDY SAGES

When better days come and we can again be planting the borders of hardy flowers, we shall hope to make some good use of these showy plants of early July. Meanwhile, from the scattered examples kept to save the stocks, it will be well to make some notes of grouping and arrangement, and to have at least a foretaste of their effects in imagination and anticipation. For a bold purple group the largest plants will be of *Salvia sclarea*, the clary of old gardens, widely branching and four to five feet high. Next to these will be a bold group of *S. nemorosa*, of a splendid purple colouring, and, towards the front, the purple-leaved form of the common sage, little known as a border plant, but of considerable value. The clary is in cloud-like masses of pale of deep mauve. The seedlings vary in colour, and as the tendency is to incline to a lighter colour, whereas the deeper is the better, we plant them more thickly than they need stand, and thin out the lighter ones as soon as the half-developed flowering shoots show colour, which they do nearly a month before flowering time. The whole colour effect is delightfully soft and nebulous. The actual flowers are bluish lavender, but they are set among a profusion of wide bracts of a true mauve colour – that of the wild mallow. This broken colouring of two tints intermingled gives, as such a combination always does, a valuable delicacy of general colouring. In the case of *Salvia virgata* there is also a combination of two colours of flower and bract, but in this the purple of the flower and the deep crimson of the bract are both powerful – one may even say intense – in colour strength, with a result of surprising richness. In the lower-growing purple-leaved sage there is yet again the bloom and bract of different tint, but though the flower is a good bright purple – brighter than that of common sage – the effect beside that of the taller *S. virgata* is a pleasant modest colouring, in perfect harmony, both in flower and leaf, with the taller plant of fuller colour and with the cloudy bloom of the clary. The purple effect will be carried further by a front planting of the dwarf lavender, a neat plant that blooms nearly a month before the ordinary tall kind, and whose flowers, on stalks barely eight inches above the leaves, are of a much deeper colour. The whole purple group will occupy several square yards. Part of the front edge will be planted with the silvery-leaved *Stachys byzantina* and with *Artemisia stelleriana* and such other grey-leaved plants as *Senecio cineraria* and *Centaurea ragusina*, and on the middle flanks will be the tall *Artemisia ludoviciana*.

SEDUM SIEBOLDII

Among the many stonecrops of our gardens *Sedum sieboldii* is one of the prettiest, but except in the south and west it is too tender to be trusted out of doors through the winter. We therefore keep it in a cold frame, break it up and plant it afresh in some ornamental pots, to be rewarded for this care by the quantity of the pretty, pale, rosy bloom in September and October, when the leaves are also suffused with a ruddy tinting that forms a delightful harmony with the tone of the flowers. Such yearly replanting tends to the production of good bloom in all the sedums, though it is, perhaps, too much to expect that one can get round all the stonecrops grown in any one garden and give them the benefit of a yearly shift; but we all know, by the flowerless sheets of growths that so constantly reproach us, that they are sadly needing this timely attention.

The roughly squared stones under the pots of flowering *S. sieboldii* are movable covers to built boxes where there are taps regulating the heat that passes from the greenhouse on the left to other houses. A hot-water pipe runs underground just inside the stone edging. The existence of this pipe prompted the making of a warm, sheltered bed on the southern face of the greenhouse wall for a few pretty plants of doubtful hardiness. In late September *Nerine bowdenii* was well in flower; earlier than this the mood white *Alstromeria pelegrina*, the pretty little soft red anomatheca, tigridias, and some other tender plants. Later we hope for pancratiums, but they are not yet grown to flowering size.

A NATURAL COLOUR STUDY (THRIFT)

Those who study colour for garden use often find admirable examples in wild places. Such a one was just now displayed in a place where a narrow strip of salt marsh comes next to the sea. It was more or less covered with thrift, and, as seen from an adjoining meadow a few feet higher, showed a perfect picture of tender beauty of colouring. It was at half-tide, or rather less, and beyond lay level lines of pale grey, muddy shore, while between the two some short seaweedy growth told as a pale bluish green, like the colour known as malachite green, lightened with white. It all lay in long, level drifts in a perfectly eye-satisfying colour harmony, helped in the foreground by near groups of a grey-leaved tufted atriplex. The colour of the thrift was in itself especially beautiful, with a kind of liveliness, though extremely tender. Going down on to the marsh to see how nature painted this miracle of colouring, it was found to be done by broken colours and infinite gradations of tint. Among the hundreds of thousands of plants of thrift no two seemed to be exactly alike, although all were paler than the ordinary garden plant. Nothing could be better instruction in planting where space can be given to the doing of one thing at a time thoroughly well. It was also noteworthy to observe the beauty of the wild plant without any so called 'improvement', although the kind of thrift most commonly seen in gardens is of a low-toned pink that is pleasant enough. But there is a garden variety in which the colour has been deepened to a kind of dull, heavy magenta that is insufferably displeasing, and that destroys all the charm of this useful little plant, so good for edgings, whether straight or informal, and, for all its familiarity, always one of the best plants in the rock garden.

SCENTS IN THE GARDEN

A GARDEN OF SWEET SCENTS

It is no new idea, that of making a garden where flower and bush of sweet scent only shall be admitted, or where, at least, they shall predominate; but it is worthy of more frequent interpretation. It would be a pleasant thing to know that somewhere in the garden there was a region where nearly everything was not only beautiful, but also fragrant; where, at every step, one would be greeted by some sweet scent – to know that whichever way the wind might blow it would waft some delicious breath of perfume new-distilled. It should be observed that flowers and leaves give off their scent in different ways – one might say, in three different ways. First, there are those that give it off naturally, so that, in passing, it is brought to us by the lightest wind, or even spread abroad in quite still air. This is done by sweet briar, azalea, cistus, azara and French honeysuckle (*Lonicera japonica* var. *repens*) among shrubs, and by wallflowers, stocks, mignonette and violets among border plants; also by three of the grandest of the lilies – the pure and stately white lily, and the gold-rayed lily of Japan and the immense *Cardiocrinum giganteum*. Some lowlier plants must be admitted, for of all the sweet scents of the year that of the dying leaves of the little wild strawberry is one of the most enjoyable; pungent yet delicate, mysterious, elusive, but wholly delightful. Roses in general give off but little scent in the open air, though a bowl of cut roses will scent a room; they are, as Bacon says, 'fast flowers of their smell'. But there is one notable exception in the type *Rosa multiflora* of the Himalayas, the parent of a number of the modern rambling roses. The warm-white flowers, not unlike bramble flowers, are not much larger, borne in great number at the end of the new shoots. Their scent is carried far and wide; as far as that of *Lilium auratum* and *Cardiocrinum giganteum*, two of the most noted of scent-distributors. *Clematis montana*, though not usually reckoned among plants of good smell, must be admitted, for when the flowers are just passing their best – when the petals, instead of being quite smooth, show a slightly ridged surface – a scent much like vanilla is given off. Secondly, there are the plants with sweet leaves – some of them have sweet flowers also – that do not give off their scent in the air, but yield it to the touch. Such are rosemary and lavender, bay, bog myrtle, candleberry gale and *Rhododendron myrtifolium* among shrubs, sweet geranium, sweet verbena and balm of Gilead among tender plants, and a number of the sweet herbs, their near relatives – balm, marjoram, thyme, savory, sage, hyssop and variegated mint. The last is the variegated form of a native plant, *Mentha suaveolens*; it is a good old garden plant that is too much neglected. Thirdly there are all the other sweet flowers that only ask for the slight effort of searching for their sweetness – roses, carnations, peonies, heliotrope, jasmine, sweet peas, lily of the valley and many others. The names are given only as examples, not as complete lists.

It would be well to arrange the garden of sweet scents as a double border, with a path of turf leading to a summerhouse or arbour, which might be covered with honeysuckle and jasmine. The path would be of wild thyme, with, for better wear, a mixture of some of the finer fescue grasses with wiry leaves, that mow and roll into a close short turf. The border would be backed by a planting of sweet briar and two of the cistuses, namely, *C. laurifolius* and *C.* x *cyprius*, the kind that is usually sold as *C. ladanifer*. Next the grass, the better to be brushed by foot or skirt, would be bush thyme, winter savory, sage, lavender cotton, catmint and hyssop. Sage should be oftener used as a plant for border or rock garden. It is one of the best of the grey-foliaged plants, and its bright purple bloom is as good as that of any flower of the same colour that blooms at its time of year. The main planting of the border would be of roses, lilies, peonies, lupins, tulips, rockets and daffodils, the sweetest of which are the poet's daffodil, single and double, the yellow campernelle and the tazettas. Of tender plants there will be heliotrope in plenty and sweet geraniums, and all the sweetest of the annuals, such as sweet peas, mignonette, sweet sultan, night-scented and other stocks, wallflowers and the low-growing *Lobularia maritimum*. Mignonette should be on the sunny side, as the sun brings out the scent. Night-scented stock (*Matthiola longipetala* subsp. *bicornis)* should be freely sown in empty places, not necessarily at the front, though it is a smallish plant, because it has no special beauty. Its delicious fragrance is only given off when the day is dying and through the night. *Nicotiana alata* is another, much larger, plant of the same character, giving off its sweet scent at night, when its flowers expand fully. Lavender and rosemary must also have a place, and *Daphne pontica*, so lavish of its sweetness in the early year.

Lilium auratum by the steps leading to the North Court.

If there is a wall or a wooden fence, there would be the place for the wintersweet, that gives its sweet, small blooms in the winter months. Such a garden might be still better done if the place were of the more formal type, with the terminal summerhouse of the small temple or pavilion kind. In this case the path would be paved, with here and there an open joint for the planting of the creeping wild thyme, that is so sweet when trodden underfoot. Or the sweet garden may be on quite free lines, that would give a better opportunity for displaying the larger of the scented shrubs. There might be small groves of magnolias and azaleas, of daphne and rosemary, and in some places quite narrow pathways or merely slight openings between the shrubs, so narrow that anyone passing must needs brush up against the plants and bushes. Here would be the place for rosemary and *Rhododendron myrtifolium,* and especially for candleberry gale (*Myrica cerifera*), whose leaves, crushed or bruised, give off an incomparable scent, such as can hardly be matched by that of any other growing thing.

SHRUBS WITH SCENTED LEAVES

In wintertime, when the general interest of the outdoor garden is at the lowest point, the sweet-leaved shrubs have special charm and value. In passing, a little branch of rosemary is drawn through the hand and all the sweetness of summer is there, for no summer scent can surpass the wonderful incense-like fragrance that may be had for the touching, even in the deadest months. Then among the cistuses there is hardly a day in winter, except in actual frost, when one is not met by invisible clouds of balsamic sweetness, freely given off; while even in the worst weather the scent may be had for searching among their leafy tops. This giving off of scent from leaves is a rare quality among evergreen shrubs, for usually one has to provoke it either by purposely crushing or bruising the leaves, or at least brushing through them. But, besides the cistuses, the cypresses have the same merit: in their case, however, the quality of the scent, though pleasant, is less fragrant. Sometimes, it becomes overpowering, and a case has been known where some Lawson's cypress had to be removed from near a bedroom window. But out in the open it is a joy suddenly to meet and inhale the almost pungent breath of the sun-baked cypress. As far as the present writer has observed, Lawson's cypress and the American arbor-vitae are the ones that exhale their scent most freely. It would be worthwhile, for the sake of winter delight, to plant a little wood or thicket of the evergreen sweet-leaved shrubs, with paths so narrow that one must needs brush against them or push gently through them. The main planting should be of the candleberry gale (*Myrica cerifera*), sweetest of all persistent leaves when slightly bruised, with its congeners the fern-leaved gale (*Comptonia peregrina* var. *asplenifolia*) and the native bog myrtle. Then the dwarf *Rhododendron myrtifolium,* lavender and rosemary. Further back would come tree box, *Cistus laurifolius* and *C.* x *cyprius,* the latter being the kind usually sold as the gum cistus (*C. ladanifer*). Myrtles would, of course, be among this sweet-leaved company if the climate allowed, and choisya for its pleasant rue-like leaf smell, and, enclosing all, the sweet cypresses.

SWEET-SCENTED SHRUBBERY BEDS

So often, even in the deadest of wintertime, a delicious whiff of sweetness comes from some plant or shrub, that it is well worth looking up the sweet-smelling things and planting them together, the better to enjoy their perfume. There is one class of sweetness that seems rather to belong to late autumn and winter, of which the typical scent is that of dying strawberry leaves, those of the alpine class being the best. The foliage of the great St John's wort smells very nearly like it, and a little yellow-flowered potentilla, a neat plant carpeting bare ground, has just the same refreshing smell. It is rather a charming quality of these sweet scents that they seem to come when they will, and cannot be had from intentional sniffing.

Another powerful scent of the same class is that of *Cistus laurifolius*, the strongest and best winter-smelling plant I know. Then all within the same class of perfume we have *Escallonia rubra* var. *macrantha*, bog myrtle, *Comptonia peregrina* var. *asplenifolia*, and the dwarf *Rhododendron myrtifolium*; but these need to be brushed up against to give off their scent, and, sweetest of all, *Ledum palustre*. Here we have already a number of plants and shrubs, all evergreen, suitable for beds or clumps at all season, and especially enjoyable for winter sweetness.

It is to be noticed that of the many flowering plants and shrubs that are sweet scented, there are not a great number that give off their scent, but of these the one that stands first in my recollection is the common yellow azalea – all other azaleas, too – but the yellow best of all. The scent of sweet briar is mainly or entirely from young leaves, when they are just getting to be full grown, but are still of tender texture. Lilies are lavish of this scent. Lilacs, syringas, honeysuckles and a few roses give off their scent when the sun brings it out. Of all annuals, mignonette gives out most of its delicious smell. Rockets and stocks perfume the air in the evening.

The daphnes, especially *D. cneorum*, are liberal of their sweetness, and the vanilla-like scent of *Azara microphylla* carries a long distance. These are only a few instances out of many that a well-stocked garden furnishes, but they may serve to remind some who are planting of one of the delights of plants and shrubs. It is the same with trees; everyone knows the sweetness of a lime tree in flower. The young-leaved branches of larch smell like lily of the valley, and anyone who goes shouldering about among cypresses, junipers and box trees becomes acquainted with subtle and delicious scents that cannot too often be repeated.

CLIMBING PLANTS

HARDY VINES ON HOUSE WALLS

There is hardly any vigorous shrub or plant that is a more satisfactory wall covering than one of the strong-growing vines of the sweetwater class. The best of these is the 'Royal Muscadine', hardy and beautiful of foliage and admirably suited for the wall of any house of the large cottage type. The popular name is a little misleading as it suggests – quite erroneously – some connection with the tender Muscats. It is the popular chasselas of the French, largely grown for market at Thomery, a little south of Paris, and sold in the markets and on barrows in the street of the capital. Its use in England is not for fruit, though there are varieties that fruit well on a warm wall, but for its free growth and handsome foliage. As with all its kind it likes a strong soil with the addition of anything of a limy nature.

Another good, hardy vine for wall covering is the claret vine, a fine thing for a garden wall where a background of dusky, reddish foliage is desired. Then there is the parsley vine, a name not properly descriptive, for though the leaves are small and deeply indented they cannot be said to resemble parsley. But it is a capital thing of free growth, good either for wreathing a garden doorway or for covering an arbour or trellis.

SIMPLY PLANTED PERGOLAS

The pergola is now so much used in garden design and has proved a source of so much pleasure and advantage that some suggestions as to the employment of special plants less commonly used may be of service. In many cases it may be desirable, for the sake of a large, simple effect, to plant it entirely with one kind of climbing shrub. Of these the most obvious is the grape vine, for, though the grapes do not ripen in England under such treatment, yet the foliage of vines of the sweetwater and chasselas types is the most beautiful that can be had, and gives an ample shade. Then there is the wisteria, a whole covering of which makes a pergola of extraordinary beauty, and gives three distinct effects at different seasons of the year. First the masses of lovely bloom in earliest summer before the leaves are developed; then the important and always graceful foliage; and in winter the mass of interlacing grey stem that in itself gives an aspect of constructive carpentry, and is, in fact, of considerable structural strength. The weakest point in the employment of wisteria is that the plants are, at first, slow of growth; but by the third year after planting the increase is rapid, and the yearly growth thereafter faster still.

The long pergola at
Hestercombe, framing
the view over the
Taunton Weald, with
planting designed by
Miss Jekyll.

A vine-smothered pergola.

A pergola of laburnum only is also most desirable. The small trees, when young, can be trained to any form; they are, in fact, so docile to guidance, and their own wood of trunk and branch so firm and strong, that they do not absolutely need a well-built pergola such as is usual in garden design. They adapt themselves admirably to the pleached alley treatment of our old Tudor gardens, where a slight wooden framework is first set up, to which the young trees are trained. Split chestnut two inches thick suffices for this, for by the time the laburnums have been guided into shape and have grown enough to cover the frame they form their own walls and roof to the shady tunnel. Seedlings that have not been trained to the usual standard form are the best for this use, as they branch low down. Timely cutting back of these branches ensures well-filled walls, and continued pruning good flowering spurs, so that at the end of May there is a sheet of the graceful, tender yellow bloom, and for the rest of the year a dense covering of the neat three-parted leaves.

For a short pergola on quite a small scale nothing is better than the box thorn or tea tree (*Lycium chinense*, or *L. barbarum*, as it is often called). It is quick and free of growth, and the abundant shoots and neat foliage form a close, compact covering. It is one of the best of plants for forming an arbour, but the very neatness and smallness of detail make it less suitable for a full-sized pergola. The small flower is inconspicuous as to general effect, but, with its modest purple colouring, pretty veining and handsome centre of protruding stamens, is always a delight to examine in detail.

CLIMBING PLANTS FOR COTTAGE GARDENS

Foreigners visiting England for the first time, if they have the opportunity of driving about in the country in summer, are always full of admiration for the little wayside gardens in the

Vine over the Mushroom House door.

few yards of space between the road and the cottage door. And indeed these gardens are a wonderful means of adding interest and beauty not only to the dwelling itself, but to the whole village.

Many small houses have some kind of little porch which asks to be clothed with a pleasant flowering plant; or if there is no porch such a thing is easy to make with four rough pieces of pole put upright, with some small branching stuff fixed across to form a top. Even if a cottage is of the plainest brick with a slated roof, such an addition, well covered with a good climbing plant, will not only redeem it from plain ugliness, but will give it a certain dignity and inevitably some kind of beauty.

As to the choice of suitable plants, the first that comes to mind is the sweet white jasmine. After the first year it gets on quickly, and when the growths have covered their supports and have been tied in so as to be properly spreading, then in later years it should have the lateral shoots pruned back in winter to within a few eyes of the branch; then in July it will give a mass of short sprays each with its deliciously sweet flowers. Even when not in bloom the foliage is of much beauty. A denser-growing porch plant is the old tea tree or box thorn; the botanical name is *Lycium barbarum*. It is quick to grow and easy to train; the flowers are not showy, their colour is a low-toned pink shaving to buff, but they are pleasant for anyone to see while waiting for a knock on the door to be answered. Even with a very slight support this accommodating plant can be trained to form a porch in itself; it is also a capital thing for making a shady arbour in some other part of the garden.

When there is nothing of the nature of a porch one of the best plants for flanking the doorway is *Kerria japonica*, commonly called Jew's mallow; the double form is the one usually grown. It is a mass of flower in April and May; every three years the oldest shoots should be cut out. I have seen a capital green porch to a cottage made by planting a common laurel on each side of the door. The very slightest framework is needed for guiding and training; when they have grown to cross overhead they can be pruned to form a perfect arch, and no support is needed. Laurustinus and laburnum can be treated in the same way. The old Dutch honeysuckle grows only too quickly, but if cleverly managed can be made to form a good arch. For the same use there is also the variegated Japan honeysuckle, which is nearly related to the still sweeter French honeysuckle (*Lonicera japonica* var. *repens*). Rambling roses can of course be used, but they want very careful treatment to make good arches. Perhaps the best rose for a cottage door is the old cottage white rose in the double form, or its pretty pink variety 'Maiden's Blush'.

CLIMBING PLANTS FOR COTTAGE WALLS

For any bare wall spaces one of the best shrubs that may be treated as climbers is *Chaenomeles speciosa*. The fine red flowers come early; after blooming it should be pruned back to within a few eyes of the older wood. If the wall is of red brick one of the paler varieties can be chosen; there is a fine one named 'Apple-blossom'.

The winter jasmine (*Jasminum nudiflorum*) is a valuable wall plant. The yellow flowers come quite early, in February and through March. It is a rapid grower, soon covering a wall with its yard-long drooping branches. For a warm place against a cottage wall a trained rosemary is a delightful thing, especially if it may be accompanied by a bush of the old pink China rose. In the southern counties, and especially near the sea, myrtles may be grown, either in bush form or trained to the wall, where they will cover quite large spaces.

The pretty *Fuchsia* 'Riccartonii' is used in the same way. These two delightful shrubs are too tender for our immediate neighbourhood, unless they have some protective covering in winter, though they do well in the southern parts of Sussex, Kent and Hampshire.

The large two-flowered pea (*Lathyrus grandiflorus*) is more often seen in cottage gardens than in those of larger places. It delights in any narrow border against the house, in a rather warm place. The flowers, in pairs of two shades of crimson, are the largest and handsomest of any of the cultivated peas. It grows about five feet high, and if it is given a couple of pea sticks they will soon be covered. The better-known everlasting pea likes the same treatment; the white variety is an improvement on the common pink kind.

Forsythia suspensa is an admirable wall plant, and though perhaps not often used in this way, it is so well adapted to it that it should not be overlooked. It can be trained close to the wall, when it throws out long arching growths, laden with charming yellow bloom quite early in the year. These should be pruned back to a few eyes from the stems after flowering.

There is no lack of free-growing shrubs for covering larger spaces. One of the best known is Virginia creeper, whose leaves turn such a fine colour in the autumn. Then there is its near relative, *Parthenocissus tricuspidata* 'Veitchii', whose rootlets cling like ivy. It grows so freely that it should be carefully kept in check as to the amount of space it is allowed to cover.

The beautiful white-flowered *Clematis montana* will also cover a large space – a whole house front if that should be desired. The sweet Dutch honeysuckle is also a rampant grower, but easily kept in check by reasonable pruning. It should never be planted in a warm exposure or it becomes covered with blight, but is quite happy facing north or north-east. There is often a place where a woodshed or some such place is rather an eyesore, but it may be converted to a thing of beauty by planting a guelder rose and partly training it to the wall. Even a bit of corrugated iron roofing can be made a pleasant object by training over it the wild clematis (*C. vitalba*), which is so common in chalky places, but that will grow freely anywhere.

IVY AND ITS MANY WAYS

Things that are extremely familiar are often apt to pass almost unnoticed. Such a one is our common ivy; for it is only when one gives it a little careful thought, or something more than common observation, that one perceives what a wonderful and precious plant it is, and what an important part it plays in the clothing and adornment of our winter landscape. Indeed, it may truly be said that no one kind of vegetation can do so much for us when summer-leafing trees are bare.

When one is travelling about country roads in winter, ivy is often the only green thing to be seen. The fields are brown plough, woods and hedges are bare and leafless. Even pastures and roadsides are not green, for what short grass there is, is of a dull grey colour, and partly obscured by the buff and brown of last season's bents. But any turn of the road may bring into view deciduous trees richly mantled with ivy, a sight that rejoices the heart of any true lover of nature's beauties. For it is in the depth of winter that the ivy leaves are at their glossiest and that their bowery masses not only look their best, but also give the most comforting assurance of that cosy warmth and safe harbourage so friendly and beneficent to the varied forms of bird life.

Often some handsome arch of tree limb bending over the roadway would pass unnoticed were it not overgrown with ivy; but the bushily branching, dark green clothing, accentuating the tree form, reminds us how often it is that trees, and especially oaks, assume this graceful form over roads, and thereby give the impression of protective sympathy towards those who pass by. This is the more noticeable in that the oak is not always graceful in form like the birch or the ash.

The small ivy of the hedge bank is beautiful too; in winter, and on poor soils especially, taking on wonderful colourings of brown and bronze and red, some leaves even approaching a scarlet colour. In the trailing or creeping stage, and when it first begins to climb, the leaves are of the typical five-pointed form. But as soon as it has climbed enough to make a distinct trunk, and to throw out the woody side branches that will produce flower and fruit, the form of the leaf changes to the plain shape with pointed end, only varying more or less in width. This rule, with one exception, is invariable. As long as it rails on a bank or spreads over the floor of a wood, or only begins to climb, the leaf is wide, either five- or three-pointed, or, at any rate, wide-shouldered; in the mature state it has none of these leaves. The exception is where, as on walls, the ivy is clipped every year, and is prevented from making the woody side shoots. In this case the leaves remain of the wide shape.

Other trees – for ivy is a true tree, having a woody stem and branches – have the same way of producing leaves of two patterns. The most familiar is the holly, though in this case leaves both prickly and smooth-sided are seen on the same tree. The ilex also has the leaves prickly edged in a young state, and plain, almost olive-like, when older.

CLEMATIS MONTANA AND ITS MANY USES

Although it is one of the most commonly seen climbing plants, this Indian mountain clematis can never be too largely used. Its freedom of growth and wealth of bloom fit it for the covering of any unsightly building or rough wooden fence. It will ramble up dead trees and over banks, it will cover arbour or pergola, and it is specially suitable for training over any succession of arches and swinging garlands. It is equally suitable for a cottage porch, or, with due restraint, for association with careful architecture: it is not fastidious about soil or situation and will submit to almost any treatment. Although its nature is to ramble a good thirty feet, it will even allow itself to be cut back close, and to form a tufted plant covered with bloom. In this case a plant self-sown came up in a joint of the stone pavement at the

foot of a step; to let it grow here would have been inconvenient, the walk above being already well covered; what this plant will do in future years remains to be seen. We have it also in a flight of garden steps, and were able to guide it along the foot of each step; the effect of a flowery garland trimming each step-foot was very pretty, and it was only given up because in winter some of the strands came loose and threatened to trip up anyone passing up or down the steps.

   A favourite use of this good clematis is to grow it with guelder rose, the clematis running at will through and through the viburnum. They flower at the same time. The combination is especially pretty with the addition of the early Dutch honeysuckle, whose soft, pale yellow colouring appears pleasantly from the white bloom-masses of its companions. *Clematis montana* is a native of the Himalaya. It is grown from seed and has been improved as a garden plant by selection of plants with wide-petalled flowers. For the reason that plants from seed are apt to vary and tend to revert to the type, comparatively poor flowers are often seen, and care should be taken to secure plants from a good strain.

WINTER JASMINE

Useful as this fine winter-flowering shrub is when trained on a wall or fence, I always wish to see it on some very steep, wild rocky bank, where its habit of flinging itself about and trailing downward would be displayed to the greatest advantage. It is also charming when grown in some wild brake among stiff, twiggy bushes, such as blackthorn and hawthorn, which give it both support and protection.

OPPOSITE
LEFT A pyracantha trained espalier fashion at York Gate, Adel, Leeds.
RIGHT The North Court, decorated by *Clematis montana*.

Winter jasmine cascading over a wall in a Yorkshire village, as Miss Jekyll describes.

SMALL GARDENS

COLOUR IN THE SMALL GARDEN

Where space is limited and there is no opportunity for working out schemes of colour in the most complete way, which is by having separate gardens or borders for special seasons, something may still be done by keeping to the same principles of arrangement. This consists mainly in grouping together plants whose colours harmonize, and passing by degrees from one colour harmony to another in such a way that all may be represented and a good progression secured. As an example [shown below], we may suppose that there is one main border for hardy perennials, with certain additions of tenderer summer flowers. The most convenient way of accommodating all the colours will be to begin at one end with a grouping of purple, white, pink and grey, to let this lead to palest yellow, then to deeper yellow and orange, and from that to the fullest and most gorgeous scarlets and crimsons. After that the scheme of colour would go on again through orange, yellow, pale yellow and white to the pure blues, with a setting of grey and glaucous foliage.

There should, if possible, be a separate place for spring flowers, preferably in a strip or border with a cool aspect. So many of them are bulbous that it is not convenient to have them in the main flower border, where they could only show in detached patches with but poor effect; then, when they die down and their place is wanted for summer flowers, the bulbs are sure to get stabbed or injured by fork or trowel. But if a special place cannot be given, daffodils and crocuses at least can be planted in grass or among deciduous shrubs or fruit trees. If it should happen that an old hedge bank forms one boundary of the garden, there will be a capital site for the spring flowers, for no place is more suitable for columbines, Solomon's seal, anemones, daffodils and scillas, for snowdrops, wood sorrel, myosotis, tiarella, woodruff and blue-eyed Mary (*Omphalodes verna*), to be followed by white foxgloves

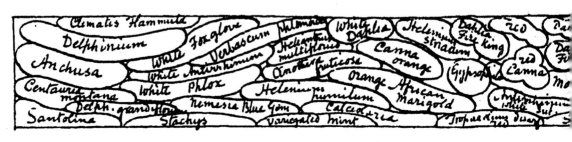

and hardy ferns for summer. Or any border that is slightly in shade or that has a cool aspect may be devoted to the spring bulbs and early flowers, so long as it is not actually invaded by the roots of trees. It is best if they are planted in long-shaped, diagonal drifts alternating with corresponding drifts of hardy ferns. The flowers will be over before the ferns are fully grown and will cover the whole space for the summer and autumn.

To return to the main flower border and to follow the rule suggested, beginning with purple, white and pink flowers with grey foliage, they would be: first, as to the taller, pink Japan anemone, *Campanula persicifolia*, *C. macrocarpa*, *C. lactiflora* and the fine white form of *C. latifolia* var. *macrantha* 'Alba'; the purple form of *Thalictrum aquilegiifolium*, globe thistles, white foxglove, white dahlia and white everlasting pea; in the middle, the fine purple *Salvia virgata*, *Eryngium giganteum*, flag irises of purple and white colourings; white phlox and the fine white daisy *Leucanthemum* x *superbum*, and, quite to the front, white and pink pinks, catmint, white alyssum sown, and stachys and *Senecio cineraria* for grey foliage.

Then, passing to the pale yellows, at the back of the border would be yellow dahlias and the pale form of *Helianthus* x *laetiflorus*, the tall yellow *Thalictrum flavuma*, the perennial *Verbascum chaixii* and the biennial *V. phlomoides*; to the middle pale yellow snapdragons and *Achillea eupatorium* and yellow irises, with *Oenothera macrocarpa* and intermediate yellow snapdragons at the front edge.

Then, passing to the stronger yellows, at the back of the border, double *Helianthus* x *multiflorus*, the fine tall form of *H.* x *laetiflorus* named 'Mrs Moon' and *Rudbeckia laciniata* 'Hortensia', with *Coreopsis lanceolata* in front; these middle yellows deepening to the splendour of orange African marigold and the deep richness of French marigold, with a front planting of the dwarf or miniature marigolds and the best form of that fine plant the annual pot marigold (*Calendula officinalis*). This leads to the strongest colouring of rich reds: at the back, blood red and darker hollyhocks, scarlet dahlias of the 'decorative' class, cannas and penstemons, and to the front, scarlet salvias and bedding geraniums. The colouring then returns through orange, full and pale yellow, to near the further end, where palest yellow and white is the best setting for flowers of purest blue. Delphiniums of the usual tall kinds will

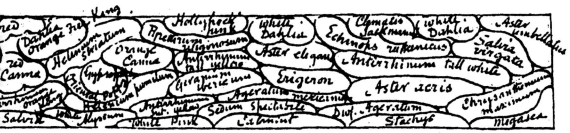

A plan for a well-coloured border.

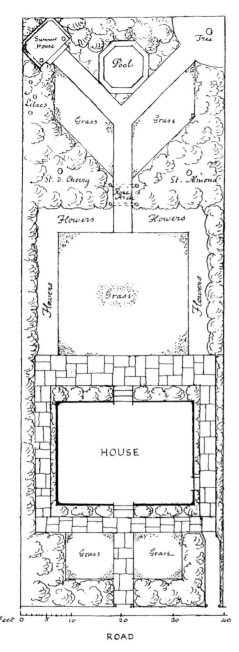

A suggested treatment for a small garden.

be at the back, with white dahlias, then anchusas and more delphiniums of the branching intermediate kinds. There should be a plant of *Clematis flammula* quite at the back to train over the stems of the delphiniums when they stand four to five feet high after the soon-seeding bloom has been cut away. Then in the middle space will be white phlox and tall white snapdragons, and to the front the low-growing *Delphinium grandiflorum*, with white foliage of *Senecio cineraria*, *Artemisia stelleriana* and *Stachys byzantina*.

To use all the plants named in groups of reasonable size would require a large space, but from among them enough may easily be chosen to suit individual taste and the space at disposal. The use of some of the best half-hardy annuals and biennials can hardly be too strongly advised, such as the marigolds and nasturtiums already named, China asters, stocks (especially where the soil is chalky), snapdragons of several kinds and the dwarf ageratums. These are sown in greenhouse or frame, pricked off in boxes and planted out at bedding time, which is usually in the last days of May. It is then that the weak or empty spaces of the border can best be seen, and can be filled, according to colour, with the plants prepared.

THE ORDINARY GARDEN

A FEW SUGGESTIONS FOR MAKING IT OUT-OF-THE-ORDINARY, WITH A PLAN [LEFT]

When travelling by train, and passing from the outskirts to the centre of a town, it is commonplace to note the treatment, or lack of treatment, of the average suburban plot. It is true that the possibilities are limited alike by the conditions of the site and probably by limitations of time and expense which can be devoted to the layout and upkeep of the garden. Nevertheless, much more could be done by a little knowledge and imagination. By way of example, let us take a small house standing back, say, twenty or twenty-five feet from the roadway at the front, and having at the back a piece of ground perhaps seventy-five feet in length and about forty feet in width. The entry to the house may be centrally placed, or it may be at the side. We will assume the former, and there will, of course, be a side path to the tradesmen's entrance.

The plot of ground is assumed to be divided off from its neighbours by a wood fence, and though for the most part it may be devoid of natural features of special interest, we will assume that at one corner there is a small beech tree, with two or three lilacs on the opposite side of the garden. It is further assumed that the front of the house faces south-west. With this preliminary data before us, we will proceed to see what can be done.

It is always well in planning a garden, whether large or small, to keep everything quiet on the entrance side. It gives a certain sense of reserve and dignity, and is an all-the-better preparation for the enjoyment of the bright, flowery garden on the sunny side. It is also in character with the slightly ceremonious sentiment on the part of the visitor in the act of ringing at the front door and asking to be admitted. Then comes the welcome and, following it, the joyous aspect of the lawn and flowers. Therefore on the plan which accompanies these notes the entrance front has only shrubs and two little grass plots, and it is best for the shrubs to be mostly evergreen. Laurustinus, box, yew, aucuba, Portugal and ordinary laurels will give an ample choice; in fact, these are too many for any one little front garden. Some of the smaller of these may be against the house. Laurustinus can be trained to the wall or to the fence in the narrow spaces at the sides. Other suitable plants for the house front will be the Japanese *Skimmia japonica* 'Oblata' and the beautiful Alexandrian laurel (*Danae racemosa*). These could be filled in with the broad-leaved saxifrage *Bergenia cordifolia*, preferably removing the early bloom, which is of a harsh magenta pink colour, the better to benefit by the handsome and persistent foliage, which is always so good near any masonry. Where the planting space is extremely narrow, as against the fence by the tradesmen's entrance on the right, one of the many good forms of ivy will be the right plant.

Stone steps are always of good effect in a garden, and it often happens that there is a small fall in level from the house on the garden side. Here steps will come well. It does not matter if the fall is so slight that each step only rises four inches. More steps than needful are shown on the plan; two will probably be enough, especially as it is all the better for them to be as wide in the tread as possible. For the planting against the house on the sunny side, small shrubby things are preferable to soft plants. Rosemary, lavender, little bushes of pink China rose, *Olearia phlogopappa* and santolina, all sun-loving things, will be the best plants here, and for climbers a white jasmine, and, if there is room for it, a wisteria, which in time would cover the whole front above the first-floor windows, and perhaps ramble some way along the sides.

When a garden consists of a narrow strip, it is well to make at least one cross division so as to lessen the insistence of the strip feeling. The little lawn shown in the plan, with its backing of shrubs, will do this. The shrubs to right and left of the rose arches should be of the more dark and solid character, such as laurustinus and Japan privet; those on each side of the lawn next to the fence should be beautiful flowering things, such as weigela, bush lilacs, deutzias, philadelphus, ribes and so on. These, or shrubs of some such character, would be repeated in the further shrub planting next to the two diagonal spaces of grass. Two standard flowering trees should be in the middle of these shrub clumps, and would show finely from the house. It may be objected that the square lawn and its side planting give no convenient access by a hard path to the further garden. That this is so is one of the inconveniences of a narrow plot of land. Of course, a path could be taken right down the middle, cutting the lawn in two, but it would be a pity, and various small ingenious methods would get over the difficulty. For instance, if it is urged that the grass is too wet to walk over, it does not seem to be generally known that it dries almost immediately after a few strokes of a birch broom. The broom breaks up the drops that hang in the grass, they fall into the earth and the blades quickly dry.

At the junction of the Y-shaped paths at the end of the garden is a pool or tank, octagonal in shape, backed with solid evergreen foliage, such as that of the broad-leaved laurel. Smaller shrubs, such as the alpine rhododendrons, *Hebe odora* and *Euonymus fortunei* var. *radicans*, would come in front, where the shrub planting is shown a little more lightly on the plan [on page 140].

One of the arms of the forked path leads to the tree which has been assumed as existing at one corner of the garden – here a seat could appropriately be set. The other path leads to a summerhouse – always a pleasant thing in a garden, and especially useful when treated and used as an outdoor room.

The suggested plan [on page 140] is, of course, only one of many which might be put forward; and though it may not fit every case, it may offer some ideas that can be adopted in the layout of a suburban plot of ground.

SMALL LONDON GARDENS

There must be in London hundreds of houses of the better and best classes that have an unsatisfactory outlook from the living rooms at the back. In many cases there is nothing really large enough to be called a garden, for it is often nothing but a kind of well, or narrow rectangular space with buildings on every side, with walls grimed and blackened by an old sooty deposit. Such spaces have generally been neglected, but there is no reason why they should not be taken in hand and made into something that is a pleasure to look at instead of being as now depressingly dull, if not actually eyesores. It is all the more to be desired because, with the great increase of modern traffic, London grows more and more noisy, and the rooms that are furthest from the roadway are necessarily more quiet and restful. But then there is the dispiriting outlook, which has either to be endured for the sake of daylight, or must be screened by blinds or some other device that more or less intercepts the light that is so precious in London, especially as the days grow shorter and winter approaches.

It is obvious that any form of gardening that would be right in larger areas would here be unsuitable and that the treatment must conform to the near conditions and be of the nature of something built. But we know from the many examples of the Italian Renaissance, both small and great, how finely the work of architect and sculptor may minister to the needs of a garden, even of the smallest size, or to confined spaces between buildings that it is desirable to treat ornamentally.

A small walled court, panelled in brick and stone, at the far end, steps on either side, leads to an upper terrace that has stone seats on the two landings and a wrought stone balustrade.

Lindsey House, a modern view, after the garden was restored.

Lindsey House, 100 Cheyne Walk, Chelsea, a garden designed by Sir Edwin Lutyens and planted by Gertrude Jekyll for Sir Hugh Lane in 1910.

Lindsey House, looking through the 'screen' towards the old mulberry tree.

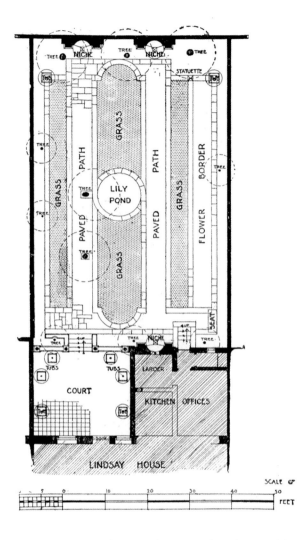

Garden plan for Lindsey House.

On this upper terrace is a central wall fountain. The water from this is conducted to a point from which it falls into the pool below between the middle pair of caryatid pilasters. Such an idea may be varied almost infinitely. As in garden design where area is not limited, so also in these restricted spaces: every place must be treated on its own merits and in conformity with its own conditions. But it is well to press the point of having at the far end some distinctly ornamental object of interest. None is better than a wall fountain, for in the first place it demands beautiful design in itself; then the sound and sight of falling water are both delightful, and the pool or basin is of practical use for dipping.

With regard to planting, even though the space is small it is well to keep it on broad lines, and to have the growing things distinctly contained in stonework. Any borders for planting will be the more handsome for having a bold stone curb and it is all the better for this to be high enough to give the bed a raised appearance. For the actual planting, by far the best way is to have a good proportion of foliage of rather large size, such as acanthus, hostas and the best of broad-leaved saxifrages. For flowering plants, as the object is to have a continuous summer display of bloom in perfect condition, and as this could not be secured by permanent planting, it would be best to have spaces, the depth of an average pot, between the acanthus and other foliage masses, so that potted plants can be dropped in and changed as they pass out of flower. Lilies will be among the best especially *L. longiflorum*, *L. candidum* and *L. speciosum*, and of the last, for preference the pure white and the pale pink punctatum. Pots of hosta, aspidistra and fern will be useful to arrange with flowers so that no pots are actually seen. If it is desirable to have any hardy things permanently planted, the best choice would be Solomon's seal, common male fern and some of the irises. Of the last among those most desirable will be the native *Iris foetidissima*, which scarcely deserves its uncomplimentary name. It has the advantage of being evergreen and of forming handsome pods of orange berries. The foliage is dark green, shining and persistent. Of the June-flowering irises the best will be the grand *Iris pallida* subsp. *pallida* [formerly *Iris pallida* var. *dalmatica*], desirable not only on account of its large size and the beauty of form of its light lavender bloom, but because the great glaucous, sword-like leaves remain in good condition all the summer, whereas in the greater number of the bearded irises they wither and turn brown. Clove carnations are also suitable town plants, with good winter foliage. There is another large-leaved plant, less well known, that does well in London, namely, *Trachystemon orientalis*; it is of the borage family; the flowers, which come early, are of no importance, but they are quickly followed by large and handsome foliage.

There are also many places with an equally unpleasant view, looking out upon leads that roof basement rooms, where any stone paving or building of brick or stone are not possible. I have in mind a small house in Mayfair, well known to Londoners of the last generation. The principal rooms are at the back, with wide windows, looking out upon a dingy prospect of blackened walls all round and leads below. Even this could be made into something pleasant to look at, with some simple carpenter's work of board pilasters with caps of existing mouldings, and perhaps a series of arches between, and a decent entablature – all of thin wood clapped on, but designed and clapped on just rightly. The whole would have two coats of oil paint and then a yearly coat of lime white, slightly tinted with ochre, in the spring.

In connection with the same subject there is a kind thing that owners of good London houses might do for their servants. The view from the kitchen windows on to the wall of the area a few feet distant is not exhilarating, though the wall may be often whitewashed for the sake of extra light. But a broad panel of the wall could be made into a fern garden, by having two pilasters of brick standing on end, cemented to the wall, enclosing a space six or eight feet wide, and up to within eighteen inches of the foot pavement level. Wire netting of coarse mesh is stretched across this space, leaving behind it the depth of the brick, which is two and a half inches. Here and there a large-headed spike is driven in, the head wired to the netting, so as to keep it fairly evenly away from the wall. The space between the wall and the netting is packed with a peaty compost, with moss in front. Small plants of male fern, with any lesser kinds, are planted in (a bit of the wire can always be cut out where desired), and other little plants, such as London pride, musk and moneywort and the bright green tiny soleirolia, are planted between. The whole is thoroughly syringed and then kept fairly moist and becomes an enjoyable wall garden.

SHRUBS AND THEIR USES

SMALL EVERGREENS FOR POOR SOILS

Now that the summer-leafing trees and shrubs are bare, one is all the more thankful for those with good evergreen foliage. There are people who deplore having to garden in a poor, light soil, but it is just the kind of ground that is most favourable to some of the best evergreens – holly among those of larger growth, arbutus of medium size, but, above all, to some of the smaller shrubs that are so valuable in regions where garden joins woodland or any other rougher ground, besides their many other good uses. One of the best among these is *Skimmia japonica* 'Oblata', about three feet high, with bright green leathery foliage. It should be remembered that skimmia is dioecious, so that at least one pollen-bearing plant should be among a group of those that will bear the bright red berries. Besides its value as a handsome small shrub, a few twigs without berries are good to use with cut flowers, for they are fresh looking, bright green and long lasting. Those who have blooms of stephanotis will find some short cut twigs of skimmia the best possible accompaniment to the flowers arranged in some shallow bowl. The handsome *S. japonica* 'Veitchii' is a good deal larger than the type of the broad-leaved *S. japonica*, both in leaf and berry and general growth and, like its congener, is one of the indispensable evergreens.

Nothing is better in winter in poor sandy soils than *Leucothoe axillaris*. As an informal shrubbery edging or at the sides of a woodland path it is always charming. It is in some kind of beauty the whole year through, only excepting three or four summer weeks when the new shoots are forming. But it is as a winter plant that it is most enjoyable. It likes a cool place in slight shade, but in light soils will do almost anywhere except on a dry sunny bank. In winter much of the foliage is prettily spotted or marbled with red colouring, and here and there some shoots are entirely red.

The dwarf *Rhododedron ferrugineum* (alpenrose) is a precious plant in poor soils, and, though it likes a bit of peat, it is not at all fastidious and will even thrive in quite heavy ground. Its very near relative *R. hirsutum* is a limestone plant, and is therefore precious in gardens on the chalk, where all other well-known rhododendrons are forbidden. The very useful small shrub known in nurseries as *R. myrtifolium* is no doubt a hybrid. The leaves have the sweet myrtle-like scent when rubbed or crushed; it is a good deal larger than *R. ferrugineum*, whereas the true plant is smaller.

Though scarcely a shrub, the plant commonly known as Alexandrian laurel, more properly named *Danae racemosa*, should be mentioned among the lesser shrubs of good winter greenery. Either indoors as cut branches or as living fountains of graceful growth, it is alike admirable. The tufts should be kept clean and perfect by the timely removal of discoloured fronds of the last year's growth. It does fairly well on light soils, though it prefers something of better quality, and it likes some degree of shade. Conditions that suit Christmas roses suit Alexandrian laurel, and nothing can better than a combination of the two in some place devoted to outdoor winter flowers, especially if they have an irregular front planting of *Bergenia cordifolia* or of asarum.

FLOWERING SHRUBS IN THE FLOWER BORDER

In places at the back of the flower border where this is of good size, such as a width of ten or twelve feet, it is as well to have a few of the shrubs that will give a good mass of flower that lasts well. The ordinary hydrangea is always welcome, though perhaps best as pot plants, to drop in when earlier blooming things are gone over. It is the garden form of the North American *Hydrangea arborescens* with the addition of 'Grandiflora'. It has multiplied the sterile florets in the same way as our familiar guelder rose, so that instead of being almost flat has become a well-filled ball-like mass. Another shrub that is welcome in the back of the border is *Ceanothus* x *delileanus* 'Gloire de Versailles'. Grown to a height of from five to six feet, it submits to a hard yearly pruning, flowering profusely in August on the young wood. Its grey-blue colouring is of much value in combination with white and tender pink, as well as with the strong purple of *Clematis* 'Jackmanni' which is trained through it and hangs out in rich masses to meet gypsophila, phloxes and heliotrope.

In the part of the border where there are plants of white and yellow colouring the gold-variegated privet is of great value as a background shrub, and another is the gold-leaved elder. This has a yearly pruning, and, like the ceanothus, makes vigorous young growths nearly pure yellow in colour. That rather rampant plant *Rudbeckia laciniata* 'Hortensia' is planted at its foot, and the bright yellow flowers are led into the elder, looking as if they were its own bloom. A white everlasting pea is also of use for planting at the back and training over earlier-flowering plants.

SOME FLOWERING SHRUBS OF LATE JULY

By the third week of July there are not many shrubs in flower, but it is worthwhile to group together some of the few that are in bloom with other plants of the season and some of fine foliage. *Holodiscus discolor*, a large bush some twelve feet high and as much in diameter, is just opening its graceful drooping panicles, though the greater number of these are still in the creamy bud state. Beyond it is a tall bush of *Hebe brachysiphon*, loaded, as it appears to be everywhere this year, with its milk-white bloom; further back is a spike of *Yucca gloriosa*. The general prevalence of cream-white bloom is carried down to the grass by some well-established clumps of *Clematis recta*; while between them and the shrubs are some spikes of the white *Campanula latifolia* var. *macrantha* 'Alba'. The mass of white bloom is well set off by a foreground of the handsome foliage of acanthus and clumps of the bold leaves of the large form of *Bergenia cordifolia*.

SHRUBBERY EDGES

Nothing appears to be more commonly neglected in gardens than the opportunity of doing some good planting at the edges of shrubberies, whether these adjoin a lawn or a path. Flowering shrubs look much better when they stand a little way back, and it is just that bordering space of a few feet that deserves more careful consideration than it commonly receives.

In the first place it is desirable to have nothing of quite small size or petty effect. Plants of rather large and distinct foliage are wanted, or if any with small leaves are used they should be in quantity enough to show as a fairly large breadth. Small bushes would be well in place, and of these the greater number, such as rosemary, cistus, hardy fuchsias and heaths, would be rightly placed on the sunny side. Here also would be the bush garden roses, damask, Provence, gallica and the rest. The noble acanthus will also be here in place, for though in its South European habitats it is found in shady ravines, yet in our northern gardens it is glad of a place in full sunshine. The handsomest is *A. spinosus*. *A. mollis* is a fine thing, especially in the handsome form Latifolius Group, but it scarcely has the splendid vigorous 'drawing' and beauty of detail of *A. spinosus*, which is also better than the more prickly and finely divided *A. spinosus* Spinosissimus Group.

For the shadier side there is a larger choice, especially in soils that are of a light character – sandy or peaty, and free from lime; for here will be the best possible places for leucothoe and for the larger of our hardy ferns – male fern, lady fern and dilated shield fern, for the beautiful Alexandrian laurel (*Danae racemosa*) and for the fern-like sweet cicely, for the noble foliage of veratrum and for that of several of the bergenias and hostas. Besides these there are two plants that deserve special notice for the splendid green of their foliage; they are the large-leaved *Trachystemon orientalis*, and the crested tansy. The trachystemon has unimportant flowers that come before the foliage, but the leaves that follow more than make up for the insignificance of the bloom. One cannot pass a well-grown group of the plant without admiring the rich quality of colouring or observing how good a setting it makes to the branching shrubs behind. The leaves, all radial, are of a noble, simple form, boldly heart-shaped at the insertion of the stalk and pointed at the tip, a foot long and eight to ten inches across; they have also an unusual marking of dark-coloured veins. The crested tansy is striking from having the same quality of rich green. It should be kept for the green alone; the ends of the shoots, which would develop into bloom, should be cut out in the middle of June. Sweet cicely (*Myrrhis odorata*) is essentially a plant for the shrubbery border

Shrubbery edges planted with lilies and ferns.

and may be carried far in between the bushes where there are empty places. It comes to its best early in May; soon after this the large umbelliferous bloom will be turning to seed pod. It is a good plan, at this stage, to cut it boldly down, right to the ground; in a very short time it makes fresh growth which remains good all the summer. The native gladwin (*Iris foetidissima*) should also be planted in the shrubbery edge for the sake of its handsome sheaves of deep green leaves; it is a fine thing in mass. Though the flowers have no effect they are followed in the late autumn by the opening pods of brilliant berry-like seeds that are so useful for indoor decoration. Solomon's seal is another most suitable plant, beautiful not only when in bloom, but for the foliage through all the summer months.

It is not to be supposed that these large-leaved plants will take care of themselves without attention year after year. Acanthus, veratrum, myrrhis and hosta will stand a number of years, but before they are planted their places should be deeply trenched and well enriched. Cultivation is specially needful in the near neighbourhood of shrubs, whose roots are sure to invade and would quickly impoverish the border. Although these plants of handsome foliage are specially recommended, it is not meant that flowering plants should be excluded. There are classes of flowers that suit well in shrubbery borders. Lilies in bold groups, Oriental poppies, the early peonies of the officinalis class, columbines, white foxgloves and the larger campanulas, such as *C. latifolia* var. *macrantha* and *C. persicifolia*; but they are all seen at their best with a wide setting of the foliage plants so that the flower groups are more or less isolated, and so that the effect gained is one that is quite distinct from that of a mixed border. The intention is quite different; the flower border should be a complete picture of flower beauty visible as a whole from either end, if it is a double border with a path between, or from some front point of view if it is a single border adjoining a lawn, while it is also lovely and interesting to examine closely. The shrubbery border may well be a succession of plant portraits, beautifully and suitably framed in their bold setting of handsome foliage.

FOLIAGE PLANTS FOR SHRUB EDGES

Where there are groups of flowering shrubs nearly abutting on lawn there are apt to be spaces between and in front of them that require furnishing. Small plants, and any that have the rather weak habit of so many of the annuals, or the usual plants for summer filling, would look inadequate; the places demand some growths of more important aspect. Two plants may be recommended. *Trachystemon orientalis* is early in bloom, but the flower is not of much importance. It is followed by the handsome foliage that remains good all summer. The leaves are a full, deep green, with a harsh texture that seems to be uninviting to insects, for the mass of foliage remains uninjured. It forms a pleasant groundwork for the bloom of the bush of *Viburnum plicatum* that is just above it. It is a strong-growing thing and does well in London gardens.

Another desirable plant for shrub edges is *Acanthus spinosus*, which is the best of the family for garden use; it is more interesting than *A. mollis* and its varieties, and not so overmuch cut up as *A. spinosus* Spinosissimus Group. This, by the side of the trachystemon with its sharply cut and glossy leaves, is a good companion to the polished foliage of the Japan privet which is just above it. The same happy association of sharp-cut form and glossy foliage is used where the acanthus fills the space between a green holly and a garden path. Later in the year this fine plant throws up the great spikes of its hooded, purplish-tinted bloom, of majestic and monumental aspect.

Both this and the better kinds of *A. mollis* are fine things for clothing any rough or rugged places in outlying parts of the garden, where the great fleshy roots can be thrust deep down and remain undisturbed. In their native places in southern Europe they are usually seen in cool, rocky places, and though they stand well in open in our northern gardens, they are grateful for a little shade, for in times of drought, unless they can be thoroughly watered, the great leaves are apt to wilt.

A PLEA FOR THE LAUREL:
ONE OF THE NOBLEST OF EVERGREEN SHRUBS

The wholesome reaction from pernicious influence of the all-pervading bedding system of nearly half a century ago had one effect for which there was no right or fair foundation. Many people came to the conclusion that the scarlet geraniums, yellow calceolaria and blue lobelias, that had been done to death in stiff beds and, still worse, in unending ribbon borders, were bad things in themselves, whereas they are, and always will be, among the best of our summer flowers. It was not their fault that they were used in dull and tiresome ways, but as for a long time they had been connected with a wearisome form of gardening, it was not unnatural, when better ways were becoming known, that they should be looked at askance if not altogether condemned by the general gardening public. Even quite harmless words may by association come in for the same kind of superficial distaste. The name Whitehall has dignity, standing as it does for noble buildings of exalted purpose; Whitechapel is a name no less beautiful in itself, but because it means a dingy and slummy part of London we lose sight of its intrinsic value. So, whether we are thinking of a word or a flower or a shrub, let us clear away any unfavourable impressions that may have gathered round it and try to take a fair view of it on its own merits. The common laurel has come in for much the same kind of unmerited condemnation as the best known of the bedding plants, and it has suffered all the more by reason of its many good qualities. It is cheap to buy, easy to grow, undeniably handsome, and it can be put to many kinds of use; but just because it is so patient and accommodating, and has been used as such a common hack, we have come to look upon it with a kind of distaste that with some people amounts to disgust. But if one considers it quite fairly and without any kind of prejudice one cannot but see that, in spite of the many base uses to which it has been put, it is one of the noblest of evergreen shrubs. Let us think for a moment – if we had never seen a laurel, if it had now been only newly imported, what a stir it would make in the world of horticulture; what a rush there would be for the grand new thing; how it would gain honours in Vincent Square; how people would flock to Kew and Wisley, the only places where as yet they could see that wonderful new shrub, *Prunus laurocerasus*; how proudly within the next year the garden owner would exhibit to his friends the thriving young plant for which he had paid a guinea (and cheap at the price!); what admiration for its lustrous leaves of strong substance, its fine straight shoots, its pleasant look of prosperous cleanliness! What visions of how in the future, when it had become more plentiful, it could best be used, as a handsome shrub by itself, as hedges of important foliage, as arbours and green arches, as a worthy accompaniment to refined architecture of terraces, flights of steps and balustrades, as background with niches for sculpture! We seem to have lost sight of all these worthy possibilities, and yet there is the patient laurel only awaiting the time when its good qualities shall again be recognized and its worthy use shall again be carefully studied. Excepting our native yew, there is no evergreen that can be adapted to so many uses as the laurel. It makes a perfect hedge, to be carefully trimmed with the knife – never with the shears; it can readily be trained into any form of bower or arbour, and where there is space, as in outlying parts of pleasure grounds, it is a grand thing when let to grow as it will.

There are three stretches of woodland near my home in south-west Surrey, on three adjoining properties. In each of these there are a number of large old laurels that have never been pruned. I have not been able to find any record of their planting, but they must be near a hundred years of age. It looks as if three neighbouring squires had agreed together at the same time to try them as woodland shrubs for game shelter. In the wood nearest to me, where there is one roughly circular grove, I do not think these laurels can be less than fifty feet high from where they are rooted to where, far and high overhead, their utmost shoots reach the open daylight. Their trunks, elephant grey in colour, are something like ten inches through. Many of them grow in a fantastic way – the stem rising and then bending down and running along the ground some ten or twelve feet before rising again and shooting up to the light. In the dusky dimness of the grove they look like great grey serpents writhing about and then rushing upwards. To see them like this and also growing naturally in rather open woodland is to receive some quite fresh ideas as to the possible uses of this much neglected and ill-used shrub.

SOME AMERICAN PEAT SHRUBS

The middle of June brings many beautiful flowers, but one of its best delights is the blooming of *Kalmia latifolia*, without doubt one of the very loveliest of flowering shrubs. Not only is it of the first importance in the garden, but, although so hard-wooded, it is long lasting as a cut flower, and it is a delightful thing to examine closely in order to admire and wonder at its marvel of design and colouring. It varies a little in colour from a tender pink to nearly white. The tinting is stronger on the outside, so that the buds are always pink. Looking inside one sees a dainty rosy ring near the centre and the ten stamens bending over outwards with the anthers resting in little pits, which on the outside show as rounded prominences and give a starry effect to the bud when seen full face. The stamens are sensitive, and when the flower is mature will, at a slight touch, spring up in the direction of the pistil. It is often advised that kalmia should be grown in shade, but experience proves that it flowers best in nearly full sun, but it should be in a bed of peat and delights in moisture at the root. Besides kalmia, we are indebted to the North American continent for the greater number of the good bushy plants that flourish in a peaty soil – nearly the whole of the andromeda group, the gaultherias, ledums, pernettyas, the rhododendrons of the catawbiense class and many of the rhododendrons that we should call azaleas in gardens. It seems a strange thing that with such a wealth of shrubs of the heath order (*Ericaceae*) heaths themselves should be absent, though the nearly allied cranberry order (*Vaccinium*) is represented by several ornamental bushes.

Among the many American azaleas perhaps the most beautiful is the *Rhododendron occidentale* of California. Unless it is that in some years it is shy of blooming, it is difficult to understand why it is so seldom to be seen in our gardens. It should be planted with kalmia, for it blooms at the same time, a good fortnight later than the Ghent azaleas, and enjoys the same conditions. Both in bloom and leaf it is better than any of the Ghent kinds, and in both has a singular refinement of aspect. The flowers are for the most part pure white, with a yellow stain in the upper petal; the outside of the tube is tinted with pink, faint in the case of the whitest blooms, but much stronger in some others. The flowers vary much in size, but the best have well-filled trusses of bloom as large as the best of the Ghent varieties. This diversity of size comes from their being grown from seed, and for the same reason it is important that they should be seen in bloom in the nursery and then and there chosen and marked. The foliage is distinctly better than that of any other garden azalea, bold and handsome, of a full, deep green and with a polished surface.

SHRUBS FOR WINDOW BOXES

The season being now with us when the summer flowers in window boxes are over, and must be replaced by something of a hardier character, and where window gardening is carried out the whole year round, either in pots or boxes, shrubs of an evergreen character play an important part during the winter and spring months. A brief list, therefore, of some of the most reliable may be acceptable to those who have not had the opportunities of testing their respective merits, for it is not all kinds of even those whose growth is suitable that submit to the ordeal of lifting and potting without showing any ill effects therefrom. Those that have a mass of fibrous roots are the only ones that will answer the purpose, and they must have in addition short, stubby growth, feathered to the ground with healthy foliage. Happily, most shrubs of an evergreen character are in full feather, so to speak, in winter, as if to compensate somewhat for the bare look of such as are deciduous. Amongst the following sorts are many that have variegated or mottled foliage, but plain green-leaved sorts are the prettiest. Aucubas of all kinds are most useful, their foliage being good, and they stand dust and smoke better than most plants. If the precaution is taken when they are in bloom to artificially fertilize them, or even to plant the male aucubas amongst the others, they will produce a crop of berries and be very ornamental. They should be placed under glass at this season to get their berries well coloured. Box of different sorts are pretty, neat-growing shrubs, and, being exceptionally hardy, very suitable for exposed positions where tender ones fail. Lawson's cypress (*Chamaecyparis lawsoniana*) and its varieties are also very pretty, especially when young, being very graceful in habit of growth. The elegant Japanese cedar (*Cryptomeria japonica*) is another handsome conifer, and is very beautiful in a young state, forming dense bashes consisting of delicate growths that rival ferns in appearance, and which, in winter, assume a deep-bronze tint that enhances their usefulness. The Japanese spindle tree (*Euonymus japonicus*), and the many beautiful variegata varieties of it, are a host in themselves, being dwarf, busy, and having an abundance of fibrous roots; the dark-green, shining leaves of *E. japonicus* looking extremely well along with the golden and silver variegated kinds, so that those filled wholly with euonymuses look remarkably well, and in seaside places, where the range of varieties that really flourish is limited, the euonymus comes in for a very extensive amount of patronage. It not only lives in the salt-laden breeze, but puts on that glossy look which denotes luxuriant health. Golden tree ivy, and the silver variegated variety called 'Elegantissima' [probably x *Fatshedera lizei* 'Variegata'], make very pretty shrubs for window decoration. Some of the St John's worts, too, are very pretty, and do well in shady places. Hollies, in a young state, form pyramidal little bushes that make excellent central objects in boxes or vases. The holly-leaved barberry (*Mahonia aquifolium*), too, is very pretty in a young state, having shining foliage of a deep bronzy-green colour. In spring it also produces large bunches of yellow flowers. Periwinkle, both plain and variegated, forms valuable edgings, being of a graceful habit of growth. Japanese cypresses (*Chamaecyparis*), having beautiful fern-like foliage, are very suitable for window boxes. *C. pisifera* 'Squarrosa', *C. lawsonia* 'Ericoides', *C. obtusa* 'Aurea' and *C. pisifera* 'Plumose' are

Aesculus parviflora in the Shrub Bank.

amongst the best of this beautiful family. Small bushes of the common rhododendrons are well adapted for window gardening in boxes or pots; they form quite a mane of fibrous roots, and move well at any time. *Skimmia japonica* is one of the best of dwarf berry-bearing plants, producing a profusion of brilliant berries that colour early in the season. The New Zealand hebes are also very pretty shrubby plants, producing purple or blue flowers during the winter months; but even without flowers they are well worthy of culture. Adam's needles (yuccas), too, are very effective plants in the shape of single specimens in vases, pots or boxes, *Y. recurvifolia* being especially graceful and useful for that purpose, while *Y. gloriosa* and *Y. filamentosa* form pleasing additions to any collection in which they may be placed.

AESCULUS PARVIFLORA

This beautiful shrub, the dwarf buckeye of the south-eastern states of America, grows to about ten feet high and has the appearance of a condensed and refined horse chestnut. It has the great merit of coming into bloom in the end of July, when so few shrubs are in flower. It deserves an important and rather isolated place in the garden, for it is one of the neatest-habited of shrubs, forming a well-filled half-circle like an inverted bowl, with the foliage coming well down to fill the lower space. The bloom is abundant, for it comes at the tip of every well-ripened branchlet. In the picture [above] it is unduly crowded, for it was placed before its requirements were well known to the planter.

Exochorda racemosa cascading on to the West Lawn.

ALEXANDRIAN LAUREL (DANAE RACEMOSA)

Danae racemosa, better known by the popular names of Alexandrian or victory laurel, is one of the loveliest things that can be grown in a garden. The long, arching fronds, set with stiff, glistening foliage of a perfectly refined form, are at their best in winter, and, where a few of these can be spared for cutting, form the most desirable room ornaments, whether with or without flowers. These gracefully arching sprays must not be cut too freely, for each one takes two years to come to maturity; also those who plant it must have patience, for it is slow to grow at first. Botanically the leaves are not true leaves, but are flattened branches, termed cladodes. The flowers, which come near the ends, are inconspicuous. It likes a place in cool, rather moist soil in slight shade. The growth is more luxuriant in rich loam, but it does well in any lighter soil moderately enriched.

EXOCHORDA RACEMOSA

This is one of the flowering shrubs of supreme beauty that is in every nursery and yet, strangely enough, is not to be seen in every garden. It is allied to spiraea, but the flowers are much larger than those of any other spiraea, as they have a diameter of one and a quarter inches. They are borne in racemes of seven or eight from the axils. When they are in bud it is seen how well justified is the popular name 'pearl bush', for the row of unopened bloom is like pearls loosely strung. It forms a handsome bush of roundish form. It is a little uncertain about flowering, some years blooming freely, in others only sparingly. The late Mr G.F. Wilson advised rather severe pruning after flowering; this may be wise counsel to follow, as the fault of the shrub is to become too open and straggling in habit.

FUCHSIAS AS POT PLANTS

Four Neapolitain pots of a good old design stand at the edge of a paved terrace just above a tank. Some years they are filled with geraniums, but the last year or two we have found that fuchsias are satisfactory. The kind is 'Ballet Girl', red and white, the white sufficiently doubled but not overdone, as in some other kinds. An equally good fuchsia of the same colouring is 'Delight', a pretty plant raised in Messrs Cannell's nursery. It is much like the old 'Mme Cornellison', but dwarfer in habit. Possibly it may be a seedling from that graceful and useful old fuchsia.

KALMIA LATIFOLIA

One of the many joys of June is the flowering of *Kalmia latifolia*. Following the azalea and the greater number of the rhododendrons, and allied to them as a member of the great family of *Ericaceae*, it is a complete flower feast in itself. The compact busy growth and polished foliage is good to see at all times of the year, but June brings its triumph of beauty, with its clusters of lovely blooms of tenderest pink shading to a deeper tone, with its rosy buds and tufts of young leaves of freshest green. The flower is interesting to observe in detail. Seen partly in profile it shows as a five-pointed cup standing on a short stem. Each of the five divisions is strengthened by a shallow rib with a projecting knob at the base and with another such knob between each, making ten in all. Looking at the inner side these projections are accounted for by little cavities. Just above each of these is a dash of deepest crimson. The ten stamens rising from the short tube arch over outwards, so that the anthers rest in the little cavities. They are sensitive; a sharp touch causes them to fly back to the centre, at the same time flinging the pollen to a distance of three or four inches. On trying this I do not find that each flower fertilizes itself; the pollen flies clear of its own bloom, but is sure to reach the pistils of some of its near neighbours. The inside of the flower is further decorated with a zigzag ring of clearest rosy red delicately pencilled round the opening of the tube.

Where the conditions of the garden are favourable no flowering shrub is more desirable. Damp peaty ground is what it most enjoys. Though it flowers well as a low bush four to five feet high, it is at its best when older, for it may grow to a height of ten feet and attain as wide a diameter, and still retain its well-filled and well-dressed appearance. It is a native of the north-eastern states of America, where it is commonly known as mountain laurel. It is said to grow in woods, but here in south-west Surrey it refuses to flower in shady places. As with date palm, it seems to thrive with its head in the sun and its feet in the wet, and though the latter requirement is difficult to establish

Magnolia stellata at the bottom of the Shrub Bank.

and maintain on a dry hill, it has been partly met, and with some success, by a specially prepared bed of peat and the beneficent nearness of a standpipe. It is one of the best flowers for cutting, lasting long on water.

MAGNOLIA STELLATA AND M. DENUDATA

The best things in the garden in the second half of April and early May are the magnolias that flower before the leaves come. A fine bush, one might almost say a little tree, of *Magnolia stellata*, twelve feet high and more in width, is so loaded with bloom that one cannot put a hand into it without touching more than one flower. The expanded bloom of ten or more petals, looking as if it was flung open, is not much more than three inches across, while there is a charming primness about the half-opened flower. It seems to delight in the light, sandy soil of the garden, for both botanists and experienced amateurs always notice it as an unusually fine specimen.

Magnolia denudata has also been unusually full of bloom this year; at Easter, when seen from a little distance, it looked like a solid mass of white, and even when large branches went for church decoration on Easter Sunday and a quantity more was cut for home use and gifts to friends, the tree seemed to be just as much loaded with bloom. Some years it is in flower within March, but here, in south-west Surrey, and probably elsewhere, everything is about a fortnight late.

MISTLETOE (VISCUM ALBUM)

Mistletoe is so closely associated with our Christmas decorations and festivities that a few words concerning it will be in season. Perhaps there is no other plant that so much impresses us with a feeling of mystery, a sentiment perhaps augmented by the tradition of its association with ancient religious rites. However this may be, it is certainly a plant that grips and holds the imagination. For one thing, the fact of its being the only parasitical shrub growing wild in England; then its curious structure and yellow-green leathery leaves, and the lovely pearl-like berries that attain their full beauty in midwinter; also the unusual way of growth, hanging in close bunches from the tree it has chosen for its host – all this setting it apart as the most curious and beautiful of winter plants.

To consider it botanically it belongs to the *Loranthaceae*. It is dioecious, the barren and fertile bloom on separate plants. I have a bush, sown by hand some fourteen years ago on a Chinese crab, which is potentially fertile, but as there is no other plant in the garden or near neighbourhood, it has no berries through all its young life and early maturity. From ignorance of what to do it remained a shapely bush of yellow-green. It was only on close examination at blooming time one March that it was found to be a female plant. A few twigs of pollen flowers were then each year obtained from a distance, with the result of a bountiful crop of berries. The bloom is borne chiefly in the axils, but also at the points between the pairs of leaves. The female flower is scarcely noticeable – a tiny green snout of four petals with a sessile stigma. The male bloom is more conspicuous – wider open, with easily visible yellowish pollen and an extremely sweet scent. Foreign naturalists have held the view that fertilization is effected by certain bees and flies, and this may be so, though recent experiment with flowers carefully protected from such insects has shown that this is not necessarily the case. Mistletoe grows most commonly on apples and allied trees of the same family, such as whitethorn and mountain ash. Curiously enough, it is said not to succeed on the pear; not that it refuses to grow, but that it roots in a strangling ring round the branch, so that branch and mistletoe soon perish together. It is abundant and very fine on limes, rare on oaks. We are so much accustomed to seeing it on deciduous trees only that it is surprising to read, in Bean's *Trees and Shrubs*, that it is abundant on Scots pines in a Swiss valley. It is interesting to experiment with it, rubbing the berries lightly in February on the underside of young wood of various trees and shrubs. It is said to be unknown in Scotland and Ireland. It infests some of the orchards in Herefordshire, and though it is an enemy of the apple, it is profitable at Christmas time in the London market, which is also largely supplied from Brittany.

THE LESSER PERIWINKLES (VINCA MINOR)

Among the many spring flowers now in bloom or already past, from none have I derived a keener pleasure than the white form of the lesser periwinkle, now at its best. I can think of no hardy flower that has a greater look of absolute purity, with its clear-cut outline, firm texture and rarely beautiful quality of white. This lovely little plant is at its happiest in half shade among low bushes. We have it at the roots of some bog myrtles on a dryish bank; the finest flowers are near the heart of the bush among its many stems. Having occasion lately to pick some, it was a double pleasure to have the sweet scent of the sweet gale. The prettiest form of the small white vinca we have is from a friend's garden in the south of Ireland; the shape of the flower is rather rounder and richer than in the wild kinds, as it has six petals, but sometimes more and rarely five. We have also a very dainty wild white, five-petalled, from the Italian lakes.

The common blue is also a lovely plant, and its double variety, as we have it, is very pretty. The doubling strangely alters the character of the flower, giving it rather a double-daisy look, as the broad blunt-ended flatly arranged petals are transformed into a strap-shaped pointed form, and the flower assumes the shape of a flattened dome. The doubling is fairly even and regular and generally constant. Our double purple or dull purple-red, on the other hand, has every shape between single and moderately good double, and the individual petals are not so narrow as in the blue. We have also one with variegated foliage whose flowers are sometimes white, sometimes blue and occasionally parti-coloured. Once I found one exactly half white and half blue, the dividing line being perfectly sharp and clear, but the parti-colouring generally takes the form of a flower mainly of one colour, with one distinct wedge of the other.

The lesser periwinkles do well in most poor soils; the only care they need is not to be left too long undivided; they are rapid growers, and should be replanted at intervals of not more than four years. If this is not done they grow into unsightly matted masses, yielding fewer flowers and leaves.

WATER GARDENING

THE WATER GARDEN

Among the more modern developments of horticulture the water garden has taken an important place. It does not matter whether the site is of large extent, as of lake and river, or quite small as in such a place as may have only a trickle of water artificially supplied; either of these, and everything between, can be adapted for good use in the display of the many beautiful plants of the water and waterside. The diversity of circumstances and way of treatment may be as great as the nature and conditions of the place, but as in all good gardening the natural possibilities of the site have first to be considered and respected, for it is out of these that is formed, in the mind of the competent designer, the conception of the best form of treatment. The nature of the site will govern the main distinction, which is whether the place is suitable for a free kind of planting on natural lines, or whether, in the case of a restricted area and where it will necessarily be near buildings, it will have to be of a purely formal character. In the first case let us suppose that the water supply is a natural one of pond and stream on the extreme outskirts of garden ground. Here, if the water has a naturally good edge, that is an edge that is easily accessible and is not much above the water level, all that is needed will be to clear adequate spaces for planting, leaving the natural growth, especially when it has any suitable character as of sedge or bur reed, undisturbed. There are plants for all degrees of moisture. The noble water lilies for water of some depth, the fine things that thrive in quite shallow water, such as water plantain (*Alisma plantago-aquatica*), the great water dock (*Rumex*), some of the irises, namely, the yellow flag, and the Japanese *Iris laevigata*, buck bean, the arrowheads, and the flowering rush (*Butomus umbellatus*). Then there are the many plants that, though in no sense aquatics, rejoice on the banks of streams or ponds, where their roots can always feel the cool moisture of water soaking through the ground. Here may be grown many of the spiraeas: the double form of our own meadowsweet (*Filipendula rubra* 'Venusta'), with tender pink bloom and much the same habit; the larger *Aruncus dioicus* of Alpine torrents, with its handsome foliage and beautiful plumes of cream-white flowers; several of the tall meadow rues (*Thalictrum*); the rosy willow herb (*Epilobium*); and the crimson loosestrife (*Lythrum*), the great yellow loosestrife (*Lysimachia*), and its smaller relative the creeping moneywort. Here also is the place for the tall yellow mimulus and for globe flowers (*Trollius*); the marsh marigold (*Caltha*), with the yellow Himalayan cowslip (*Primula sikkimensis*) having nodding sulphur bells, and the Japanese primrose (*Primula japonica*), of a rather rank magenta colouring in the type form but with varieties of good white and various degrees of pleasant pink colouring. Then there is the Siberian iris both purplish-blue and white, with some garden improvements, all happy in damp ground, and *Darmera peltatum* with its great roundish leaves.

Where spaces are large, good use can be made of the great cow parsnip (*Heracleum*); the more recently introduced *H. mantgazzianum* is an improvement on the older *H. stevenii*. The still larger foliage of the giant gunneras requires cautious placing as it is almost out of scale with ordinary vegetation. In waterside planting, ferns should not be forgotten. The best for general use are the Royal fern (*Osmunda regalis*), the graceful lady fern, and the dilated shield fern.

The shape of the bank next the water is well worth considering. It is often of a steep, rounded form that seems to plunge suddenly into the water. Such a bank is far from pretty. It gives a sense of insecurity and does not admit of convenient planting. Where there are such banks it is well worthwhile to make a complete alteration and to shape the ground afresh, so as to leave a level grassy pathway some seven feet wide, only raised enough above the water to be sound and dry; thus providing easy access, security and the best opportunity for good planting [see illustration on page 163].

A natural running stream, especially if it flows fast over a shallow pebbly bed, with sides either naturally near the water level or purposely made so, is one of the very best settings for beautiful plants. It can often be so arranged that the path shall cross it from time to time, either by well-set stepping stones or by a simple plank or log bridge. But it is most desirable, especially in places that have a natural character, such as the edges of ponds and streams, that a wise restraint should be observed about the numbers of different plants that are to be seen at a glance. If many different kinds are seen together, restful enjoyment of their beauty will be lost. One good thing at a time in fair quantity, or two at most, is the better way, as, for example, double white meadowsweet with water forget-me-not, and to let this go on for some yards, and then, after an interval, to pass on to some other grouping, either of one kind of plant, or two in combination. In stream planting also the finer of the hardy ferns should not be overlooked: the royal fern, the lady fern, and the dilated shield fern. These are best seen on the further side of the stream; in fact, the view of many of the plants will be better and more comprehensive from the opposite bank. In this way the stream has the advantage of the pond, unless the pond is quite a small one.

It sometimes happens that the only available water is a mere trickle at the bottom of a deepish ditch. When this is the case, and when labour can be expended, the sides can be cut down as before suggested and the spare soil thrown out to form raised banks, one side having the space for a path only a little above water level, while the other is varied by taking the form of an easy bank beginning at the water's edge. The little stream may also be

The lake at Vann, a garden designed by Miss Jekyll in 1911.

widened and its bed floored with small stones or flattish slabs. The path and the accompanying treatment of the banks can move from side to side so as to give different aspects and points of observation. If it is desired that the place shall be enclosed from outer view, the banks formed by throwing up the waste soil should be planted with some kind of bushy growth, for preference holly, with whitethorn, blackthorn, spindle tree and other shrubs of like character; then the bank on the path side would be an admirable place for growing some of the better kinds of wild blackberry.

When the water garden is in a more restricted space, or where, as is often the case, it is desired to have water plants near the house or in close connection with formal gardening, it will take the form of a built tank, symmetrical pool or miniature canal; or a series of tanks may be connected by a narrow rill that may be stepped over. The edges will either have a flat pavement or a raised curb of wrought stone. There is sometimes hesitation about having a tank deep enough for water lilies on account of danger to children, but there is a way of building the outer yard or two of the tank that minimizes the danger and is in any case desirable. This is to have the outer portions only a foot deep for a yard at least from the edge [see illustration opposite]. This also provides a way of having plants in pots that thrive in shallow water; such as the noble water plantain and arrowheads; or, if the wall to the deeper level is carried up so as to retain four to five inches of soil for the plants to root in, it will be all the better. In all cases where water is employed in conjunction with masonry, as in such tanks or rills or in fountain basins, it is important that the water level should be placed high and carefully maintained. Nothing is more common or has a more slovenly and uncared-for appearance than a half-empty tank. If it is used for dipping, and the supply is not automatically continuous, it should be turned on at once.

The rill at Hestercombe in Somerset.

The gardens of the Italian Renaissance show some of the finest examples of the use of water in connection with garden architecture; but it rarely happens in our islands that there is an opportunity of using such vast masses of water; for there are in Italy examples where whole rivers were turned into the garden to form rushing cataracts, water stairs, water theatres, and endless arrangements of fountain, rill, and pool – lasting monuments to the inventions of the designer and the resource and skill of the hydrostatic engineer.

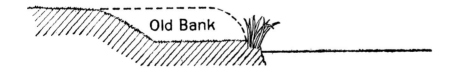

Reshaping a bank to provide a path close to the edge.

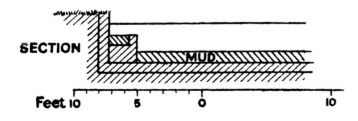

A section from a stepped pool.

SOME ELEMENTS OF DESIGN

HISTORICAL NOTES ON GARDEN ORNAMENT 1

Among all the older of the important gardens that are so numerous throughout the British Islands, there is but little that remains to us in the way of garden ornament that is of an earlier date than the first three decades of the sixteenth century. It may well be supposed that there were ornamental gardens attached to the villas built in Britain by her Roman conquerors, for the great gardens of Rome and its environment, profusely ornamented with sculpture and architectural detail, with many beautiful ways of using water, and ordered alleys of clipped evergreens, were still maintained in their original splendour. But this we can only conjecture, for there remains no existing proof or written record. We hear of a pleasure garden made in the thirteenth century by King Henry III at Woodstock, but it is an isolated fact in the history of horticulture. Manuscripts of the fifteenth century show small walled gardens with arbours, fountains and turfed seats, with trellises and covered alleys, where suitable shrubs and trees were trained over a wooden framework. It must be remembered that before the time of King Henry VIII, the great houses were still places of defence, closely encompassed by moat or wall, and that the spaces within were small, and, therefore, necessarily given to herbs and plants for use in the kitchen and pharmacy. Gardens for pleasure and beauty were thus almost unknown. But when the country became more settled, and a private house was no longer a fortress, and the windows of the main room: that formerly might only look into an enclosed court, could now be large and wide and could look abroad without fear into the open country – with this wholesome and comfortable expansion of the house came also the widening of the hitherto cramped garden spaces.

Gardens for pleasure might now be made, and every house had its roomy bowling green. Then, with increasing enjoyment of garden delights came the desire for garden ornaments. Sundials had long been in use, but now they were to be for ornament as well as utility, placed as centres and at other salient point of garden schemes. No fewer than sixteen dials were made for the King's new garden at Hampton Court. But garden expansion and the worthiest forms of ornament did not come at once for we read of much that was meretricious, such as an abundance of painted woodwork and painted wooden figures of heraldic animals; and, still worse, gilt birdcages and objects of coloured glass. Still, it is a matter for regret that no one example of this manner of gardening should remain to us, such as this garden of Hampton Court as laid out by King Henry VIII after the fall of Cardinal Wolsey, or the King's next enterprise of the same nature, the creation of the palace and garden of Nonesuch. One of the ornamental features of these Tudor gardens was the 'knotted' garden, a compact space laid out in a symmetrical design, whose character was not unlike that of the elaborate braided and corded work on the full-dress clothing of the day. That curious and perplexing toy, the maze, was also usual, both this and the 'knotted' garden being outlined with edgings of tufted herbs or plants of subshrubby growth, such as thyme, dwarf box, hyssop, lavender, rosemary and lavender cotton, though frequently the maze was of clipped trees six to seven feet high, in which case its walls were usually of yew or hornbeam. But in what remains to us in existence or record of these Tudor gardens there is still a slight feeling of cramped space – there is not yet perfect freedom. That was to follow later, as the outcome of influences from Southern Europe. Hitherto no distinct style of architecture had been known in England other than the Gothic, some of whose structural ornamental developments were carried further in our country than in any other of northern Europe.

But that extraordinary revival of learning and new life in the fine arts that we know as the Italian Renaissance, whose dawning was in the end of the thirteenth century, and whose noontide was towards the close of the fifteenth century, was destined to extend its influences to the gardens of England. Meanwhile, one of its conspicuous effects in Italy was the building of stately villas, the term 'villa' comprehending both house and garden. The garden was equally the work of the architect; indeed, in many, if not most, cases the garden was more lavishly treated with architectural enrichment than the house itself. Many of these gardens have perished, some, indeed, quite recently, but enough remain to impress us with a just idea of the sense of dignity and harmony with which the minds of their designers were saturated. No doubt they had the advantage of a simplicity of apprehension and aim which to modern designers is a thing of the past. For they had the ancient classical models and tradition alone, while we of modern days have our minds encumbered and distracted, and our sense of fitness perplexed, by a vast number of influences bearing upon questions of ornament. For to us the word ornament means decoration, not of one, but of many styles; not classical only, but of Gothic, Egyptian, Assyrian, Indian, Arab and Moorish, and numberless base hybrids of these well-defined styles. We have to allow that the marvellous discoveries and inventions of the nineteenth century and the diffusion of education have had some evil effects among their many good ones. Easy production by casting and stamping of metal by machinery, facility of communication combined with superficial smatterings of many branches of knowledge, trade competition (that greatest of all enemies to artistic production), that during the last century have flooded the world with masses of cheap rubbish, falsely called ornamental because covered with some kind of pattern – all these influences tend to debase and confuse public taste. The honest student of pure decoration, faced at every step with some one or other ignoble, if not actually vile, design in building, in furniture, in every kind of public erection and domestic appointment, has, with infinite labour and difficulty, to free his mind from all this mass of clogging impediment and to begin quite afresh; moreover, he must acquire a considerable measure of critical discernment before he can find his way through the maze of so-called ornament, false, intrusive and meretricious, that surrounds him on every side. It is sad to think of this and to know that it is an apparently unavoidable side issue of our progress – all this ill-directed effort, all this toilsome production of bad and debasing inutility.

The artists of the Renaissance had no such stumbling blocks. They had, it is true, some knowledge of Gothic architecture; but it was never rooted in Italy as was the Classical; and when the great upheaval came, when the men of wealth and influence searched for and endowed and upheld those who were already possessed of learning, industry and genius, it was to the Classical literature of Greece and Rome, to their architecture, sculpture and decoration, that the energy of these giants of the Middle Ages was directed. Then were created those wonderful gardens whose general designs have remained to us as superb models, the precious quality of whose decorative detail as garden ornament has never been surpassed or even approached. Their influence was to reach our English gardens in late Tudor days, though in the earlier Tudor gardens there were already some features that recalled some of those of the pleasure grounds of antiquity. For the maze was the direct descendant of the older labyrinth, and flower gardens were very small and closely surrounded by clipped hedges of evergreens. The 'covert alleys', too, had their ancient counterpart and the aviaries of singing birds.

English architects travelled and studied in Italy and returned with minds widened and stored with methods of taking advantage of the new freedom. Then it was that some of the greatest houses of the English Renaissance arose – Hardwick, Wollaton, Longleat – and with them the wide garden spaces and an adaptation of the methods of the gardens of Italy. But there can be little doubt that the true Italian garden cannot be rightly transplanted into our climate. It always remains exotic, and yet it so happens that in the only portions of our islands where some illusion of Italian conditions might be gained, namely, in the Isle of Wight and the southern coasts of Devon and Cornwall, it has scarcely been attempted. Those who are acquainted with the gardens of Italy at first hand cannot help feeling this comparative unsuitability. We have not the sky, or we have it only on but few days in the year; we have not the temperature; above all, we have not the endless abundance of rushing water.

The villas of antiquity and of the Italian Renaissance were almost invariably on hilly ground, needing steep terracing in some place where there was an ample water supply. There are cases where there are whole rivers of water rushing down long flights of steps, plunging at intervals into pools or basins and then flowing on in endless variety of invention for garden beneficence or garden delight. Cisterns on high ground were so arranged as to give ample pressure for fountain jets. The wealth of invention, in fountains alone, if described from known examples would fill a book. Fountains in the open formed centres of garden schemes in relation to the parterre, and were commonly known by the name of the deity whose sculptured figure formed the central ornament. On rising ground a frequent form was the wall fountain, sometimes expanded into the still more important 'theatre'. Here, in a space more or less semicircular, would be a colossal group of Tritons, or a Neptune with attendants of human shape, or water monsters, and boldly rusticated architectural forms cunningly intergrouped with masses of the living rock. Over or through the rock, only partly tamed by the guiding of the design, the water would come thundering into the great pool or basin, the sound reverberating from the wing walls and gaining both in volume and mystery. Then in another part of the garden where steps descended from the higher ground, little runnels were often built in order that the wayfarer might be accompanied on either side by the sweet tinkling and musical gurgle of the running rills. Near a seat there was always, as in the more ancient days, a fountain for the enjoyment of the pleasant, refreshing sound of falling water. In comparing the ornamental possibilities of our English gardens with those of Italy, this lack of water is a conspicuous deficiency, and it is the more to be regretted in these days when the reposeful and soothing qualities of pleasure grounds are more than ever important. For to a tired brain there is nothing more healing or refreshing than the sound of falling or moving water. It is difficult to describe the mental effect; but all who have noticed it and felt its salutary kindness will probably agree with the present writer that, even with closed eyes, it occupies the mind without strain in a way that no visible beauty can do. Other obvious delights of a garden are comparatively enlivening and awakening, but in days of summer heat the sound of water is lulling, tending to internal dreaming and refreshing brainsleep. It may be that the contemplation of flower border and parterre leads the mind to the thought of their production and maintenance and mutability, but the sound of water is final and eternal. Be this how it may, that garden is a happy one where running water may be freely used. But even when we have water we are apt to misuse it – we are strangely careless. Nothing is more frequent than to see some garden pool or fountain basin with a little water in the bottom only, and nothing looks worse or more neglectful. The proper water-level should be maintained and never relaxed; moreover, it should be near the level of the inner edge of the kerb or parapet – the nearer the better. If there is not a sufficient supply to feed the basin, the thing is a sham and a fraud, and ought not to be there. Gardens can quite well be designed without fountains or pools, but a water space which is half empty shames and debases the garden. Often in the gardens of Italy the whole basin is raised and the water level is raised with it. A fine example of such treatment is the Fountain of Neptune in the gardens of the Palazzo Doria at Genoa. The whole design is large and bold. The raised basin has an outline of eight segments of circles, four large and four smaller, with projecting bracketed plinths bearing figures of eagles. There is an inner basin whose lines are reversed. Each panel is a great hollow shell, and each pier, bearing sculptures suggesting the forms of swan and dolphin, is surmounted by an infant Triton. In the centre is the huge figure of Neptune, in his car drawn by sea horses. This is an example of the greater fountains; more frequently they were of one basin with a central figure or group, the kerb of some well-designed plan often treated with dwarf plinths and statues. Balustraded basins of considerable size were of fine effect, especially in connection with the thick groves of ilex and cypress that so usually encompassed the pleasure ground. Of these there are good examples in the gardens at Frascati.

But when such a basin is transplanted into an English garden with an open environment it only shows how bald and dull such treatment may be in itself. An example of this is at that fine place, Montacute in Somerset. There is an important fountain at Hewell Grange, a copy of the one in the marketplace of Perugia. It has a good deal of panelled decoration, and is set in a basin of fair size. But the surroundings are quite inadequate, especially the very plain and wearisomely monotonous rounded kerb. Such examples show the dangers that beset the imitation and importation of isolated objects. It is bad enough in England, but far worse in the northern states of America, where the pleasure grounds seem still less fitted for the reception of Italian garden ornaments. If in England they often look out of place, in the States they have the appearance of unhappy exiles. It is true that there is a certain measure of success in the case of some of the Italian gardens in England, but this success may be nearly always traced to the strong individuality of some highly cultured owner whose mind had become saturated with the spirit of the older work, and who was, therefore, able to reproduce it. Some notable examples (among others) that come to mind are the gardens made in recent years by Mr John Morant at Brockenhurst in the New Forest, the parterre and other portions at Castle Ashby in Northamptonshire, and those of Balcarres and Balcaskie, both in Fifeshire. But even in these one misses the delightful *abandon* of the design, the way the Renaissance artist let himself go, bursting with the wealth of his fancy and the over-mastering force of his conviction.

The Italian garden designers of the fifteenth century, imbued with the spirit of the ancient work and with their own traditions of nearly two centuries, showed an astonishing boldness of conception and fertility of invention. The whole thing was done with a kind of passion, of spontaneous exuberance. It came straight out of the artist's mind and is instinctive with his vitality of imagination, his sense of beauty and fitness insisting on adequate and unrestrained expression. We, on the contrary, import a Venetian *pozzo* and put it as a centre ornament *on gravel* in the middle of a hybrid parterre in an open garden, where the poor exile cries aloud for its old environment of wall-encompassed courtyard and flagged pavement; or, if we are more ambitious, we bring over a pair of highly decorated marble vases and erect them on plain plinths with a very slight and thin moulding at the base, as an ornament to the top of a short flight of unmoulded garden steps!

Such are the usual results of our attempts to introduce the Italian character into our gardens, although there is now and then a glimpse of the true Italian feeling, as in the well-designed box-planted parterre at Balcarres, and the view up the south walk at Chatsworth. In the latter case, and one or two others, the pleasant southern effect is gained by the straight outline of the masses of trees, recalling the *bosco,* the woodland frame that commonly surrounds the picture in the gardens of Italy.

HISTORICAL NOTES ON GARDEN ORNAMENT II

My last article closed with a reference to the difficulties to be met in the introduction of an Italian character into English gardens, especially by way of the fountain. Another of the many uses of water in the Italian gardens was in the grotto, to which the hillside building readily lent itself. Sometimes these grottoes were actual caverns in the mountain, sometimes hollow places under terraces – entirely artificial. In some cases they were not accessible, the floor spaces being pools, with hidden mysteries of falling water, faintly visible – distinctly to be heard. Or they were cavernous cool retreats for hottest summer, with sprays of water rising from the floors and spouting from the sides, and strange hydrostatic toys – water organs. The pool and tunnel grotto at Albury in Surrey, part of the garden design of John Evelyn, were adapted from his recollection of the grottoes of Italian gardens. He probably set the fashion for grottoes in English pleasure grounds, for many still remain. They had their predecessors in ancient days, when in places near the sea they were sometimes lined with sea shells worked in patterns, or mosaics, or designs of curious stones. In the grottoes of the Renaissance gardens we see audacious mixtures of natural and artificial rock, and roofs adorned with bold masses of stalactite, so cleverly combined with architectural form and so completely harmonized by the water mosses and other growths that there is no sense of incongruity; only one of admiration for the boldness of the artist's invention and the skill with which he has brought order out of chaos.

Stairways are always beautiful in garden design; nothing gives a more distinct impression of nobility than a perspective of a succession of always ascending flights of steps rising into higher ground. Especially is this so where the individual steps are long and shallow, with a moulded edge that gives a shadow below, and when they are bounded by a balustrade of refined design. Then the balustrade runs out to right and left, crowning the retaining wall of the terrace, and leaving the best of places below for well-arranged groupings of plants in the flower border, itself one of the best of garden ornaments. There is something peculiarly satisfying in stairways descending to water. There is a fine example at Stoneleigh Abbey in Warwickshire, where there are important water stairs and a stone embankment with balustraded parapet. Such stairs were also worthily designed in the Italian villas that adjoined water, as in those of the Italian lakes.

Flagged terraces with porches were beautifully treated in the time of the English Renaissance; of these there are good examples at Bramshill in Hampshire and Fountains Hall in Yorkshire. Careful planting will always enhance the value of beautiful architecture, but it must, indeed, be careful, and in some cases studiously restrained. Nothing is more frequent than to see good architectural detail smothered and obscured by masses of climbing plants. Here and there a cluster rose may be allowed to fling its long branches over the sculptured balustrade, or a clematis, jasmine or honeysuckle may lightly drape it; but to keep them within due bounds they need the most careful watching, guiding and regulating. It is the work of the artist-gardener.

Only too often handsome gate piers may be seen choked with ivy, and walls of ornamental brickwork, with important copings, completely obliterated. But there is many a garden on sloping ground where delicate architectural forms would be out of place, but where the steps are needed and also the retaining wall. Here is the opportunity for making the stonework grow its own ornament by laying the walling dry, that is to say, without mortar, but with

earth joints, to be planted with all the good things that are suitable.

The parterre of the Italian garden took a firm hold in England, and showed a distinct development on diverging lines. It grew into a design of bright flower masses rather than one of firmly drawn outline. In the Italian parterre the pattern was in strong lines of box bordering, from two to three feet high and wide. Frequently the whole design was planted in box. The garden at Balcarres shows one of the best examples in our islands of a box-planted parterre; there are others in English gardens, but perhaps none that is so good in design or so entirely Italian in feeling. In the gardens of antiquity we learn that the parterre was also solidly edged. Here it was always small. For one thing, they had but few kinds of flowers – rose, iris, jasmine, poppy, violet, narcissus and not many others. The gardens of Italy were nearly always encompassed by masses of trees – ilex and cypress for the most part. It is interesting to observe that with us also those gardens are the most beautiful and restfully satisfying that have bounding encirclements of large tree form, the trees distant enough to allow plenty of air and sunlight, and for the flowers to be safe from the most far-travelling roots, but so closely associated with the garden scheme that they frame it distinctly, and do not allow the eye to travel into distant landscape.

Parterre and wide, far-away view are too much material for one picture. The mind is distracted between the two. But the tree-girt parterre is one complete picture; and before or after it the distant landscape, also suitably framed by trees, acquires its own value and becomes far more enjoyable. One of the weaker points of the development of the parterre when the beds were set in gravel was that the gravel spaces became much too large, quite out of proportion with the design. This is a frequent fault in our gardens. It is not only unsightly in itself, but a waste of one of the best features of our pleasure grounds, namely, their delightful expanse of that fine turf that comes to greater perfection here than in any other country.

Except in the case of bounding or sheltering walls of greenery, chiefly of box and ilex, which were kept closely trimmed, there was very little of topiary work in the gardens of the Italian

Renaissance. In ancient time much more was done, and the topiarius was a chief among the slaves. But the clipping of evergreens, either into neat walls or some symmetrical or ornamental pattern, has always been a distinct feature in English gardens, perhaps because our native yew is of all evergreens the most docile to such treatment. There are great hedges of clipped yew in old English gardens that are not only delightful objects in themselves, but most beneficent for shelter. They are also the best of backgrounds to masses of flowers, and delightful companions to great stretches of velvet-like turf. At Cleeve Prior in Worcestershire there is a remarkable double hedge of continuous arches of clipped yews. It ranges along on each side of the flagged entrance path, each opening giving pleasant garden views. At

Fountains Hall, designed by Robert Smythson in 1611, is a study in simplicity: grass, paving and yew hedges.

Golden yews and lavender in the Dutch garden at Orchards.

Topiary at Levens Hall.

Topiary in yew and golden yew at Levens.

Elvaston are some extraordinary specimens of topiary work in yew. One example, called the Moor's Arch, has a symmetrical figure carried on two green-clothed stems. From the shoulders of the green roofing mass rises a well-designed crown, and between the arches of the crown are rounded lugs, reminding one of those on the monolithic roof of the Mausoleum of Theodoric at Ravenna. This garden is rich in cut yews; many are shaped into crowned cones, others into peacocks and architectural forms. Some of the most curiously shaped yews are at Levens in Westmorland, a garden full of charm, where the best of hardy flowers are seen most happily against a background of yew, clipped into strange and fantastic shapes. The form of the garden and its topiary work cannot have been that of the designer. It is a charming *scherzo* that has run riot through the centuries in its own sweet way. This curious place must be regarded as an exception, for there is no real excuse for topiary work except in the case of definite design, when living vegetation is treated as walling and when trees are cut into points of distinctly architectural effect. But where such design is absent, and where trees stand isolated, serving no purpose of wall, arch, arbour or perspective, they should not be trimmed into bosses or fantastic forms. All that should be done is to watch their growth and so restrain or regulate it as to keep it in harmony with what is near.

Of sculptured ornament set up in gardens, the shaft of the sundial belongs most typically to the pleasure grounds of the British Isles, and it is among those of pillar or baluster form that we find the most satisfactory examples as garden ornaments. The eighteenth century gave us some admirable ornaments in lead, a material better suited for our garden sculpture than stone or marble. There is a well-known figure – for it occurs in several gardens – of a kneeling black slave supporting a table bearing a sundial. These figures belong to a phase of ornament of a certain date, originally Italian, and for the most part Venetian, for in Venice the blackamoor as a subject for decoration was overdone. The gardens of Melbourne in Derbyshire are rich in lead sculpture of a fine type; Powis Castle, too, has some good examples of the French classical-pastoral type. There are also remarkably fine leaden vases. A large one is at Melbourne; others at Hampton Court and elsewhere. Sculptures in stone and marble are in many of our larger gardens – much of it brought from Italy. In the Renaissance gardens, the architectural niches in which many of the figures stood were often in England replaced by niches cut in yew hedges. This has an excellent effect, but has the drawback that the niche, from inaccurate clipping, often gets out of shape and proportion.

The orangeries for the winter housing of tender plants in tubs were usually of good design and took their place among the ornamental features of the eighteenth-century gardens. The tubs themselves, of round or square pattern, were probably painted of the pleasant, rather light green that has become traditional in France. They are often disfigured in our gardens by being painted a crude raw green colour and the hoops coloured black, a quite needless ugliness. A quiet green of rather neutral tone all over is the best in England, care being taken to keep the green lower in tone than any foliage near it.

Stone seats of good design are not often seen in English gardens, but there are good examples at Danby and Hackwood. The garden temple or pavilion is only suitable in large plan of classical design. A fine one occurs in the Palladian Bridge at Prior Park, near Bath.

There is grave risk in the overdoing of decorative accessories. Many a garden of formal design is spoilt by a multiplicity and variety of ornament, for there is danger in the employment of treatment that embraces the use of geometrical form and yet lacks unity and cohesion. And there are other gardens of this class in our country whose effect is chilling and unsympathetic. The design may be good, the details correct, and yet the thing that is most important wanting. You have the body without the soul.

SOME GARDEN ORNAMENTS AND ACCESSORIES

For the best example of outdoor ornament we must look to the old gardens of Italy. They may well have been prototypes of all later decoration of the kind, for they were designed and carried out by the greatest living architects and sculptors of the time. Only a few of these gardens remain intact: many have passed into the hands of impoverished owners who have been glad to sell anything that could be removed, while some have gone into complete neglect and ruin, and others have been entirely destroyed. Stray items – urns, vases, carved seats and fountains – have come into the hands of dealers and have been widely dispersed.

Vases, tazzas and urns originally stood as accentuating ornaments on the piers at the tops and bases of flights of steps, and on those that occurred at intervals in ranges of stone or marble balustrades. These vases were for the most part also of stone or marble, but some were of terracotta with a good deal of ancient classical feeling in the ornament. Sometimes the design is something of a compromise between that of sculpture and the terracotta tradition, for the form and detail of ornament belong to the terracotta, but the handles are unusual in this medium. It is impossible to say whence this vase, and many such examples that one meets with here and there in gardens, may have strayed from; the only thing evident is that it looks lost and out of place without anything definite to stand on, though this is less of a necessity than if the form and ornament had been more of the vase or tazza character. Tulips are but a weak kind of filling: the important aspect of garden vases demands something stouter or more woody. Two-year-old pelargoniums or well-furnished fuchsias are among the best plants for vases, the pelargoniums especially, for they thoroughly enjoy the sun warmth that penetrates the whole body of vase and earth.

Sundials and other solid ornaments are often misplaced. In the old gardens for which they were designed they were always given a definite position, either in the centre or at the end of some distinct garden scheme, and they stood on some kind of base, generally of one or two wide steps. A large vase or urn on an imposing plinth would be placed at the end of a vista, sometimes, and always with good effect, in a mass of dark greenery. In modern gardens it is not unusual to find these ornaments placed in or about a lawn for no apparent reason and, worst of all, without any base and therefore looking, as they needs must, as if they had lost their way and felt forlorn. It is almost better to have no ornament than to have a good ornament badly placed. Another common defect is when one sees a number of vases, or whatever it may be, of different kinds and sizes scattered about a garden. These objects belong to formal design and well-considered proportion, right and perfect in their

LEFT Putti at Melbourne Hall, Derbyshire.
CENTRE Early eighteenth-century urn at Melbourne Hall.
RIGHT Adam period vase at Kedelston Hall, Derbyshire.

LEFT An eighteenth-century birdcage at Melbourne Hall.
RIGHT An eighteenth-century urn at Polesden Lacy in Surrey.

LEFT Barley-twist column sundial at York Gate. A modern copy of an eighteenth or nineteenth-century original.
RIGHT An astrolabe in the herb garden at York Gate.

CLOCKWISE FROM TOP LEFT Metal seat at Naumkeag, Stockbridge, USA; an eighteenth-century wooden seat at St Nicholas, Richmond, North Yorkshire; bee-hive seat at York Gate; a modern wooden bench seat at Kiftsgate Court, Gloucestershire; a garden bench designed by Sir Edwin Lutyens at Sissinghurst Castle, Kent.

original places, but not at all easy to use properly in a different environment. Such a mixture gives the same uneasy impression as is received on entering a room furnished with Louis Quatorze escritoire, an old English farmhouse linen hutch, an eighteenth-century card table and chairs of any period from Cromwell to Queen Victoria. Each piece may be genuine and good of its kind, but there can only be a sense of painfully clashing incongruity when they are brought together.

The same general considerations are applicable to garden seats. A great house of palatial character will probably have architectural features in any part of the garden that is near the main building. Here there will be wrought stone seats with sculptured detail as to supports and bench ends. A balustraded terrace in an upper level may have projecting bastions; places between these will be found for specially designed stone seats, and others will come at the ends of terraces and at other distinct points, as on the landings of wide stairways. An eighteenth-century manor or dower house will be well suited with a wooden seat of slightly more complex pattern than the norm, or with one of the seats of French design of the same period that are still made and can be imported. For ordinary houses there are garden seats of good simple design made of hardwoods from old wooden ships. When a painted seat is used it is best to avoid the very harsh white that is so commonly employed, for it often happens that the glaring white of the seat attracts undue attention. It is easy to modify the colour so that it tells as white, if white is desired, and yet is not obtrusive. Plain oak weathers to a beautiful colour, a kind of silvery grey, if untouched. The maker will probably want to oil or varnish it, but this should be firmly resisted. It is delightful to have seats at many points in any region of home woodland that are near the garden. Here they should be of the very simplest form, merely planks nailed to four stout stumps that can be let into the ground. If a back rest is required, the back rest should be chosen from a branching tree, the branch that is to support the back rail only slightly diverging from the line of the trunk if it is to give suitable support, for nothing is less comfortable than a hard wooden seat that throws the sitter too far back. Seats are often fixed in summerhouses, but seldom with the care for detail as to height and width and slope of back that makes for simple comfort. If one may judge by the evidence of illuminated manuscripts of the Middle Ages, it would appear that our far-back ancestors were content to sit on grass banks, for so they are represented in the curious 'Romance of the Rose', which contains some of the earliest-known illustrations of pleasure gardens.

Where a garden has the advantage of water in small or moderate volume there is no better way of employing it than in the narrow rill with little tanks at intervals. The width is of more than fifteen to eighteen inches, so that it is easily stepped over. The sides of the rill, which passes through any space of lawn, are built in stone or brick with a flagstone top level with the grass. The water is shallow for the accommodation of such plants as the beautiful natives, the water plantain (*Alisma*) and the flowering rush (*Butomus*), which grow by river banks in water a few inches deep. This kind of built and planted rill was first designed by Sir Edwin Lutyens for the garden at Sonning. The tanks are built deeper than the rill to admit of the planting of water lilies. The steps that lead to the higher level have a very slight rise of about four and a half inches, and are wide in the tread. Steps of such proportions are not only pleasant to walk, or even run up and down, but are also agreeable to the eye and mind, suggesting ease and slight effort. Where there are steeper slopes there may still be easy steps, for where it is not too steep for them to go conveniently up and down a landing can be built straight forward and the steps be taken down to right or left or both, with a second landing and another square turn of the steps. In the case of some tanks that might be dangerous to children, a space about two feet wide can be built up inside. The space is filled with earth to the level of the inner wall for aquatic plants. Another way which is always beautiful is to build the whole tank in wide underwater steps, the successive depths showing in an interesting way by the deepening colour of the water.

IRON GARDEN GATES

When garden walls are going up and ways of entrance are being considered, the possibility of a beautiful feature is often overlooked – this is an iron gate of good, simple design. Such a chance is lost when, as is so often seen, a garden is shut in with heavy wooden doors. There may be cases when the wooden door is a necessity, as where a cold draught of wind may be injurious or where there is something unsightly that it is desirable to hide. Though in these notes it is only some simpler form of gate that is being considered, it is well to remember, and to see when occasion allows, any of the fine old gates that exist at entrance grounds or gardens of our great houses, or such as are accessible to everybody at Hampton Court.

Iron gates were in England in the reigns of Elizabeth and James I, but the art of making them flourished from the end of the seventeenth century for about a hundred years. That wonderful designer and practical smith Jean Tijou was at work in England in the reign of William and Mary; he was followed closely by Bakewell of Derby, and by clever smiths from Wales and the West Country, and a number domiciled in and about London. Some Italian gates were imported early in the eighteenth century. Their general design was quite different from that of the English smiths, for it was more free in line and was composed of much scrollwork, with a further enrichment of acanthus foliage and flower forms. There are examples of such work by the clever Welsh smiths the brothers Roberts, who wrought in the earlier decades of the eighteenth century; but they never acquired, or possibly never attempted the almost riotous freedom and sumptuous enrichment of the true Italian work.

The usual gate had a general filling of vertical bars; the filling thickened at the bottom with additional rods known as dog bars. These served a double purpose: the practical one of keeping out dogs, and the other, of pleasing the eye by giving extra weight and solidity to the base of the gate. Then, at convenient hand height, came the lock rail, often with some filling of ornament, and also satisfying the eye with a distinct horizontal treatment at about one-third of the height; the remainder upward being of plain bars. In the more important gates there was a finely designed and wrought overthrow, with scrollwork, and the initials or some heraldic emblems of the owner. But in the simpler gates this was omitted altogether.

CLOCKWISE FROM TOP LEFT Wrought-iron gates into the kitchen
garden at Orchards, Surrey, designed by Sir Edwin Lutyens; another gate
at Orchards by Luytens; a gate composed of circles at York Gate,
West Yorkshire; fine wrought-iron gates from the eighteenth century at
Fountains Abbey, North Yorkshire; a wooden gate in Thomas Church's
garden, San Francisco, California, USA; simple iron gates at
Hidcote Manor, Gloucestershire.

CLOCKWISE FROM TOP LEFT
Small pavilion, of seventeenth-century design, at Montacute House in Somerset; small classical summerhouse of modern construction at Barnsley House, Gloucestershire; an open loggia at Tintinhull Manor, Somerset; another version of an open loggia in more rustic form at York Gate, West Yorkshire; one of a pair of chinoiserie pavilions at Hidcote Manor, Gloucestershire; summerhouse at Kedleston Hall, Derbyshire. designed by Adam.

Where there are iron gates there should be brick or stone piers, if not of importance, at least of some size and solidity. In the finest examples they were of elaborate architecture with sunk panels or niches, and sometimes with a complete entablature. These would be surmounted by stone or leaden urns or heraldic beasts. In the case of lesser types of gate the piers were commonly finished with stone balls.

There are many places where really fine piers have become completely smothered with ivy or ampelopsis. If the gates and their piers have merit, such overgrowth should never be allowed. This may be generally known now, but it is well to repeat the warning, because these rampant things grow quickly and, though they may have been cleared a few years ago, they may again be threatening to obscure good building. There is no reason to forbid any reasonable planting that may partly come over the piers, but it should be carefully watched and either guided or checked, as may be desirable.

Iron gates have to be painted. In our climate the most generally satisfactory colour is a dark grey inclining to a bluish tone. There is no harm in what is sold ready mixed as 'dark slate', but it is the better for a fair admixture of dark blue. The French commonly paint their garden ironwork with red lead; it is good for the iron, but not pleasing to the eye. The pretty pale green with which they paint garden tubs and seats is also unsuitable for iron, for which, at least in England, the dark blue-grey is much to be preferred.

THE GARDEN SUMMERHOUSE

A pleasantly placed and planned summerhouse is so great a gain in a garden that it is well worth considering how it may best be made useful, besides serving as an attractive feature in the garden landscape. The planning of the grounds will govern its position, but it is generally understood that it is a place of temporary rest from which there is a good outlook on flowers and pleasure ground or on some beautiful distant view. It may be anything in quality or degree from the banqueting house of our Tudor and Jacobean ancestors to the simplest structure of slab and thatch; but nothing is more desirable in any garden than a really comfortable summerhouse, such a place as may be used as a quiet retreat for reading or writing in the summer months. There may often be seen some little building, say of ten feet square, that might well serve such a purpose, but that is quite useless because it is not properly lighted. If the light comes only from the entrance opening, it is never comfortable, but a window at the back or side makes all the difference. It is all the better if the little house can be entirely closed and have a fireplace, for then it becomes available as a teahouse – pleasant for grown people and a delight to children. Whether opened or closed, if the walls cannot be all of brick, there should be a brick base that comes three courses out of the ground; a wooden framework is then built, to be covered outside with elm weather-boarding. The roof may be also of weather-boarding or of thatch or tile. Thatch is warm in winter and cool in summer, but is apt to be much pulled about by sparrows, and is difficult to repair, though it has a good appearance. Tile is best – permanent and well-looking. The inside should also be boarded, the boarding continued on the underside of the rafters. This is also best of elm, and if properly done makes the whole snug and completely weather and draughtproof. 'Slab' is the word used in timber yards for the outside of the tree trunk first sawn off; slabs also make a good side walling for a summerhouse; their edges are first trimmed straight and they are then nailed on upright to the framework; oak are the best, and if set on the brick base will last for many years, though they are rather less durable than weather-boarding. The floor should be of flagstones, paving brick or tile, or cement. If there is a fixed seat its proportions should be carefully considered; but the following measurements may be advised: the seat itself seventeen inches from front to back and fifteen inches from floor to its upper side. The back of such seats is usually made to slope too much, so that it does not rightly support the spine; if it slopes back one inch in six it will be enough.

There are many examples throughout the country of well-built summerhouses, both open and enclosed, dating from the time of Elizabeth to the early years of the nineteenth century. In the case of palatial places some of them were purely for decoration, such as the pillared pavilions or domed temples of Palladian architecture, the purpose of which was solely to secure a dignified full stop to a garden vista. But in both earlier and later, as well as contemporary, examples there were delightful little houses of one room, of stone or brick, as carefully planned and built as the main house, and closely related to it in character and decoration. In some of the larger places they stand as a finish to the end of a raised terrace, giving a commanding view of the parterre below, or they were reared at the four angles of a great wall that enclosed the flower and vegetable garden. These are commonly of two storeys, the ground floor serving as fruit room or root store or some such purpose, and entered from the garden level, while above is a beautifully finished room with access from a raised terrace or 'mount' and perhaps directly overlooking the moat.

There are but few good examples of garden houses from the earlier part of the nineteenth century till lately, but, with the revival of interest in gardening and a more intelligent comprehension of all that it embraces, the need of a better class of summerhouse or gardenhouse has been felt, and the architect is now called upon to design them, more especially as so many people now take a wholesome pleasure in having their meals served in the open air.

SOME PRACTICAL IDEAS AND SOLUTIONS

SOME HORTICULTURAL INDISCRETIONS

When one sees some native plant showing conspicuous beauty or some kind of charm, it is natural that one should wish to bring it into the garden. It may be either of unusual size or colouring, or something that, though quite well known, is not common in one's district, or a plant that has not been seen for a long time and that brings back happy memories of early days. It may be any one of these influences that creates the temptation. But if one who has suffered by giving way may save others from regretting rash action, these notes may not be without use.

The common wood sorrel (*Oxalis acetosella*) is certainly one of the loveliest of lowly plants and is all the more attractive because it grows in delightful wild places, and especially in sylvan mysteries of natural woodland. But I have never ceased regretting its introduction to the garden, for not only does it increase rapidly, but it has a way of worming itself into the crowns of plants and ferns so that it is impossible to dislodge it without breaking up the plant and washing it out. Precious, narrow horizontal ledges, sacred to small alpine campanulas, attract it irresistibly and there is no way of saving the lawful occupant except by moving the stones and washing it free from the intruder and providing new soil for fear of seeds being left.

Another pretty thing that has become a persistent weed is the field scabious (*Knautia arvensis*). During a summer ramble in some pleasant wild ground some plants were found that for colour and size of bloom stood out distinctly from their hundreds of fellows. They were marked and dug up later and put in the garden border, where they throve amazingly. After the first season, as they had been placed too near the front, they were dug up and put further back. But it became evident that every bit of root tip that had been left in the original place had formed a fresh crown, for the next summer the patch was stronger than before, and all further attempts to clear it out completely failed. Moreover it has strayed into other parts of the garden, where the same trouble goes on. Enchanter's nightshade (*Cireaea lutetiana*), though by no means a conspicuous plant, has a certain modest charm that is enhanced by the places where it grows – cool, shady near water – dimly lighted – mysterious. But when brought into the garden it positively ramps, with white roots running into other plants and greedily taking up much more space than it was offered. Tansy, which is so handsome in dense masses by the waterside, is much too 'rooty' to be safely admitted to the garden, but is admirable for wild, watery places.

By far the worst offender, however, is the great yellow loosestrife (*Lysimachia vulgaris*), a pest that, once established in light soil, has proved impossible to be rid of. It is not common in my district though frequent on many river banks. But it is associated with some happy days of half a century ago – summer days spent fishing with my father on the banks of a charming little sequestered river. The yellow loosestrife grew in good company, with water plantain and flowering rush and skull cap, and I greatly delighted in the clean-looking upright growths crowned by the heads of good yellow bloom. But I have never ceased to regret the day when, in recent years, I brought it into the garden. For, besides the place where it was originally planted, it has spread, by what means I cannot guess, as it is never allowed to seed, to a number of different positions. We try to fork it up, but small invisible pieces of root must remain, for it reappears again and again when one thought it must have been got rid of. It seems so hopeless that now we merely tug it up wherever it has grown high enough to present a good hold. Many people are baffled by goutweed, but goutweed has, at least, visible white roots, and I can undertake to clear it in any open ground, though not when it has got into the roots of shrubs that may not be disturbed.

THE PAINT POT IN THE GARDEN

The colour of garden paintwork does not by any means receive the consideration it deserves, and as the dry days of March are at hand, it may be well to think of the doors, gates and railings, the seats and the tubs, that will be thankful for a coat of paint, and to consider with

White-painted seat of eighteenth-century pattern at Kelmarsh Hall, Northamptonshire.

some care what colour the paint should be. In some places it seems to be an inflexible law that the paint must be dead white. It has to be admitted that white paint makes for a kind of clean, neat appearance, and in the case of movable garden seats that are bought ready made, it would seem reasonable that the maker, with a proper pride in his work, should wish them to show up as sharply as possible. But often the white-painted seat become disastrously prominent and asserts itself with a harsh discordance in the garden landscape. One may go into a garden where all is well designed and where there are borders of beautiful flowers, but where a gleaming white seat at the end catches the eye and painfully compels its attention to the exclusion of every other consideration. One turns a corner and again a white seat shrieks at the eye and commands its undivided notice. One goes away, and the recollection of the garden become a kind of nightmare of white seats. There are places where one may even see a pitiless white-painted bench placed against the dusky splendour of a yew hedge or glaring out of some other place of dark foliage, so that the cruel contrast robs the eye of all the value of the many tones of quiet green, just as the true colour of yew or any evergreen is absolutely lost when the snow lies on the ground at its foot. It is a kind of wanton or, at the best, unheeding desecration. Another matter that one notices about the use of white paint on gates is that the painter follows some kind of rule that constrains him to paint the hinges black. If white paint can be made more glaring and pertinacious, more crudely conspicuous, it is by the contrast with black.

All these mistaken uses of good paint come from the fact being either unknown or generally ignored that all effect of colour is relative. No paint should be of such a kind or tint that it either wars with what is near or unduly attracts to itself. If we take the case of plants in tubs, there is an unhappy convention that the tub must be a bright green and the hoops black; the greener the green the better the painter is pleased. He only thinks of the tub, not knowing that whatever its colour may be it should be quite secondary to that of the plant. It is a safe rule that no tint of green should go on the tub that is cruder or greener than that of the leaves, and there is no need to paint the hoops another colour; in fact, it is better, besides being a considerable saving of labour, to paint it all out of one pot.

If it is asked what colour other than white it is best to use for seats, a neutral grey may safely be advised; such a grey as may be matched from the bark of young stems from three to four inches in diameter of Spanish chestnut or from many kinds of tree bark. This at any rate would be safe. But anyone who is careful in the matter of colour would have some pieces of board painted in a series of such tints and see which would suit the actual place, according to its aspect and its own special conditions. The lovely silvery grey of oak unpainted, as in an oak park paling, or of old elm weather-boarding can hardly be matched in paint because its quality is a matter of surface texture as well as of actual colour, but something of the kind might be attempted. For simple board seats fixed on stumps in woodland a useful colour is that of a scale of Scots fir, a warm grey. But in all painting of seats the considerations that matter are that they should be visible enough but not unduly prominent, and that their colour should harmonize with what is near, but should never compete with it.

An illustration of the mischief of wrong colouring with foliage comes to mind and may be worth mentioning, though it does not concern paint. At some of the great flower shows green baize is provided for covering the stands; when new it is of a rather ruthless green, but with age it fades, and finally acquires an almost neutral tint that is not only harmless but is actually becoming to foliage. There was a winter show, and one exhibitor, who brought a few choice orchids, was allotted a bench covered in new baize. The exhibit did not take up the whole space, and a good deal of the baize showed between the pots. The leaves of orchids are hardly ever a bright green; for the most part they are low in tone and of a dull yellowish tint. The effect of the raw green baize was to exaggerate this weakness of colouring, and what should have been an exhibit of green refinement became a sad example of how bad it was possible to make it look.

The painting of the conservatory and other glasshouses should also have more careful consideration, for here also the white paint pot has generally reigned supreme, and the glass structures, usually unsightly rather than desirable to see, have been made as obtrusively prominent as possible; whereas if the paint was well toned down with umber and a little black they would be comparatively innocuous. Some firms have a habit of finishing their glass-houses and frames with a paint even worse than dead white – a ghostly blue-white – and they colour the inside ironwork a crude blue!

There is a certain sense in keeping the paint inside a greenhouse white, or nearly white, on account of saving all possible light, but even here a very slight warming with umber does not harm and is a great gain both in general good effect and in colour harmony with vegetation.

GARDENING AMONG STONES

The form that any kind of rock garden is to take will necessarily be suggested by the area and conditions of the space most conveniently available. As such gardening aims at being a more or less following of the planting of nature in wild places it is best to keep it right away from the house or any kind of building. If there should be woodland adjoining the garden, a space between the two will be all that can be desired.

The most usual faults of rock gardens are that they are too fussy and complicated, and that too many stones are used. The stones should be as the jeweller's setting of gems – so placed as to give the plant a firm and comfortable roothold, but not so as to be themselves obtrusive. The best, and at the same time the simplest, form that the rock garden can take is that of a little shallow valley, with one path, gently winding, but not needlessly wriggling, and with sloping banks on either side. It is tempting to make a raised rocky mound with the path on both sides, but the simpler form will be found to be not only the more convenient to make and keep in order, but to be the one that will be the best for the display of the plants. Simplicity of aim and some measure of restraint are good influences in this and all other kinds of gardening, and where these virtues are not practised the full enjoyment of the beauty of plants is in danger of being lost by the mind being distracted by too many objects of interest in view at the same time.

It is always best to place the stones with some feeling of stratification: that is to say, to let them show as if they were a natural outcrop. In doing this they will, naturally, come in consecutive ranges more or less parallel, an arrangement that favours the placing of a sufficient group of one kind of plant at a time. If the front base of the stone is to show, it should be a little underground, so fostering the illusion that it may be of considerable or unknown depth. If the ground is of a heavy nature the path had better be of rough flags, but it should be remembered that such paths are difficult to weed. If the soil is light, a sand path is always pleasant. Many natural sands bind well, and as the edges become mossy and self-sown seedlings of near plants invade them, they give no impression of undue formality. The intentional planting of the joints of pavements has of late been overdone. A paved path is for comfortable access and unrestricted progress, and if those who pass along it have to be looking at their feet in order not to trample on some floral treasure, the comfort of the place is lost, and attention is distracted from the more important plants to right and left.

A background of shrubs is always desirable; they should be of small stature next to the rock plants, with taller ones behind. Best of all are such low shrubs as *Rhododendron ferrugineum* (the alpenrose), then the larger of the heaths and the shorter of the leucothoe. Then at the back taller shrubs, preferably evergreen, in order to shut out all other aspects of the garden.

For smaller spaces the best way is not to attempt a whole rock garden on a reduced scale, but to have a few large stones well placed and a restricted number of the best rock plants. These will include the lovely *Lithodora diffusa* and iberis, both of them evergreen and therefore a good rock clothing at all times of the year. This is a matter worth thinking of, for the greater number of the best rock plants are early blooming, and the rock garden, even when showing but little flower, should retain some sort of comeliness. The alpine species of pinks, the useful hybrid rock pinks and cerastium have this merit of keeping good foliage; the useful thrift also (both white and pink), alyssum, arabis and several of the stonecrops and saxifrages. There will be spaces between these for a few of the best plants that either lose their foliage or look tired or overworn in the later year, among them the indispensable aubrieta, a plant that should be cut back close after flowering, and some of the dwarf phloxes – *P.* x *procumbens*, *P. bifida cedraria* and the best of the subulata group, such as the charming pink 'Vivid' and the white 'Nelsoni'.

There is yet another way of stone gardening that has many delightful features and is capable of beautiful treatment – namely, dry walling. In many a garden where there is a change of level there is a dull slope of grass, difficult to mow and of no beauty. If a line is taken along the middle of the slope and a dry wall built and planted, a good bit of gardening is the result. The wall is built with a slight inclination backwards, and the stones are laid tipping back so that every drop of rain that falls upon it runs into the joints. The conditions are highly favourable not only to rock plants but to many of larger size; in fact, in many cases these do better in the wall than in the carefully prepared flower border, the roots delighting in the contact with the cool underground stone surfaces. A dry wall can also be built of brick, though it is a little less convenient to form and to plant.

In building a dry wall workmen should have impressed upon them the necessity of ramming the earth well behind the stones. Those who are not used to dry walling will try to raise a wall against a scarp of hard sand or chalk. Such a wall is quite unsafe and is likely to come down when heavy rain gets in at the back. Nepeta and the red valerian (*Centranthus*) are specially happy in dry walling, but the conditions are admirably suited for nearly all rock or border plants.

A PLACE WHERE 'NOTHING WILL GROW'

There are often bare corners in gardens and shrubberies that are left bare because their condition is considered hopeless. Their owner will say, 'Oh, that is a place where nothing will grow!' Such a place, condemned in much such terms three years ago by many who saw it, thoughout the past winter has been the best clothed bit of the garden, with its healthy-looking clumps of *Helleborus argutifolius, H. foetidus* and *Iris foetidissima* and Irish ivy beginning to cover the paling at the back. The soil is the poorest possible – a dry sand, and under the shade of fir trees. A bank was thrown up to conceal a road, and the hellebores, then young seedlings sent by a friend by post, were planted in groups. On other parts of the same bank are varieties of minor periwinkle, Solomon's seal and common hardy ferns – all doing well.

PLANTS FOR EDGINGS

Though there is nothing that can compare with the dwarf box for neatness and durability, there are often in a garden places where something is desired that will serve as a pretty edging but that is less distinct and hard in appearance. The two most obvious alternatives are the old white pink, neat at all times and specially good in its winter dress, and in June a mass of its sweet bloom; and London pride, one of the easiest plants to grow. These two serve well in exactly opposite conditions, for the pink delights in an open, sunny place and will stand a good deal of drought, while the saxifrage is thankful for cool or even moist soil, and does not object to slight shade. But besides these two, both so well known that they scarcely need a reminder, there are a number of others that make good edgings and that are not often used. Of these the best known is the common thrift with its pale pink bloom. There is a deeper-coloured form, but not so desirable as the type, for the colour is rank and unpleasant; but the best is the small white, a very neat plant, with foliage unusually dark and glossy. A plant that deserves more general use and was employed as an edging in Tudor days is hyssop, delighting in a dry, sunny place in warm soil. It stands for several years, and though if left untrimmed it will grow two feet high, it can be kept down to any desired height and good shape by annual clipping. It should also be more used as a border plant, for it not only gives an abundance of good purple bloom, but in the later summer days is singularly attractive to butterflies. A much-neglected good edging plant is *Teucrium chamaedrys*, a close-growing mass of neat, glossy foliage and low-toned reddish purple bloom. It does well in the poorest soil. Another suitable plant with handsome polished leaves is *Asarum europaeum*, good at all times of the year except for about three weeks in spring. The dark red-leaved bugle (*Ajuga reptans*) is a capital edging for a cool place, but is best renewed every year.

There is a small form of *Vinca minor* with white flowers, a plant collected wild in northern Italy, that proves excellent as an edging. The usual fault of the lesser periwinkles is that they run so freely and soon get out of bounds; but this good little plant is neat and tufted and stays at home, making hardly any runners. In a warm soil in the southern counties a beautiful edging may be made with the golden lemon thyme. No place is too hot and dry for it; and for the same kind of poor, dry ground the common ling (*Calluna*) can be kept by yearly trimming to a perfectly shaped edging. For a grey bordering plant there is nothing better than *Stachys byzantina*, but as it is a larger-leaved plant than any of the foregoing it should only be employed where a wide edging – nothing less than a foot – will be suitable. It should be transplanted every two years, and the only care it requires is that the flowering growths, which show as upright shoots in May, should be removed, when all the strength of the plant is directed to the forming of the flat silvery carpet.

GARDENING ON CORRUGATED IRON

It often happens in and about a garden that it would be extremely convenient to use corrugated iron as a roofing material for some of the many sheds and shelters that are always wanted, or even for a summerhouse. This ugly material has two good qualities: it is cheap and it can be laid at a very low pitch, often a matter of importance when a shed is to be built as a lean-to against a wall that has no height to spare. But the thing is so unsightly that often the use of it is considered to be out of the question. The case, however, is not so hopeless as it may appear, for by the exercise of a little ingenuity the hideous expanse of corrugated iron can be made not only not unsightly, but actually a thing of beauty. It is done by putting four to six inches of soil on the iron and growing on it such plants as will thrive on a shallow bed that is likely to become more or less dry. To guard against the danger of heavy rain causing the soil to shift before it has become consolidated and more or less matted with the roots of the plants, something, either of wood or iron, is fixed horizontally across the middle of the roof, or two such bars, if the roof measures much more than twelve feet from eaves to top. Angle iron, of a depth of not less than two inches, does well, but in such a roof in the present writer's garden the bar is a piece of wood about two and a half inches square in section. Another such piece is fixed just over the eaves to stop earthy debris from falling into the gutter. These bars were well coated with the thick paint refuse that painters call 'smudge' to prevent rotting. The soil used was sandy peat, because it was more likely to be free from weeds than ordinary garden soil. A thin slab of fir with bark on is fixed just in front of the gutter so that both the gutter and the corrugated edge are hidden. The earth, being tightly packed together and consolidated by treading, was planted with stonecrops – the three varieties, crimson, pink and white, of *Sedum spurium*, the pink *S. ewersii* and the yellow *S. rupestre*. The effect is charming when the stonecrops are in flower, and when they are out of bloom the quiet colour of the leaves and the small grasses that grow between, and what is seen of the earthy surface, so exactly matches that of the tiled roof of the old barn, to which it is a lean-to, that it quite escapes notice. The common stonecrop (*Sedum acre*) or any other of the genus, can, of course, be used, but acre is not recommended as it is apt to become a troublesome weed in the garden.

If the soil on the iron roof is of more loamy nature or partly calcareous the houseleeks will do well. The common houseleek (*Sempervivum tectorum*) will make large patches while the smaller Alpine kinds, such as *S.* x *barbulatum* 'Hookeri' and *S. arachnoideum* subsp. *tomentosum*, will be quite at home. Wallflowers and snapdragons will also flourish, and will make a bright show in their seasons. All this supposes a roof with a southern or western aspect. If it looks to the north or east other plants would be used, the first that comes to mind as the most desirable being the common polypody fern, which would in time entirely cover such an iron roof. Anywhere in the south-western counties the interesting, round-leaved wall pennywort might well accompany it.

ROCK-WALL EDGINGS

The better ways of gardening are chasing away some of the old horticultural bogies. Among these, one of the most prevalent, and by no means yet extinct, is the unnecessary turf slope. It is just possible that in some forms of garden design, where there are large lawns and spaces, a glacis of turf may be desirable, although the change of level that gives rise to it is probably always the better for being treated as a terrace, with a retaining wall, and such superstructure of parapet or balustrade as the calibre of garden and its general design may demand. But there are hundreds of thousands of smaller gardens where the turf bank, so uninteresting in itself and so troublesome to mow, can, with little trouble, be replaced by a dry wall of stone or brick, which can itself be made a garden of delight. Where such walls are made between stretches of turf, and where the wall top finishes level with the upper ground, it is well to have, at the top of the wall, a border of not less than three feet wide for plants, and especially for small bushy forms, such as berberis or Scotch briar. It not only serves to accentuate the break of level, but is a safeguard against possible accident by walking over. It is better not to have a border at the foot of the wall, the more easily to enjoy and tend the plants in the joints, as well as the nearest on the higher level; they can thus all be seen and enjoyed to the full. Also there are a number of flowers that are specially beautiful when seen against the sky, such as *Yucca filamentosa* and many of the irises; these can thus be conveniently seen from below. The planting should be done so that the wall and border are united by bringing some of the border plants and bushes into the upper joints of the wall and letting some of the wall plants run up on to the level. If the change of level is but slight, only a foot or eighteen inches, a great deal of good effect may be gained, and especially if the pathway is also of stone.

Much pleasant gardening may be done by such treatment, and it will easily be seen how the same may be applied to many a place where there is still a dull turf bank. Moreover, for the growing of the hosts of spring and early summer flowers – aubrieta, alyssum, rock pinks, saxifrages, cerastium, iberis and their congeners – no place is more suitable. Even if the rock wall is in shade, the mossy saxifrages, small ferns, mimulus, tiarellas, smilacina and Welsh poppy will thrive to perfection.

In many places there are local quarries where flat stones, well suited for steps and pavements, may be had. In laying them it is best to keep them as large as possible, and to give time to fitting

October borders at
Munstead Wood.

them together as they are, rather than to knock them into shape with the hammer that the
dexterous workman is only too fond of wielding.

WAYS AND MEANS IN THE GARDEN

During a long life of gardening, all kinds of minor problems have presented themselves for
solution, and indeed it is one of the many satisfactions of practical gardening to devise means
of meeting the many little difficulties that arise and to invent ways of getting over them. One
of the most frequent is the need of some kind of support. We have to remember that, though
plants in a wild state have the strength of the stems so rightly adjusted that they stand well by
themselves, yet in our gardens, where they are in richer ground, the growth is stouter and
heavier, and for a good number of plants some kind of staking is necessary. The great thing is
to do it in good time. Nothing is more deplorable than to see, as one often does in other
people's gardens, such plants as Michaelmas daisies, full grown and perhaps already beaten
down by heavy rain, and then, at the last moment, when just about to flower, bunched up to
one stake and looking like an old gamp umbrella. These grand autumn plants we stake in June
when they are barely half grown. In the winter, when a few trees and a certain amount of
brushwood is cut, we take out suitable branching stuff on purpose. It may be of oak, chestnut
or hazel; or sometimes we use last year's hazel pea sticks with the thinner lop cut off. These
are stuck away among the growing asters, in such a way, according to the special need of each
kind, which will best support the stems, while allowing for the display of the natural free
growth. By August the greater part of the staking is hidden, but if any is still visible, it is cut out
with the secateur. Also about the end of June or a week or two into July, we look at the whole

Delphinum Belladonna
Group in the Grey Garden
with arches of *Rosa*
'The Garland' beyond.

aster border to see if the form of the front cannot be improved by lowering some of the growth nearest the path, either by bending them down and readjusting the supports by putting them behind instead of in front, or by boldly cutting the stems back about a third of their height. Doing this does not retard flowering, but encourages the number of short blooming tips to each cut stem, and so gives the plant a slightly altered character.

A number of our hardy border plants have a certain sappy tenderness of growth in their earlier stages, though the stems stiffen as they become mature. This is why the early support is so important. Such a plant as alstroemeria has luscious young growth that is easily laid flat by heavy rain and should be staked early; and others such as *Gypsophila paniculata* and the herbaceous *Clematis recta* must be kept in proper shape by a timely staking with stiff, branching spray.

Cutting back, or what gardeners commonly call 'stopping', comes in usefully on many occasions. The handsome, tall *Campanula lactiflora* sometimes sows itself in places where its normal height of five feet would be quite unsuitable, but by cutting it back when it is about half grown, or even earlier, it can be made to flower at a foot from the ground, or at any intermediate height that may be desired. One of the best grey plants for use when grey is the underplanting of our special borders for pink and purple colouring is the tall *Artemisia ludoviciana*; near the back of the border but just in front of pink hollyhocks, globe thistle (*Echinops*) and purple *Clematis* 'Jackmanii'. We let it grow to its full height of about four feet six inches, and to develop its pointed spikes of bloom in the natural way, for the flower itself is greyish in colour, though not so silvery as the leaves. But in other parts of the borders, where it accompanies snapdragons and China asters, it is cut down to just the height that best suits its flowering companions, and, at the front edge, right against the path, its height is reduced to two or three inches. A good many annuals can be treated in the same way and it is a useful corrective to the rather thin and leggy habit of such plants as cosmos. The handsome striped Japanese maize (*Zea mays*), if the main stem is cut when it is half grown, branches out from the ground and forms a bushy mass about two feet high that is very useful in connection with a group of the same plant full grown further back. In the grey, purple and pink borders one of the plants we rely on for a fine violet-purple colour is a good form of the annual *Consolida ajacis*. It comes up freely self-sown and would naturally bloom in June, but we do not want it until August, and therefore cut it back two or even three times, when the flower buds are showing; the result of this stopping is a much denser mass of bloom.

One of the contrivances that I have found most successful is the pulling down of tall plants to take the place of others that have gone out of flower. The fine sea hollies (*Eryngium* x *oliverianum*) and the biennial *E. giganteum* have lost the beauty of their wonderful metallic colouring of blue steel and silver by the end of July, while peonies only last through June. At the back of the wide border where these are grouped in the middle space, there is a patch of *Helianthus salicifolius*, a plant that, if left to its own way, would not be worth having in the garden, for it is tall and lanky with only a wisp of yellow bloom at the top. But we pull it down as soon as the flowers in the middle of the border are over, and spread its many long sterns in fan shape and almost horizontally, about two feet above the ground. The effect of this, as with many other plants, is to induce it to throw out flowering shoots at nearly every axil, so that in the late summer each bare red becomes a wand of pale yellow bloom and the whole space covered again with a flowery mass. Delphiniums are out of bloom by the end of July; they make such a quantity of seed that to save them from this exhaustive process the flowers are cut as soon as the best of the bloom is over. This leaves leafy stems four feet or more in height. A *Clematis flammula* is planted just behind and is trained to come over the delphinium patch. It does this most satisfactorily; the fast-growing shoots rest on the tops of the cut delphinium sterns and are further supported by any desirable adjustment of the stiff branching spray that held up the larkspurs. Early in September the space of some three or four square yards, that two months earlier was a glory of pure blue spires, has become a dense cloud of foam-coloured, sweet-scented bloom. At the other end of the border, where there is again a group of delphinium, the mantling plant is a white everlasting pea, which is trained over the cut stems in the same manner.

The strong perennials that are the main occupants of the border will all be well grown by the end of May when we put out the tenderer plants. Any gaps, or places purposely left, will then be filled with dahlias and penstemons, cannas, snapdragons, French and African marigolds, and any other tender plants or half-hardy annuals; but there will still be something to be provided for – this is to have reserve of plants in pots. There are such plants as clary (*Salvia sclarea*) which are of large size and much beauty in the end of June; but when the best of the bloom is over the considerable space they occupy is wanted for something to succeed them. They are easily raised from seed and should be treated as biennials. It is a good plan to have one or two in some reserve place where they are likely to sow themselves and so provide young plants without trouble. As a caution it may be well to mention that the old name clary is rather

Francoa sonchifolia by the tank.

carelessly used by English seedsmen, who sometimes apply it to the smaller purple bracted *Salvia viridis*: it should be made clear when ordering seed that *S. sclarea is* the kind required. When the best of the clary bloom is over we clear the plants right away and put in their place hydrangeas in pots sunk in the earth.

For the same kind of use there is nothing better than lilies in pots; *Lilium longiflorum, L. speciosum* and *L. auratum* are among those that are most effective and easy to manage. *Francoa sonchifolia* is another good plant for dropping in and some pots of fine foliage, such as *Hosta plantaginea* var. *japonica* and *H. sieboldiana* and hardy ferns, will be found of much use. Where there is glasshouse accommodation, the fine white *Brugmansia* (or *Datura*) *suaveolens* and others of the same family dropped in, or as gardeners say 'plunged', makes a fine effect in the back of the border, as do also pot-grown plants of the tall chimney campanula (C. *pyramidalis*) and its white variety.

The devising of such expedients adds much to the interest of the daily garden work, a part of which should be the critical observation of the flower border, noting where a gap needs filling or an overblown plant wants cutting back, or where those soon to be in bloom may require regulating as to the position or fresh placing of their outer branches; also where something that is for foliage only, such as the silvery *Stachys byzantina,* or the deep green-crested tansy, should have their blooming shoots cut out or any growth shortened.

Such critical observation becomes an education in itself, doing much to stimulate invention, and it will be found that though many matters can be attended to at once for present benefit, there will be others that can be noted for further improvement, such as may involve such changes as can be carried out only towards the end of the year.

REGULATING THE FLOWER BORDER

Besides the obvious duties, such as staking, weeding, mulching when needed and watering when drought threatens, there are many things that have to be seen to if an important flower border is to show its best. At intervals during the summer we go through it attending to the various matters that are the urgencies of the moment. Now, in the end of July, beginning at one end where the flowers are blue and white and pale yellow, the delphinium bloom going fast to seed is cut down to about four and a half feet from the ground. A strong plant of *Clematis flammula* planted some years ago and now in full growth is trained so that it will rest on the cut delphinium stalks and form a sheet of bloom over their place in September. Close by, that fine perennial mullein *Verbascum chaixii*, now going out of bloom, is cut right down. It leaves rather gappy places at the base, but these are filled by plunging some pots of hydrangea just in good bloom, and nothing is more useful for such a purpose. A little further along near the back of the border is a patch of the tall *Helianthus salicifolius*. If this was left to grow naturally it would shoot up to a height of seven to nine feet and bear a bunch of its pale yellow flowers at the top only. But we pull it down and peg it over some of the middle plants of the earlier summer, and it will develop flowers at every axil. Some of it is so tall that it nearly reaches to the front of the border and looks like some quite uncommon plant. A longish patch of crested tansy at the front edge, put there for the sake of its rich deep green foliage, must have the tips of the shoots pinched out for the third time; this keeps it to a foot in height and preserves the richly cut foliage in the best order. Just behind the tansy is a long drift of *Helenium* 'Pumilum Magnificum'. Through not tall, it is of a heavy sappy nature; when heavy rain comes it is apt to be thrown down in a lumpy way that is difficult to set right. We therefore support it with the branching tips of last year's pea sticks. Now, in looking at it from a few yards distance, the group looks a little too regular and formal. This is corrected by shifting a few of the bits of spray and as the plant has now hardened into maturity, some of the flower-laden growths are pulled a little out to give more play and freedom to the outline of the group. The same thing is done with a nearly adjoining group of *Leucanthemum* x *superbum*, as the mass of white daisy flowers, all nearly of a height and covering two square yards of space, was too much of a solid patch. The border towards the middle of its length has a careful arrangement of hollyhock, dahlia, garnet and dark snapdragon, and needs no present attention except that in one or two places where there was a gap a dahlia stake has been altered to bring the plant forward to fill the empty place.

The biggest job was with a white everlasting pea of many years' growth and now a mass of heavy bloom. Its earlier regulation had not been taken in time, so that though it was supported with strong pea sticks it had not been properly divided and the growths

The Main Hardy Flower Border.

separated. It was in one dense, heavy mass of bloom lying all together in one solid ridge. We drove in two stout dahlia stakes about five feet apart behind it and slit up a phormium leaf in half-inch wide strips – a string would have cut the easily broken stems – and passed the band as nearly as might be halfway, longitudinally through the mass of plant and pea stick, and drew it back carefully, separating the head part by hand, and made the ends fast to the stakes. Luckily, nothing was hurt, and now the fine old pea, instead of being a shapeless shelf of crowded white, is suitably diffused and in good shape, and looks as if the newly released and separated blooms and branches were enjoying their restoration to air and light. The pea is now, near the end of July, in full flower, but in another ten days will be going over. As it occupies a prominent place in the border and cannot be made to look well after blooming, a strong-growing hybrid clematis planted just behind it will cover and hide it, and will make another sheet of bloom in the late summer. The clematis is a natural hybrid that occurred in the garden; the parentage is evidently *C. vitalba* x *C. tubulosa*. The same cross has taken place in other gardens and, I believe, has been given a name, which at the moment I do not recall [probably *C.* x *jouiana*]. Further in the border is a range of the purple-leaved sage, whose quiet purple-grey colouring is delightful with pink and purple flowers. It is being cut back, partly to allow of the dropping in of more hydrangeas and also to promote its own young growth.

   As to all these lesser cares of a flower border, some may say, 'What a lot of fuss and trouble!' Yes it is, but then, that is gardening!

THE MAKING OF POT-POURRI

There are two ways of making pot-pourri, namely, by the dry process and by the moist. The dry way is the easiest and quickest, but the product of the moist method is so much sweeter and more lasting that it may be worth describing in detail. The chief ingredient is half-dried rose petals, and, roughly speaking, this should constitute a proportion by bulk of something like four-fifths of the whole. Then if the remaining fifth is still further subdivided, it may be of two-thirds sweet geranium and the remainder bay leaves and lavender. These proportions are given as a kind of type, but they need not be constant, for in some years it may be convenient to use less of rose and more of sweet geranium, and it will make good pot-pourri. We make it every other year, enough to fill a big tub that holds nearly two hundredweight. It is not made every year because the preparation takes a good deal of time and trouble, and the quantity suffices for the usual two years' distribution; moreover, it is better the second year than the first, as it ripens slowly to a more complete maturity.

The roses are picked when open at their widest; they must be quite dry and must not have been rained on since they were in bud. They are best collected on a sunny day any time between twelve and three. If they are picked at all damp they will not dry properly, but will go mouldy, and the batch will only have to be thrown away. We pick about two bushels at a time, and they are at once taken to a big, airy room, a temporarily disused studio, where a large cloth, a dust sheet or a bale wrapper, is laid out on the brick floor; on this the petals are picked off and separated. If this cannot be done at once the roses must not be left in the basket or even be laid to wait in heaps, or they would soon heat and spoil; they must be laid out, not more than two or three roses thick, on the wrapper. There are three old oak tables in the studio, eight or nine feet long, and the rose leaves are laid out on cloths on these. If the following day is fine and sunny they are taken out and laid on their wrappers in the sun on the little paved court just outside; but if rain comes on or even threatens we rush to the rescue and bring them indoors and put them again on the tables. If they have been in the sun the second day they may be ready to go into the preparation jars on the afternoon of the third day, but the time they take to dry to the proper state is better understood by the barometer than by the rose grower, who has to learn it by experience; but the petals have to shrivel to about half their bulk and be not dry, but tough and leathery. Meanwhile, a store of salt mixture is held in readiness; it is half bay salt and half common salt. The bay salt is sold in lumps; it has to be roughly pounded so that the greater part is broken up small, leaving a certain proportion in knobs about the size of marrowfat peas.

The preparation jars I had made on purpose at Doulton's Lambeth Potteries; they are of strong buff stoneware with covers of the same, of plain cylindrical shape; they stand twenty-two inches high and have an inside diameter of nine inches. Each has a loosely fitting disc of lead, weighing fourteen pounds, with a flattish handle. Three moderate or two large handfuls of rose petals are thrown in and are rammed down with a wooden rammer made of the upper part of an old spade handle let into a rounded wooden block; then an easy handful of the salt mixture is sprinkled over the layer, another three handfuls are thrown in, and so on as long as that batch of rose leaves lasts; the heavy leaden disc is then lowered in to keep the mass tightly pressed down. The sweet geranium leaves are treated in the same way, but in the case of the most commonly grown kinds, namely, 'Radula' and 'Radula Roseum', each leaf is first torn up into three or four pieces. Sweet verbena is very desirable, but unless the quantity of pot-pourri made is small there is not usually enough to make a material addition to the bulk. It need not be dried, but can be put into the jars and salted at once. The young bay leaves of the year are not hard and mature till quite the end of July, and are still better in August. Lavender is ready in the last days of July or the first week of August; it should be gathered while the upper part of the spike is still in bud. Lavender and bay leaves are both of a dry nature and go straight into the salting jars without any preliminary drying. The sweet geranium is not gathered till well on in September, or according to the season, the object being to enjoy it in the open for as long as possible and to cut it just before the plants would naturally be destroyed by frost. A very precious ingredient, the earliest prepared in the year, is orange peel stuck with cloves. In March, when Seville oranges are to be had, the peel is taken off in halves and cut into strips the up and down way of the orange, so that they are about half an inch wide in the middle, and they are stuck all over with cloves. This is put into a jar with salt by itself and only pressed down by hand, as it is too tender to bear being rammed.

Thus, the collecting and preparation of the pot-pourri material begins in March and runs through the summer and early autumn, so that the time of the final mixing does not arrive till October, when the seasoning of spices and other sweet things should be prepared. The tub has a capacity of from sixteen to eighteen gallons and the weight of pot-pourri made is somewhere near 224 pounds. For the seasoning of this I use the following ground spices, gums, etc.: five large packets of Atkinson's Violet Powder – this is better than using the alternative of plain orris-root – 1 pound cloves, 1 pound allspice, 1 pound mixed spice, ½ pound mace, 1 pound gum benzoin, 1 pound gum storax. This is all mixed together and put in a pail. There is, besides, 1 pound whole cloves and 1 pound whole mace. From these weights the amounts wanted for smaller quantities can be computed.

October having come and all the materials being ready, we proceed to the mixing. In the case of the rather large quantity made, it is done on a well-swept place of the brick floor of the studio. The rose leaves in the jars are now so tightly compacted that they have to be loosened by stabbing with an iron weeding fork; they come up in close, thick flakes that have to be broken up by the hand, and are then thrown upon the floor. It is best for three or four persons to work together, one of them having the pail of spice mixture, so that as the heap on the floor rises, the various ingredients are already more or less mixed. When the jars are empty and the spices exhausted, the whole is turned over backwards and forwards on the floor with a shovel, and if it appears to be a little too dry, a slight sprinkling of water is given with a fine-rosed can. Of this new mixture none is used till the following March or April, and it is all the better if it remains for nearly a year in the tub untouched.

I have collected and studied a number of old recipes for pot-pourri, but find in many of them either some want of definite instruction or some obvious inaccuracy; but it has not been difficult to gather from them what is essentially useful, and so, with the added experience of many years, to establish a more or less regular course of operation.

SOURCES

THE JOY OF SPRING
Lent Hellebores, *Country Life*, 10 March 1923, page 326.
A Nut Walk, *The Garden*, 11 March 1916, page 128.
A Primrose Garden, *Country Life*, 28 April 1923, pages 568–9.
A Garden of Spring Flowers, *Bulletin of the Garden Club Of America*, January 1920
  (No. 2 NS), pages 3–7.
An April Garden, *Country Life*, 27 April 1912, pages 611–12.
Wallflowers in the Spring Garden, *The Garden*, 27 May 1922, page 246.
Aubrietas in the Spring Garden, *The Garden*, 12 December 1914, page 598.

A SUMMER'S LEASE
A June Border of Irises and Lupins, *The Garden*, 21 December 1912, page 639.
Midsummer in the Garden, *Country Life*, 28 June 1924, pages 1055–6.
Summer Flowers Carefully Arranged, *Country Life*, 9 September 1916, page 303.
The Flower Border, *Bulletin of the Garden Club of America*, March 1920 (No. 3 NS),
  pages 5–8.
The Use of Grey Foliage with Border Plants, *Country Life*, 7 October 1916, pages 401–2.
Bedding Out, *The Garden*, 24 June 1922, pages 305–6.

MISTS AND MELLOW FRUITFULNESS
Planting for Autumn Effect, *The Garden*, 15 April 1916, page 183.
September Flowers, *Country Life*, 11 November 1916, pages 580–1; *The Garden*, 13 September 1919,
  page 438.
Guelder Rose in Autumn, *The Garden*, 11 November 1916, page 544.
Michaelmas Daisies, *The Garden*, 18 September 1915, pages 460–61.
The Survivors, *The Garden*, 3 November 1917, page 472.

THE BLEAKNESS OF WINTER
The Last Week of January, *Country Life*, 10 February 1923, pages 186–7.
Early February, *Country Life*, 24 February 1923, pages 239–40.
Hardy Ferns in Winter, *Country Life*, 21 December 1918, page 586.
Some Winter Effects of Flower and Shrub, *Country Life*, 21 January 1911, pages 104–5.
The Conservatory or Winter Garden, *Bulletin of the Garden Club of America*, January 1921
  (No. 8 NS), pages 2–4.
Evergreens for Decoration, *Gardening Illustrated*, 20 December 1930, page 827.

SOME IDEAS ON GARDEN PLANNING
Garden Planning: Aims to be Kept in View, *Black's Dictionary of Gardening*, page 408.
An Outdoor Sitting Place, *Country Life*, 12 April 1924, page 581.
Planted Banks as Hedges, *Country Life*, 13 March 1915, pages 333–4.
Planting in Dry Walls, *Country Life*, 8 August 1913, pages 189–90; *The Garden*,
  3 October 1914, page 484.
Garden Craftsmanship in Yew and Box, *English Life*, 1925, Vol. 5, pt 6, pages 436–9.
The Yew Cat, *Gardening Illustrated*, 15 October 1927, page 641.

AROUND THE HOUSE

Planting a Carriage Drive, *Country Life*, 7 February 1914, page 190; *The Garden*, 16 October 1915 page 508.

The Way In, *Gardening Illustrated*, 2 June 1928, page 347.

Borders Round a House, *Gardening Illustrated*, 2 February 1924, page 68.

From Indoors – Looking Out, *Gardening Illustrated*, 3 December 1927, page 751.

Wild Thyme on the Steps, *Gardening Illustrated*, 22 October 1932, page 637.

Grey Foliage on a Low Wall, *Gardening Illustrated*, 19 February 1927, page 113.

The Court and its Planting, *Gardening Illustrated*, 29 October 1932, page 655.

Plants in Steps and Pavements, *Country Life*, 2 June 1917, pages 553–4; *The Garden*, 29 September 1917, pages 407–8.

Rosemary Growing in Masonry, *Gardening Illustrated*, 17 December 1927.

Plants in Steps, *Gardening Illustrated*, 30 June 1928, page 410.

Plants in Pots, *Gardening Illustrated*, 1 January 1927.

SOME THOUGHTS ABOUT COLOUR

Colour in the Flower Garden, *The English Flower Garden*, pages 280–86.

Colour in the Flower Garden I and II, *Country Life*, 22 March 1919 , pages 308–9, and 29 March 1919, pages 348–9.

The Blue Border, *Country Life*, 19 August 1922, pages 218–19.

Colour Names and Descriptions, *Gardening Illustrated*, 3 August 1929, pages 525–6.

ROSES

Some Garden Roses and their Uses, *The Rose Annual*, 1921, pages 97–101.

Some of the Sweetest Roses, *Gardening Illustrated*, 9 July 1927, page 424.

Some Tea Roses, *The Garden*, 4 October 1919, pages 470–1.

Good Climbing Roses, *The Garden*, 5 June 1897, page 415, reprinted from *The Guardian*.

The Joys of Observation, *Country Life*, 12 August 1922, page 177.

Scotch Briars, *The Garden*, 31 January 1920, page 57.

The Rose Zéphirine Drouhin, *Gardening Illustrated*, 16 August 1930, page 541.

WILD AND WOODLAND GARDENING

Wild Gardening, *Bulletin of the Garden Club of America*, May 1920 (No. 4 NS), pages 5-9.

A Self-sown Wood, *Country Life*, 18 May 1912; *The Garden*, 16 January 1915.

Rhododendrons Grouped for Colour, *The Garden*, 12 April 1890, page 335.

The Azalea Garden, *Country Life*, 25 August 1923, pages 258–9.

White Flowers in the Woodland, *The Garden*, 8 August 1925.

White Foxgloves in Woodland, *Gardening Illustrated*, 9 January 1932, page 20.

Lilies in Woodland Edges, *Gardening Illustrated*, 21 November 1931, page 715.

A Heath Garden in West Surrey, *Country Life*, 5 October 1918, page 281.

Woodland Roses, *The Rose Annual*, 1920, pages 29–31.

BULBOUS PLANTS AND THEIR USES

Grouping of Hardy Bulbs, *Country Life*, 3 February 1923, pages 156–7.

Hardy Crinums, *The Garden*, 23 September 1922, page 482.

White Crinum x powelli 'Album', *Gardening Illustrated*, 15 October 1927, page 642.

Bulbous Plants in Grass and Woodland, *Country Life*, 3 October 1914, page 465.

A River of Daffodils, *Gardening Illustrated*, 14 June 1924, page 363.

Carpeting Bulb Beds, *The Garden*, 5 December 1885, page 577.

SOME HARDY PLANTS

The Taller Campanulas, *The Garden*, 6 May 1922, page 210.

Some of the Lesser Campanulas, *The Garden*, 13 May 1922, page 227.

How to Grow Hollyhocks, *The Garden*, 22 February 1913, page 99.

Iris unguicularis in Algiers, *Gardening Illustrated*, 5 March 1932. [**page no.?**]

That Blue Pea, *Gardening Illustrated*, 13 September 1930, page 595.

Mulleins Pulled Down, *The Garden*, 18 June 1921, page 306.

Some Uses of Grey Plants, *Country Life*, 2 February 1920, page 196.

Some of the Hardy Sages, *The Garden*, 27 July 1918, pages 289–90.

Sedum sieboldii, *Gardening Illustrated*, 6 December 1930, page 790.

A Natural Colour Study (Thrift), *Country Life*, 18 July1913, page 87.

SCENTS IN THE GARDEN

A Garden of Sweet Scents, *Country Life*, 7 January 1911, pages 8–9.

Shrubs with Scented Leaves, *Country Life*, 7 May 1910, page 678.

Sweet-Scented Shrubbery Beds, *The Garden*, 22 February 1890, page 169.

CLIMBING PLANTS

Hardy Vines on House Walls, *Gardening Illustrated*, 1 August 1931.

Simply Planted Pergolas, *Country Life*, 12 June 1915, page 808.

Climbing Plants for Cottage Gardens, *Busbridge Parish Magazine*, June 1928.

Climbing Plants for Cottage Walls, *Busbridge Parish Magazine*, July 1928.

Ivy and its Many Ways, *Country Life*, 10 June 1905, pages 833–4.

Clematis montana and its Many Uses, *Country Life*, 2 February 1918; *The Garden*, 22 February 1919, page 80.

Winter Jasmine, *The Garden*, 17 February 1912, page 87.

SMALL GARDENS

Colour in the Small Garden, *Our Homes and Gardens*, June 1919, pages 20–21.

The Ordinary Garden, *Homes and Gardens*, 6 April 1925, pages 395–8.

Small London Gardens, *Country Life*, 8 October 1921, pages 458–9.

SHRUBS AND THEIR USES

Small Evergreens for Poor Soils, *The Garden*, 14 December 1918, pages 461–2.

Flowering Shrubs in the Flower Border, *Gardening Illustrated*, 1 October 1932, page 596.

Some Flowering Shrubs of Late July, *The Garden*, 19 August 1916, page 405.

Shrubbery Edges, *Country Life*, 22 July 1916, page 105.

Foliage Plants for Shrub Edges, *Gardening Illustrated*, 29 January 1927, page 68.

A Plea for the Laurel: One of the Noblest of Evergreen Shrubs, *The Garden*, 5 February 1921, page 68.

Some American Peat Shrubs, *Country Life*, 11 August 1917, pages 139–40.

Shrubs for Window Boxes, *Gardening Illustrated*, 22 October 1887, page 455.

Aesculus parviflora, *Gardening Illustrated*, 11 February 1928, page 78.

Alexandrian Laurel (Danae racemosa), *Gardening Illustrated*, 5 May 1928, page 271.

Exochorda racemosa (Exochorda grandiflora), *The Garden*, 22 June 1918, page 240.

Fuchsias as Pot Plants, *Gardening Illustrated*, 17 August 1929, page 565.

Kalmia latifolia, *Gardening Illustrated*, 23 July 1927, page 450.

Magnolia stellata and M. denudata, *Gardening Illustrated*, 7 June 1930, page 381.

Mistletoe (Viscum album), *The Garden*, 27 December 1919, page 614.

The Lesser Periwinkles (Vinca minor), *The Garden*, 25 April 1885, page 359.

WATER GARDENING

The Water Garden, *Black's Gardening Dictionary*, pages 1149–51.

SOME ELEMENTS OF DESIGN

Historical Notes on Garden Ornament I & II, *Country Life*, 4 November 1911, pages 662–4, and 11 November 1911, pages 701–702.

Some Garden Ornaments and Accessories, *The Garden*, 26 April 1924, page 282–3.

Iron Garden Gates, *The Garden*, 11 July 1925, pages 390–91.

The Garden Summerhouse, *Black's Gardening Dictionary*, page 416–7.

SOME PRACTICAL IDEAS AND SOLUTIONS

Some Horticultural Indiscretions, *The Garden*, 24 November 1923, pages 607–8.

The Paint Pot in the Garden, *Country Life*, 3 March 1917.

Gardening Among Stones, *Homes and Gardens*, September 1923, pages 119–20.

A Place Where 'Nothing Will Grow', *The Garden*, 13 April 1889, page 331.

Plants for Edgings, *The Garden*, 10 May 1919, page 216.

Gardening on Corrugated Iron, *Country Life*, 1 April 1911, page 466.

Rock-Wall Edgings, *Country Life*, 2 July 1910, pages 29–30.

Ways and Means in the Garden, *Bulletin of the Garden Club of America*, September 1920 (No. 6 NS), pages 4–7.

Regulating the Flower Border, *The Garden*, 12 August 1922, pages 397–8.

The Making of Pot-Pourri, *Country Life*, 4 August 1917, page 115–16.

INDEX

Page numbers in *italic* refer to illustrations.

Acaena microphylla, 69;
  A. novae-zelandiae, 114
acalypha, 48
Acanthus, 61, 144, 148, 149;
  A. mollis, 148, 150;
    A.m. 'Latifolius Group', 148;
  A. spinosus, 148, 150;
    A.s. Spinosissimus Group, 148, 150
achillea, 139
Aconitum carmichaelii Wilsonii Group, 76;
  A. japonicum, 37, 41, 76
Aesculus parviflora, 154, *154*
ageratum, 24, 26, 32, 33, 35, 36, 39, 40, 77, 140
Ajuga reptans, 17, 72, 73, 187
Albury, Surrey, 168
alder, 98
Alexandrian laurel
  see *Danae racemosa*
Algiers, 46
Alisma plantago-aquatica, 160, 176
alpenrose
  see *Rhododendron ferrugineum*
Alstroemeria, 68;
  A. chilensis hort., 120;
  A. pelegrina, 125
alternanthera, 72
Alcea ficifolia, 119
alyssum, 64, 139, 186, 189
Amaranthus hypochondriacus, 29, 72
amaryllis, 48
Amelanchier canadensis, 54, 95
Anchusa, 25, 29, 31, 78, 140;
  A. 'Opal', 78
andromeda see *Leucothoe catesbaei*
Anemone, 138;
  A. apennina, 70, 96, 110;
  A. blanda, 96;
  A. coronaria, 109;
  A. coronaria (De Caen Group) 'Die Braut', 110;
  A. hepatica, 70;
  A. nemorosa, 70, 96;
  A. sylvestris, 70;
  anemone wood 97
Antennaria dioica var. *hyperborean*, 72, 114
anthericum, 25
Anthurium 'Orange King', 35
arabis, 17, 186
Arbutus unedo, 59, 146
arctotis, 80
Arenaria balearica, 114
Aristolochia, 71;
  A. microphylla, 89
Arkwright, Revd Edwyn, 120

arrowheads, 160, 162
Artemisia, 29, 81;
  A. lactiflora, 33;
  A. ludoviciana, 26, 33, 75, 124, 191;
  A. stelleriana, 26, 32, 33, 122, 123, 124, 140
Aruncus dioicus, 25, 78, 160
Asarum europaeum, 65, 73, 147, 187
ash, 97
Asphodelus ramosus, 25
aspidistra, 48, 144
Asplenium scolopendrium, 19, 45, 47, 63, 65;
  A. trichomanes, 45, 48
Aster amellus, 36, 39, 40;
  A. 'Archer Hind', 40;
  A. 'Beauty of Colwall', 40;
  A. 'Climax', 40;
  A. 'Cloudy Blow', 37;
  A. 'Collerette Blanche', 39;
  A. 'Coombe Fishacre', 78;
  A. cordifolius 'Elegans', 40, 41, 78;
    A.c. 'Diana', 40;
  A. 'Ella', 40;
  A. 'Esther', 40;
  A. 'Flora', 40;
  A. 'F.W. Burbidge', 36;
  A. 'Hon. Edith Gibbs', 40;
  A. 'J. Dickinson', 40;
  A. 'Lady Lloyd', 37, 40;
  A. lanceolatus
    subsp. *lanceolatus*, 33;
    A.l. subsp. *simplex*, 37;
  A. lateriflorus, 39, 40;
  A. 'Lovely', 40;
  A. 'Magnet H. Adams', 40;
  A. 'Margaret', 36;
  A. 'Mme Soynuce', 40;
  A. 'Mrs Tynam', 40;
  A. novae-angliae, 39, 41;
    A.n. 'J. Bowman', 40;
    A.n. 'Constance', 40;
    A.n. 'Lil Fardell', 40;
    A.n. 'Mitchellii', 40;
    A.n. 'Ryecroft Pink', 40;
    A.n. 'Ryecroft Purple', 37, 40;
    A.n. 'Ruber', 40, 77;
  A. novi-belgii, 39, 93;
  A. puniceus, 37, 40, 76;
  A. 'Queen', 40;
  A. 'Robert Parker', 36, 40;
  A. sedifolius, 36, 37, 39;
  A. thomsonii, 40;
  A. 'Top Sawyer', 40;
  see also Michaelmas daisies
Atriplex hortensis, 29, 125
Aubrieta, 17, 20, 21, 115, 186, 189;
  A. deltoidea var. *graeca*, varieties of, 21, 115
aucuba, 45, 49, 141
August borders, *32*

auriculas, 68
azaleas, 38, 59, 68, 93, 95, 96, 98, 105, 126, 129, 152, 156;
  garden of, *102*;
  Ghent, 59, 95, 101;
  named Ghent hybrids, 101–2
Azara microphylla, 126, 129

Bakewell of Derby, 177
Balcarres, Fife, 168, 170
Balcaskie, Fife, 168
balm of Gilead
  see *Cedronella canariensis*
banks as hedges, 53–4
Banksian rose
  see *Rosa banksiae*
Barbary ragwort
  see *Othonna cheirifolia*
Barnsley House, Gloucestershire, *179*
Barr, Peter, 10, 21
bay, 46, 70, 126, 196, 197
Bean's *Trees and Shrubs*, 158
bedstraw, 62
beech, 38;
  as hedges, 52
Begonia rex, 48
Berberis, 10, 49;
  B. darwinii, 18
Bergenia, 19, 30, 148;
  B. cordifolia, 30, 141, 147, 148
blackthorn, 54, 95, 97, 137, 162
bluebells, 9, 92, 97, 103
Bodichon, Eugene Dr, 120
Bodichon, Mme, 120
bog myrtle, 129
bougainvillea, 48
box, 46, 49, 52, 57, 60, 63, 70, 97, 129, 141, 153, 165, 170, 187
Brachyglottis (Dunedin Group) 'Sunshine', 122
bracken
  see *Peridium aquilinum*
Bramshill, Hampshire, 169
Brimeura amethystine, 114
Brockenhurst, Hampshire, 168
broom, 53, 54, 97
Brown, Lancelot 'Capability', 6
Brugmansia suaveolens, 48, 193
bryony, 55
buck bean, 160
buckthorn, 98
Butomus umbellatus, 160, 176

caladium, 48, 80
calanthe, 48
Calceolaria, 47, 71, 72;
  C. amplexicaulis, 26, 33, 34, 37, 41, 75, 79
Calendula officinalis, 139
Caltha, 160

Campanula, 11, 81;
  C. alliariifolia, 117;
  C. carpatica, 117, 123;
  C. cochlearifolia, 118;
  C. fragilis, 118;
  C. garganica, 25, 118;
  C. glomerata, 116, 139;
  C. isophylla, 118;
  C. latifolia, 32, 103, 116, 139, 191;
    C.l. 'Eriocarpa', 116;
    C.l. var. *macrantha*, 29, 116, 149;
    C.l. var. *macrantha* 'Alba', 139, 148;
  C. macrocarpa see *C. glomerata*;
  C. medium, 117;
  C. persicifolia, 25, 103, 116, 139, 149;
  C. portenschlagiana, 25, 118;
  C. punctata, 118;
  C. pyramidalis, 117, 193;
  C. sarmatica, 118
campions, 97
candleberry gale
  see *Myrica cerifera*
cannas, 26, 29, 34, 36, 48, 75, 76, 139, 192
Cardiocrinum giganteum, 126
Castle Ashby, Northamptonshire, 168
catmint
  see *Nepeta*
Ceanothus × *delileanus* 'Gloire de Versailles', 79, 147
Cedronella canariensis, 62, 126
Centaurea ragusina, 72, 124
Centranthus ruber, 25, 186
Cerastium tomentosum, 68, 72, 186, 189
Chaenomeles speciosa, 134;
  C.n. 'Apple Blossom', 134
Chamaecyparis lawsoniana, 153;
  C.l. 'Ericoides', 153;
  C. obtusa 'Aurea', 153;
  C. pisifera 'Plumose', 153;
  C.p. 'Squarrosa', 153
Chamerion angustifolium, 103
Chatsworth, Derbyshire, 168
cherries, 97
Chimonanthus praecox, 42, 46
China asters, 26, 33, 36, 37, 81, 140, 191
China asters, Ostrich plume, Comet, Victoria classes, 'Mammoth' formerly 'Vick's White', 36, 37
China roses
  see *Rosa* × *odorata* 'Pallida'
Chionodoxa, 18, 96, 109, 112;
  C. luciliae, 109, 114;
  C. sardensis, 109
choisya, 43, 49, 128
chrysanthemum, 70
Church, Thomas, *178*

cineraria, 47
Circaea lutetiana, 182
Cistus, 25, 126, 148;
  C. × *cyprius*, 55, 101, 104, 106, 127, 128;
  C. × *florantinus*, 101;
  C. ladanifer, 106, 127, 128;
  C. laurifolius, 101, 104, 106, 127, 128, 129
claret vine, 89
clary
  see *Salvia sclarea*
Cleeve Prior, Worcestershire, 171
Clematis flammula, 30, 32, 37, 41, 71, 76, 79, 87, 95, 140, 192, 194;
  C. 'Jackmanni', 26, 29, 33, 71, 75, 117, 147, 191;
  C. montana, 71, 87, 95, 126, 135, 136, 137, 136;
  C. paniculata, 41;
  C. recta, 25, 78, 148, 191;
  C. tubulosa, 195;
  C. vitalba, 41, 54, 135, 195
climbers, 87, 88, 89
clove carnation, 144
Coelogyne cristata, 48
Colchicum, 113;
  C. autumnale, 109, 112;
  C. speciosum, 109
coleus, 47
colour, theory of, 66, 68, 69
Colour in the Flower Garden, 7, 18
columbines, 11, 70, 138, 149
Commelina tuberosa Coelestris Group, 79, 81
Comptonia peregrina var. *asplenifolia*, 128, 129
conservatories, planting of, 47, 48
Consolida ajacis, 26, 33, 70, 192
Coreopsis, 29;
  C. lanceolata, 139
Coronilla orientalis, 114
cornus, 47, 98
Corydalis cheilanthifolia, 19;
  C. lutea, 65;
  C. ochroleuca, 20, 65;
  C. solida, 110
cosmos, 37
Cotinus coggygria, 58
Cotoneaster, 19;
  C. frigidus, 95
Country Life, 6
cow parsnip, 55
crab, 97
cranesbill
  see *Geranium*
Crataegus coccinea, 95
Crinum × *powellii*, 26, 34, 38, 61, 110;
  C. × *p.* 'Album', 61, 111
Crocus, 18, 43, 60, 96, 109, 112;
  C. sieberi, 44;
  C. speciosus, 113

croton, 48
crown imperial
  see *Fritillaria imperialis*
Cryptomeria japonica, 153
cyclamen, 70, 113
Cynoglossum amabile, 81
cypress, 46, 129, 170
Cypripedium insigne, 48
Cytisus 'Andreanus', 54;
  C. 'Dallimorei', 106;
  C. × *praecox*, 54, 106
Czar violets, 46

Daboecia, 105
Dadamsvarrt, *67*
daffodils, 17, 61, 70, 95, 96, 108, 109, 127, 138;
  river of, *113*;
  see also *Narcissus*
Dahlia, 26, 29, 30, 34, 36, 37, 75, 76, 80, 139, 140, 192, 194;
  D. 'Amethyst', 80;
  D. 'Lady Primrose', 34, 40;
  D. 'Porthos', 80;
  D. 'Victoria', 34
Danae racemosa, 42, 46, 49, 141, 146, 147, 148, 155
Danby, 172
Daphne cneorum, 129;
  D. mezereum, 19, 44, 46, 110;
  D. odora, 48;
  D. pontica, 127
Darmera peltata, 161
daylily
  see *Hemerocallis*
Deanery Garden, Sonning, Berkshire, 176
Delphinium, 29, 31, 71, 74, 79, 80, 139, 140, 192, 194;
  D. 'Belladonna', 25, 78, *191*;
  D. grandiflorum, 140
dentaria, 19
deodar cedar, 46
Deschampsia flexuosa, 101
deutzia, 25, 141
dilated shield fern, 45, 55, 63, 103, 148, 161
dog's-tooth violet
  see *Erythronium dens-canis*
dogwood
  see *Cornus*
Doronicum, 17, 20;
  D. plantagineum, 17
dracaena, 48
drift planting, 17
drive plantings, 58–9
Dryas octopetala, 114
Durando, M., 120

echinops, 26, 33, 36, 75, 139, 191
elaeagnus, 47
elder, 55, 97, 147

Elizabeth I, Queen, 177, 181
elm, 98
Elvaston Castle, Derbyshire, 172
enchanter's nightshade
    see Cireaea lutetiana
Epilobium, 160
Epimedium pinnatum, 44
Erica, 100;
    E. arborea var. alpina, 105;
    E. australis, 105;
    E. carnea, 44;
    E. ciliaris, 106;
    E. ciliaris 'Maweana', 106;
    E. lustanica, 105;
    E. terminalis, 105;
    E. tetralix, 106;
    E. vagans, 105;
    E. x veitchii, 105
erigeron, 29
erinus, 64
Eryngium, 29, 81;
    E. giganteum, 139, 192;
    E. x oliverianum, 192
Erythronium dens-canis,
        18, 19, 110, 112;
    E. oregonum, 110
Escallonia, 49;
    E. rubra var. macrantha, 61, 62, 129
Euonymus, 47, 153;
    E. europaeus, 95;
    E. fortunei var. radicans, 142;
    E. japonicus, 153
eupatorium, 139
Euphorbia characias, 40;
    E.c. subsp. wulfenii, 34, 42, 43, 122
Evelyn, John, 169
evergreen oak, 70
Exochorda racemosa, 155, 155

x Fatshedera lizei 'Variegata', 153
feather hyacinth, 25
Felicia, 79;
    F. amelloides, 35, 81
ferns, 18, 19, 95, 187, 189, 193;
    fern walk, 96
feverfew, 40, 75, 76
ficinus, 76
field maple, 98
field scabious
    see Knautia arvensis
fig, 26
Filipendula rubra 'Venusta', 160;
    F. ulmaria, 78
Folly Farm, 30
forget-me-not
    see Myosotis sylvatica
Forsythia suspensa, 134
Fountains Hall, North Yorkshire,
    169, 171, 178
foxglove, 29, 30, 32, 55, 56,62, 95,
    97, 103, 104, 138, 139, 149
Francoa ramose, 63;
    F. sonchifolia, 193
Frankenia laevis, 114
Fritillaria imperialis, 17
Fuchsia 65, 148, 173;
    F. 'Ballet Girl', 63, 65, 156;

F. 'Cannell's Delight', 63, 65, 156;
    F. magellanica var. gracilis, 62;
    F. 'Mme Cornellison', 63, 65, 156;
    F. riccartonii, 134
fumitory, 19

gaillardia, 25
Galanthus x allenii, 109;
    G. elwesii, 109;
    G. plicatus, 109
galega, 29
Garden Ornament, 7
A Gardener's Testament, 6
Garrya, 42
Gaultheria, 19, 152;
    G. shallon, 19, 49, 93, 100
gentians, 71, 81
Geranium, 26, 34, 35, 36, 65;
    G. ibericum, 25;
    G. robertianum, 64;
    for bedding, 29, 71, 75, 80, 139,
        155, 173;
    radula varieties, 61, 197;
    G. 'Radula Roseum' 197;
    see also Pelargonium
Geum 'Mrs Bradshaw', 25
Ghent azaleas
Gladiolus, 26, 29, 31, 33, 34, 68, 76;
    G. 'America', 36, 75;
    'Barron Hulot' 36;
    'Blue Jay' 36;
    'Lily Lehmann' 26;
    G. 'The Bride' (x colvillii), 25, 78
Glyceria maxima, 37;
    G. maxima var. variegata,
        33, 75, 79
Godetia (now Clarkia)
    'Double Rose', 36
golden lemon thyme, 188
golden privet, 23, 42, 46, 147
golden rod, 41
gorse, 53, 97, 119
goutweed, 183
grape hyacinth, 45
great knapweed, 55
grey foliage, use of, 31, 32
grey garden, 31, 32
guelder rose
    see Viburnum opulus 'Roseum'
gunnera, 161
Gypsophila, 26, 33, 36, 147;
    alpine, 115;
    G. elegans, 36;
    G. paniculata, 191

habenaria, 70
hackwood, 172
Halimium lasianthum
    subsp. formosum, 101
Hamamelis, 46
Hampton Court Palace, 164, 172,
    177
Hardwick Hall, Derbyshire, 166
hart's-tongue ferns
    see Asplenium scolopendrium
hawkweed, mouse-ear, 62
hawthorn, 47, 137

hazels, 9, 12, 16, 53, 93, 97, 190
heaths, 59, 62, 97, 101, 104, 105,
    119, 148, 188
Hebe, 154;
    H. brachysiphon, 147;
    H. odora, 142
hedychium, 48
Helenium, 32;
    H. 'Pumilum Magnificum', 194
Helianthus, 32;
    H. x laetiflorus, 139;
    H. x l. 'Mrs Moon', 139;
    H. x multiflorus, 139;
    H. salicifolius, 192, 194
helichrysum, 80
Heliotrope, 26, 36, 72, 123, 127, 147;
    H. 'President Garfield', 123
Helleborus argutifolius, 187;
    H. foetidus, 187;
    H. niger, 45, 46;
    H. orientalis, 9, 10, 43, 110
hemerocallis, 25
Henry III, King, 164
Henry VIII, King, 164
Hepatica, 19;
    H. transsilvanica, 19
Heracleum mantgazzianum, 161;
    H. stevenii, 161
Hestercombe House, Somerset, 35,
    122, 131, 163
Heuchera, 17, 19, 73;
    H. americana, 17, 23, 73
Hewell Grange, Herefordshire, 168
Hidcote Manor, Gloucestershire,
    178, 179
Himalayan ccowslip,
    see Primula sikkimensis
Archer-Hind, Mr, 10
hollies, 16, 19, 46, 47, 49, 52, 53,
    54, 58, 59, 85, 89, 93, 95, 97,
    103, 105, 106, 150, 153, 162,
    170
hollyhocks, 26, 29, 30, 33, 36, 75,
    76, 80, 118, 119, 139, 191, 194
Holodiscus discolor, 147
honesty see Lunaria annua
honeysuckle, 54, 55, 71, 89, 92, 95,
    97, 98, 129, 169;
    see also Lonicera
hornbeam, 37, 52, 98, 165
horse chestnut, 98
Hosta, 30, 63, 193;
    H. plantaginea var. japonica,
        30, 63, 193;
    H. sieboldiana, 30, 31, 193
houseleeks
    see Sempervivum
hut garden, 83
Hyacinthoides hispanica, 96
Hydrangea, 11, 33, 60, 60, 61, 62,
    63, 147, 193, 194, 195;
    H. arborescens, 79, 147
Hypericum, 129, 153;
    H. olympicum f. minus, 114, 115
hyssop, 126, 127, 165, 187

Iberis, 189;
  I. sempervirens, 68
Ilex,
  see hollies
Impatiens glandulifera, 33
iresine, 26, 34, 71, 76
Iris, 17, 23, *23*, 24, 73, 74, 144,
  160, 170, 189;
  I. 'Aurea' 24;
  I. flavescens, 24;
  I. 'Florentina', *24;*
  I. foetidissima, 55, 144, 149, 187*;*
  I. laevigata, 160;
  I. pallida subsp. *pallida*, 24, 144;
  I. planifolia, 120;
  I. pseudacorus, 69;
  I. reticulata, 114;
  I. unguicularis, 46, 119, 119, 120*;*
  German and Spanish, 68;
  flag, 139;
  Siberian, 161
Irish heath
  see Daboecia
Isatis glauca, 74
ivy, 54, 71, 97, 98, 135, 169, 187

jacobea, 36
Jacob's ladder, 69
James I and VI, King, 177
Japan quince, 71
Japanese anemones, 36, 37, 40, 70,
  139
Japanese privet, 49, 141, 150
Jasminum, 60, 71, 89, 141, 169, 170;
  J. nudiflorum, 42, 46, 134, 137, *137*
Jekyll, Frances, 6
Juniperus, 19, 46, 58, 59, 89, 97, 129;
  J. sabina, 19

Kalmia latifolia, 25, 59, 100, 152, 156
Kedlestone Hall, Derbyshire,
  174, 179
Kelmarsh Hall, Northamptonshire,
  183
Kelway's of Langport, 22
Kerria japonica, 18, 134
Kiftsgate Court, Gloucestershire, *175*
Knautia arvensis, 55, 182
kniphofia, 29, 68
knot gardens, 165

laburnum, 132, 134
lady fern, 44, 45, 59, 103, 148, 161
lapageria, 48
larch, 97
larkspur
  see Consolida ajacis
Lathyrus grandiflorus, 79, 134, 139,
  147, 194;
  L. nervosus, 121;
  L. pubescens, 121;
  L. sativus, 120, 121
laurel, 49, 52, 134, 141, 142, 150,
  151
laurustinus
  see *Viburnum tinus*
Lavatera trimestris, 36

lavender, 24, 26, 36, 62, 126, 127,
  128, 141, 165, 196, 107
Lawson's cypress, 128, 153
Ledum, 152;
  L. palustre, 129
Lent hellebores
  see Helleborus orientalis
Levens Hall, Cumbria, *171*, 172
Leucanthemella serotina,
  29, 37, 40, 77
Leucanthemum × *superbum*,
  33, 139, 194
Leucojum aestivum, 96, 108, 112;
  L. autumnale, 114;
  L. vernum, 109
Leucothoe, 46, 58, 100, 186;
  L. axillaris, 44, 49, 59, 146;
  L. catesbaei, 19, 44, 49;
  L. fontanesiana, 93
Leycesteria formosa, 41
lilacs, 25, 129, 141
Lilium, 105, 126, 127, 129, 149;
  L. auratum, 63, 104, 126, 127, 193;
  L. brownii, 48;
  L. candidum, 78, 144;
  L. longiflorum, 26, 36, 48, 63, 75,
    78, 144, 193;
  L. nepalense, 48;
  L. speciosum, 48, 63, 144, 193;
  L. sulphureum, 48;
  L. wallichianum var. *neilgherrense*,
    48
lily-of-the-valley, 70
lime, 97, 129
linaria, 36
Lindsay House, Chelsea, *143, 144*
liquidambar, 38
Lithodora diffusa, 20, 186
Lobelia, 26, 71, 79;
  L. cardinalis, 29, 34;
  L.'Cobalt Blue', 35
Lobularia maritime, 33, 75, 122, 127
loganberry, 54
London pride, 25, 145, 187
Lonicera japonica var. *repens*, 126, 134;
  L. periclymenum 'Belgica',
    95, 134, 135, 137;
  L.p. 'Serotina', 95, 134, 135, 137
Longleat House, Wiltshire, 166
loosestrife
  see Lysimachia
Lord Anson's pea
  see Lathyrus nervosus
love-lies-bleeding, 34
Luculia gratissima, 48
Lunaria annua, 17, 18
Lupinus, *23*, 73, 127;
  L. polyphyllus, 25;
  L. lupinus 'Somerset', 22
Lutyens, Sir Edwin, 6, 35, 175, 176
Luzula sylvatica, 59
Lycium barbarum, 132, 133;
  L. chinense, 132
lyme grass, 40
Lysimachia vulgaris, 160, 183
Lythrum, 160

Magnolia, 71;
  M. denudata, 157;
  M. stellata, 157, *157*
Mahonia aquifolium, 11, 46, 153
maidenhair spleenwort
  see Asplenium trichomanes
Main Summer Flower Border,
  27, *27*, 28, *28*, 30, *30*, *123*, *195*
Main Woodland Walk, *96*, *113*
maize, 26
male fern, 44, 45, 55, 59, 63, 103,
  144, 145, 148
Malus baccata, 95;
  M. prunifolia, 95;
  M. sylvestris, 81
mandevillea, 48
maples, 18
Marguerite, 34;
  M. 'Mrs Sander', 26, 75
marigold, 41, 70, 72, 140
African marigolds, 24, 29, 35, 37,
  40, 76, 139, 192
French marigolds, 24, 29, 139, 192
marjoram, 126
marsh marigold
  see Caltha
Mary II, Queen, 177
Matthiola longipetala
  subsp. *bicornis*, 127
mausoleum of Theodoric, Ravenna,
  172
meadow rue
  see Thalictrum
meadowsweet, 25, 68, 161
Melbourne Hall, Derbyshire,
  172, *174*
Mentha suaveolens, 79, 126;
  M.s. 'Variegata', 26, 33, 34, 37,
    41, 75, 76
Michaelmas daisies, 30, 36, 37, 38,
  39, 40, 77, 93;
  see also Aster
mignonette, 126, 127, 129
milkwort, 62
mimulus, 160, 189
mistletoe
  see Viscum album
monarda, 29
moneywort, 145, 160
monkshood, 70
Montacute, Somerset, 168, *179*
Morant, John, 168
mountain ash, 87, 158
mouse-ear hawkweed, 62
mulleins *see Verbascum*
musa, 48
Muscari armeniacum, 112;
  M.a. 'Heavenly Blue', 112
Mushroom House, *133*
musk, 145
Myosotis sylvatica, 11, 17, 20, 69,
  72, 81, 138
Myrica cerifera, 93, 95, 106, 126, 128
Myrrhis odorata, 16, 20, 73, 148, 149
myrtle, 60, 62, 128

Narcissus, 18, 108, 170;
  N. 'Emperor', 108, 112;
  N. 'Empress', 108;
  N. 'Horsfieldii', 62, 108, 112, 113;
  N. x *incomparabilis*, 108, 112;
  N. 'J.C. Backhouse', 108;
  N. *minor*, 114;
  N. *obvallaris*, 114;
  N. *pallidiflorus*, 108;
  N. *poeticus*, 20, 108;
  N. *rugilobus*, 112;
  N. 'Sir Watkin', 112;
  N. 'Stella', 108;
  see also daffodils
nasturtium, 70, 72, 80, 140
Naumkeag, USA, *175*
nemophila, 81
Nepeta x *faassenii*, 23, 55, 127, 139, 186
Nerine bowdenii, 125
Nicotiana alata, 60, 127
night-scented stocks, 127
Nonesuch, Palace of, 164
North Court, 62, *63*, 65, *136*
Nut Walk, 9, 11

oaks, 12, 16, 100, 105, 184, 190
October borders, *39*, *190*
Oenothara fruticosa, 25;
  O. *glazioviana*, 29, 68;
  O. *macrocarpa*, 139
Old English Household Life, 7
Old West Surrey, 7
Olearia phlogopappa, 23, 24, 60, 62, 141
Omphalodes verna, 138
Ophiopogon jaburan, 45
orange lilies, 25, 71, 104
Orchards, Godalming, Surrey, *170*, *171*, *178*
orchids, 48
Oriental poppies, 68, 149
Osmanthus, 70
Osmunda regalis, 95, 103, 161
Othonna cheirifolia, 122
Oxalis, 72;
  O. *acetosella*, *182*
Owlpen Manor, Gloucestershire, *170*

peonies, 24, 73, 74, 127, 149
paint colours, 51, 183, 184, 185
Palazzo Doria, Genoa, Italy, 167
pancratium, 125
Pandanus veitchii, 48
pansies, 66
Papaver orientale var. *bracteatum*, 25
parsley vine, 89, 130
Parthenocissus tricuspidata 'Veitchii', 134
passion flower, 71
Pelargonium, 72;
  P. 'Madame Crousse', 122, 123;
  P. 'Mme Lemoine', 65;
  P. 'Moore's Victory' 61;
  P. 'Pretty Polly', 61;
  P. 'Paul Crampel', 34

Peltaria alliacea, 22, 74
Penstemon, 26, 34, 36, 76, 139, 192;
  P. *heterophyllus*, 78
Penzance, Lord, 82, 87
pergolas, 87, 130, *132*
Peridium aquilinum, 95, 97, 104, 105
pernettyas, 45, 58, 104, 152
petrorhagia, 115
petunia, 24
phacelia, 81
philadelphus, 141
Phlomis fruticosa, 40, 62
Phlox, 29, 139, 140, 147;
  P. *bifida cedraria*, 186;
  P. x *procumbens*, 186;
  P. *subulata* 'Nelsoni', 186;
  P. *subulata* 'Vivid', 186
Phormium tenax, 26, 34, 42, 122, 195
Picea pungens, 46
pinks, 25, 42, 81, 139, 187
pink, pheasant eye, 42
Platycodon grandiflorus 'Mariesii', 123
Plumbago auriculata, 48, 79, 81
Polemonium caeruleum subsp. *himalayanum*, 25
Polesden Lacy, Surrey, *174*
polyanthus, 68, 72
Polygonatum multiflorum, 16, 20, 66, 73, 95, 138, 144, 149, 187
polypody fern, 45, 47, 55, 59, 189
Polystichum aculeatum, 45
poplar, 98
porch, *60*
Portugal laurel, 141
Potentilla brauniana, 114
pot-pourri, 63, 196, 197
Powis Castle, 172
prickly shield fern
  see Polystichum aculeatum
primroses, 9, 11, 12, 17, 43, 55, 70, 92, 96, 97, 103
primrose garden, 12, *13*, 14
Primula japonica, 160; P. *sikkimensis*, 160
Prior Park, Bath, Avon, 172
privet, 55, 98
Prunus cerasifera 'Pissardii', 34;
  P. *laurocerasus*, 151
Pseudosasa japonica, 47
punctatum, 144
purple sage, 17, 73, 74, 195
pyracantha, 71, *136*
pyrolas, 70

retinospora (*Chamaecyparis*), 46, 58, 59
Rhamnus frangula, 98
Rhododendron, 25, 44, 46, 48, 58, 59, 62, 93, 98, *99*, 100, 152, 156;
  named hybrids, 99, 100;
  R. *catawbiense*, 93, 152;
  R. *ferrugineum*, 19, 104, 142, 146, 186;
  R. *hirsutum*, 146;
  R. *luteum*, 101, 129;
  R. *myrtifolium*, 126, 128, 129, 146;

R. *occidentale*, 101, 152;
  R. *ponticum*, 46, 93;
  R. 'Multimaculatum', 98;
  R. 'Praecox', 43, 110
ribes, 141
Ricinus, 26;
  R. *communis* 'Gibsoni', 34
rills, 176, 177
Roberts-Smiths of Wales, 177
rock pink, 64, 189
rocket (sweet rocket), 25, 127, 129
Romneya coulteri, 26
Rosa, 24, 127, 170;
  R. 'Adam', 86;
  R. 'Aimée Vibert', 87, 88;
  R. x *alba*, 83;
  R. 'Alister Stella Gray', 86;
  R. 'Andersoni', 107;
  R. 'Anna Oliver', 86;
  R. 'a Parfum de l'Hay', 85;
  R. *arvensis*, 54, 84, 107;
  R. 'Austrian Copper'
    see R. foetida 'Bicolor';
  R. *banksiae*, 71;
  R. 'Blanche Double de Coubert', 84;
  R. 'Blush Boursault', 90;
  R. 'Bouquet d'Or', 86, 87;
  R. *bracteata*, 61, 84;
  R. 'Bridesmaid', 86;
  R. *brunonii*, 88;
  R. 'Catherine Mermet', 86;
  R. 'Céleste', 83;
  R. 'Céline Forestier', 87;
  R. x *centifolia*, 82, 85, 90;
  R. 'Cramoisi Supérieure', 83;
  R. 'Crimson Boursault', 85;
  R. 'Deoniensis', 86;
  R. 'Docteur Grill', 86;
  R. 'Dundee Rambler', 84, 88;
  R. 'Emelie Plantier', 87;
  R. 'Evangeline', 54, 95, 107;
  R. *filipes*, 87; R. 'Flora', 84;
  R. *foetida* 'Bicolor', 84;
  R. 'Fortune's Double Yellow'
    see R. x odorata 'Pseudindica';
  R. *gallica* 'Versicolor', 82;
  R. 'Gloire de Dijon', 86, 88;
  R. 'Glorie des Rosomanes', 85;
  R. 'G. Nabonnand', 86;
  R. 'Goubault', 85, 86;
  R. 'Hebe's Lip', 82;
  R. *hemisphaerica*, 84;
  R. 'Homère', 86;
  R. 'Lady Curzon', 107;
  R. 'Lamarque', 86;
  R. 'Lawranciana', 83;
  R. 'Macrantha', 107;
  R. 'Maiden's Blush', 83, 134;
  R. 'Madame Alfred Carrière', 87;
  R. 'Madame Berard', 86;
  R. 'Madame Lombard', 86;
  R. 'Madame Plantier', 85, 87;
  R. 'Maman Cochet', 86;
  R. 'Mme Falcot', 86;
  R. 'Mme Sancy de Pavabere', 85, 90;

R. 'Morlettii', 90;
R. moschata, 84, 95, 107;
R. moyesii, 84;
R. multiflora, 84, 107, 126;
R. multiflora var. cathayensis, 107;
R. 'Mundi'
    see R. gallica 'Veriscolor';
R. x odorata 'Pallida', 22, 23, 24,
    36, 41, 60, 62, 64, 73, 83, 134,
    141;
R. x odorata 'Pseudindica',
    84, 86, 88;
R. 'Ophelia', 87;
R.; pendulina, 85;
R. pimpinellifolia, 24, 54, 83, 90,
    91, 92, 106, 126, 129, 189;
    R.p. 'Grandiflora', 54, 91, 106;
R. 'Princesse de Sagan', 86;
R. 'Reine Blanche', 82;
R. 'Reine Olga de Wurtemburg',
    87;
R. 'Rêve d'Or', 87;
R. roxburghii f. normalis, 84;
R. rubiginosa, 82;
R. 'Ruga', 84;
R. rugosa, 84;
R. 'Safrano', 86;
R. sempervirens, 84;
R. 'Souvenir d'Elise Vardon', 86;
R. 'Souvenir d'un Ami', 86;
R. 'The Garland', 83, 84, 88, 191;
R. 'Triomphe de Rennes', 86;
R. virginiana, 16, 54, 84, 107;
R. wichurana, 84, 107;
R. 'William Allen Richardson', 87;
R. xanthina f. hugonis, 84;
R. 'Zéphirine Drouhin', 85, 86,
    90, 91
rosemary, 24, 60, 61, 62, 64, 126,
    127, 128, 134, 141, 148, 165
R. laciniatus, 54;
R. odoratus, 25;
R. parviflorus, 25
R. 'Golden Glow'
    (now R. laciniata 'Hortensia');
R. laciniata 'Hortensia', 42, 139,
    147
rue, 29, 32, 78
Rumex, 160
rush, flowering, 183
Ruskin, John, 7
Ruys, Mein, 67

St Bruno lily
    see Anthericum
St John's wort
    see Hypericum
St Nicholas, Richmond, Yorkshire,
    175
sage, 126, 127
salipiglossis, 24
Salvia, 29, 35, 139;
S. horminum see S. viridis
    var. comata;
S. nemorosa, 124;
S. patens, 31, 79, 81;
S. splendens, 75;

S. uliginosa, 79;
S. virgata, 29, 124, 139;
S. viridis, 193;
S. viridis var. comata, 29, 33, 74,
    123, 192, 193
Sanguinaria, 95
santolina, 29, 33, 55, 62, 127, 141,
    165
saxifraga, 115, 144, 186, 187, 189
scarlet oaks, 38
Scilla, 18, 42, 96, 109, 110, 112, 138;
S. bifolia, 109;
S. sibirica, 109, 114;
S. siberica var. taurica, 114
Scotch briars
    see Rosa pimpinellifolia
Scots pine, 61, 64, 96, 97, 105,
    158, 184
seats, 176
Sedum acre, 188;
S. ewersii, 188;
S. hispanicum, 114, 115;
S. lydium, 114, 115;
S. rupestre, 19, 188;
S. sieboldii, 124;
S. spectabile, 37, 40, 76;
S. spurium, 188;
S. telephinum var. borderei, 76, 123
selaginella, 48
Sempervivum arachnoideum
    subsp. tomentosum, 189;
S. x barbulatum 'Hookeri', 189;
S. tectorum, 189
Senecio cineraria
    (formerly S. maritimus), 29, 32,
    42, 68, 72, 124, 139, 140;
S. greyii see Brachyglottis
September borders, 38, 77
Silene pendula, 72
silver birches, 12, 19, 93, 95, 97,
    100, 105
Sissinghurst Castle, Kent, 87, 175
Sisyrinchium striatum, 42
Skimmia, 45, 46, 49, 154;
S. japonica 'Oblata', 49, 141, 146;
S. japonica 'Veitchii', 49, 146
skull cap, 183
smilacina, 189
Smilax aspera, 43, 49
snake's-head fritillary, 112
snapdragons (Antirrhinum), 24, 26,
    31, 32, 33, 34, 35, 36, 37, 40, 41,
    56, 75, 76, 79, 139, 140, 189,
    191, 192, 194
snowdrops (Galanthus), 42, 46, 96,
    109, 112, 138
snowflake, 42
soapwort, 32, 40
Solanum jasminoides 26
soleirolia, 145
Solomon's seal
    see Polygonatum multiflorum
Sorbaria tomentosa, 64
sorghums, 111
South Terrace, 61
Spanish iris, 25

Spring Garden, 14, 15
spruce, 97
Stachys byzantina, 32, 33, 37, 40,
    62, 72, 77, 81, 124, 139, 140,
    188, 193
stephanotis, 146
stitchwort, 55
stocks, 126, 127, 129, 140
stonecrops, 188
Stoneleigh Abbey, Warwickshire,
    169
sundials, 173
summerhouses, 28, 143, 176, 180,
    188
sunflower, 29
sweet alyssum, 22, 26, 123
sweet cicely
    see Myrrhis odorata
sweet chestnut, 29, 97, 100, 184, 190
sweet pea, 127
sweet rocket, 25
sweet verbena, 62, 126, 197
sweet William, 69
sycamore, 97

tamarisk, 58, 59
Tanacetum 'Golden Feather'
    (T. parthenium 'Aureum'), 26, 33,
    35, 37, 79
tansy, 74, 148, 182, 193, 194
Taylor, George, 6
Teucrium chamaedrys, 187
Thalictrum, 25, 29, 160
Thalictrum aquilegiifolium, 139;
T. flavum, 139;
T. minus, 65
thorn, 53, 106
thrift, 25, 125, 186, 187
thyme, 62, 92, 126, 127, 165;
    Thymus pseudolanuginosus, 114
tiarella, 138, 189
Tijou, Jean, 177
Tintinhull Manor, Somerset, 179
toadflax, 55
topiary, 56, 57, 171, 172
tormentil, 62
Trachystemon orientalis, 145, 148, 150
tree lupin, 25, 55
Trillium, 70, 95, 112
Trollius, 160
Tropaeolum speciosum, 80
Tulipa, 17, 20, 73, 127, 173;
T. 'Artus', 17;
T. 'Bleu Celeste', 20;
T. 'Clara Butt', 17;
T. 'Erguste', 20;
T. 'Gesneriana Major', 17;
T. 'La Merveille', 17;
T. 'Rev. Ewbank', 20;
T. 'Rosemunda', 17;
T. 'Thomas Moore', 17

Upton Grey, Berkshire, 83

Vaccinium, 93, 95, 100, 152;
    V. angustifolium, 100;
    V. angustifolium var. laevifoliumi, 38, 106;
    V. corymbosum, 106
valerian, 25, 186
Vann, Surrey, 162
vases, 173
Veratrum nigrum, 16, 17, 20, 73, 149
Verbascum, 29, 30, 55, 56;
    V. chaixii, 139, 194;
    V. phlomoides, 121, 139
verbenas, 72
Veronica fruticans, 114;
    V. prostrata, 114;
    V. repens, 114
Viburnum lantana, 98;
    V. opulus, 25, 54, 98;
        V.o. 'Roseum', 25, 37, 135;
    V. plicatum, 25, 150;
    V. tinus, 41, 134, 141
Victoria, Queen, 176
Vinca, 19, 153;
    V. minor, 46, 159, 187
vines, 61, 62, 71, 130;
    see also Vitis
violets, 126, 170
Viola gracilis, 17
Virginia creeper, 71, 135

Viscum album, 47, 158
Vitis coignetiae, 89, 95;
    V. labrusca, 89;
    V. thunbergii, 95;
    V. vinifera 'Royal Muscadine', 89, 130

wall planting, 55, 87, 88, 89
wallflowers, 17, 20, 60, 68, 69, 71, 73, 126, 127, 189
walnut, 98
water forget-me-not, 103, 161
water features, 144, 166, 167
water lilies, 162
water plantain, 183
weigela, 141
Welsh poppy, 189
whitebeam, 97
white bedstraw, 55
whitethorn, 54, 92, 95, 97, 158, 162
whortleberry, 59, 97, 104, 105, 106
William III, King, 177
willows, 47, 76, 92, 97
willow herb
    see Epilobium
Wilson, G.F., 156
winter aconite, 46, 112
winter jasmine
    see Jasminum nudiflorum

winter savory, 127
Wisteria sinensis, 29, 89, 130, 141
witch hazel, 46
Wolley-Dod, Revd C., 40
Wollaton Hall, Nottinghamshire, 166
Wolsey, Cardinal Thomas, 164
Wood and Garden, 7
woodruff, 66, 70, 138
wood sorrel, 138
Woodstock, Manor of, Oxfordshire, 164
wrought iron, 177
wych elm, 98

yew, 16, 18, 23, 46, 49, 52, 57, 61, 70, 97, 103, 141, 165
yew cat, 57
York Gate, Adel, Leeds, West Yorkshire, 70, 136, 174, 175, 178, 179
Yucca, 26, 29, 32, 34, 122, 154;
    Y. filamentosa, 30, 154, 189;
    Y. gloriosa, 29, 42, 148, 154;
    Y. recurvifolia, 29, 154

Zea mays, 192
zinnia, 72

AUTHOR'S ACKNOWLEDGMENTS

The book would not have been possible without the assistance of many people. Particularly I should like to thank the staff of the Royal Horticultural Society Lindley Library; the staff of the reference library at Bradford Central Library; Bingley Library; the British Library; and the staff of York Gate.

I should also like to thank Sir Robert and Lady Clark; Valerie Kenwood; Maureen Nyazai; Judith Tankard; Colin Young; and the late Mien Ruys and Graham Stuart Thomas. Grateful thanks are also due to the unseen hands who make books possible: my editor, Jo Christian, the designer Becky Clarke and all the staff at Frances Lincoln Ltd; and my agent Catriona Wilson.

PICTURE ACKNOWLEDGMENTS

With the exception of those listed below, all the photographs and illustrations in this book either belong to the author or are out of copyright. The Publishers have made every effort to contact holders of copyright works. Any copyright holders we have been unable to reach are invited to contact the Publishers so that a full acknowledgment may be given in subsequent editions. For permission to reproduce the images below, the publishers would like to thank:

Country Life Picture Library: 15, 30 right, 31, 38, 43, 123
Private collection: 23, 32, 51, 143 centre, 143 below, 144
The Royal Horticultural Society, Lindley Library: details from the workbook of Gertrude Jekyll used throughout the book
Judith Tankard: 39, 83 right